What the experts are saying about
Your Love Life and Reincarnation:

"An informative and valuable spiritual guide to explore the subject of love relationships through past life regression."

—Janet Cunningham, Ph.D., president of the International Association for Regression Research and Therapies, Inc. and author of several books, including *Caution: Soul Mate Ahead!*

"A treasury of good metaphysical advice for love and life."

—Brad Steiger, author of *Discover Your Past Lives* and *You'll Live Again*

"A step-by-step practical and spiritual guide to a better love life."

—Kevin Todeschi, author of *Edgar Cayce on Soul Mates: Unlocking The Dynamics Of Soul Attraction* and *Soul Development: Edgar Cayce's Approach For a New World*

Your Love Life and Reincarnation:

Why The Past Is Affecting Your Present and How To Fix It

includes 18 case histories and
10 meditation scripts

Stephen Petullo

Learn and Track Your Love Cycles
by Scott A. Petullo

MetaPublishing

Your Love Life and Reincarnation:
Why the Past is Affecting Your Present and How To Fix It

This book's case histories contain the actual transcripts of past-life regressions. Most of them have been summarized and edited for clarity and space considerations, but the fundamental nature of each case and the awareness gained by each client remain the same. Names and identifiable details have been changed to protect the privacy of the individuals.

All quoted material is used with the permission of the author or publisher except in those cases where they could not be reached. Every attempt was made to contact them.

Interior design and layout by Lee Lewis, Words + Design, 888-883-8347

LCCN: 2001 129187
SAN: 254-0924

Cataloging-in-Publication Data:

Petullo, Stephen.
Your love life and reincarnation : why the past is affecting your present and how to fix it / Stephen Petullo with Scott A. Petullo. -- 1st ed.
p. cm.
Includes index.
ISBN 0-9713867-5-7

1. Love. 2. Conduct of life. 3. Reincarnation therapy. 4. Dating (Social customs) I. Title

BF1045.L7P48 2002 131
QBI01-701037

Manufactured in the United States of America

MetaPublishing
3741 NE 163rd Street, #314
North Miami Beach, FL 33160

Contents

Section IV
Dealing With Other Relationship Issues

Section V
Discover, Forgive, Release

Section VI
Putting It All Together

Section VII
Other Resources to Improve Your Love Life

Dedication

To my twin brother Scott for being my friend and confidant
on this path we are traveling,
and for sharing his knowledge of the cycles of time

To all of you who make the effort to express truth
and unconditional love

Acknowledgements

I am grateful for everyone who contributed in some way
to help create this book. Thank you all—
my clients, all my teachers along the way,
my editors Lee Lewis and Matthew Gilbert,
and all others.

Disclaimer

This book isn't about finding an ideal partner or changing your current one. It's about how to improve yourself from within—which will in turn help create a foundation for a compatible love relationship. When you focus on self-improvement and take the necessary action, your relationship will improve or you'll meet the right person at the right time.

Every effort has been made to make this book as complete and accurate as possible. However, there may be mistakes, both typographical and in content. Therefore, it should be used only as a general guide and not as the ultimate source for improving yourself and your love life. Furthermore, while many concepts described within this book have been applied successfully for thousands of years, the information may only be current up to the printing date.

It isn't the purpose of this book to reprint all the information available regarding reincarnation, karma, love life, relationships, and various metaphysical subjects, but instead to compliment, amplify, and supplement other sources. You are urged to read all the available material, learn as much as possible about the above subjects, and tailor the information to suit your individual needs (see Recommended Reading). The purpose of this book is also to educate and entertain.

The authors and MetaPublishing shall have neither liability nor responsibility to any person or entity with respect to any loss or damage caused, or alleged to have been caused, directly or indirectly, by the information contained within this book. It is sold with the understanding that the publisher and authors are not engaged in rendering legal or other professional services. If legal or other expert assistance is required, the services of a competent professional should be sought. If don't wish to be bound by the above, you may return this book to the publisher.

Note to the Reader:

How This Book Can Help You

While I was preparing this book, someone said to me, "The public doesn't care about past lives anymore. That fad is over." Interest in reincarnation may have been more popular in the '70s and '80s, but if it really was only a fad, then the general public may not have had the chance to truly understand reincarnation and how it relates to their current life. I believe it's time we take the possibility of reincarnation more seriously because past-life regression works. My goal with this book is to help you realize how much your long forgotten past is affecting your present, especially your love life, and how you can fix it on your own—*even if you choose not to believe in reincarnation.*

Most of us are at least somewhat skeptical about reincarnation and karma. After all, it's difficult to believe in something that we can't physically prove true or false. Many people have actually perceived dates, names, spouse or children's names, events, addresses and so on during past-life regression which later proved to be accurate and linked together, but this still doesn't prove that they actually lived those lives.

This book is presented *as if* we really have lived past lives, and so its purpose isn't to prove or disprove reincarnation and karma. There are many other books and articles on these subjects. Nevertheless, by doing your own research and keeping an open mind in the process, you may find it difficult not to at least accept the *possibility* that they are real.

Proof of or belief in past lives is unnecessary for the process of past-life regression to work. Even if you're a skeptic, by acting as if you have lived before, past-life therapy, with a professional or on your own, can transform not just your love life but other areas of your life as well. See the Appendix at the end of this text for answers to common questions about reincarnation and karma.

During my regression and progression sessions, I instruct clients to *act as if* they have lived before and to pretend past lives are real. Whether or not the client believes in reincarnation or whether or not he or she has actually lived past lives is irrelevant. The process works as long as the participant can and is willing to follow directions. In fact, many former skeptics have found the process to be more valuable than other more traditional methods of therapy. *Even when past-life perceptions are viewed only as symbolism, the process of past-life regression and recall, when done correctly, is a powerful and effective tool for positive change.* It is more effective for positive permanent results than any other therapy I am aware of. And yes, you can do this on your own. This book will show you how.

What does reincarnation have to do with your love life? More than you may currently realize. Most people probably pay attention to physical, intellectual, and emotional characteristics when choosing a partner, but fail to consider the spiritual or karmic reasons for the relationship.

I will show you how to become aware of those karmic reasons for a relationship, recognize your personal love life karma and relationship cycles, overcome negative karma and blocks, and organize your efforts toward a happy and harmonious love life. You'll be able to live and react with less fear and more love, make better choices in love and life, and eventually live the love life that you may have only dreamed about up until now.

Real-life case histories will show you how and why the process of past-life regression has improved the love life of others. Step-by-step instructions for your own past life self-regressions are included in chapter 14. You don't need to read through each case history to use those instructions. And while you may not feel initially that some of the case histories apply to you or your love life, they all contain valuable insight gained through actual past-life regressions which may at some time help you or someone you love. Although it may appear that most of the clients discussed herein perceived lifetimes or situations that could be considered negative, uncovering such memories is often extremely helpful in resolving present-day issues or conflicts.

The answers to all our problems really are inside of us. We just need to ask the right questions, know where and how to look for answers, and then recognize, understand, and accept the truth.

— Stephen Petullo

Introduction

If you don't understand the meaning of karma and how it's directly related to reincarnation, you may not understand how it can affect your love life.

A law of energy states that for every action there is a reaction. The concept of karma means "cause and effect." Whatever you do, say, think, and even intend will sooner or later come back to you. Many of us mistakenly associate the word karma with punishment and don't realize how karma and reincarnation work together. It is common today to blame "bad" karma when explaining negative circumstances in life, and yet overlook the fact that the word karma implies *past-life* origins and that only ourselves are responsible for everything that happens to us. There is no such thing as a victim.

In light of the theory of karma, our current gifts, blessings, talents, problems, and heartaches are the result of our past deeds and experiences. The force we call "God" didn't decide by chance to bestow a talent or curse on you instead of your neighbor. To refuse to give reincarnation any credibility and then to tack on the words "karmic" and "fated" to positive life-changing experiences is only acknowledging part of the truth.

Even though the theories of reincarnation and karma have gained popularity during the last 30 years, many still feel they should be taken as seriously as Santa Claus and the tooth fairy. Those who are more open to the theories may find them interesting, but often don't understand how or why they work. And some of us do apply them to our own lives. Those of us who do understand, live, and act within the ideals of reincarnation and karma realize that our world would be a better place if everyone did the same. If we all *acted as if* everything we said and did came back to us, there would be far less murder, rape, theft, lying, manipulation and so on, and a lot more love, acceptance, compassion, and people helping each other.

Most of us have fantasized about an ideal love life:
"I want to find my soul mate and grow old with him/her."
"I am looking for a long term relationship."
"I want to spend the rest of my life with my husband/wife/ partner."

As a former professional matchmaker and now as a metaphysical counselor, I've heard these statements countless times from clients, family, friends, and acquaintances. My response is usually, "Okay, that's a goal which could potentially bring you much happiness, unless it is motivated by fears such as loneliness or poverty. But what about your relationship karma? What about your relationship cycles?" I ask the same questions of those who want to improve their existing relationship. I usually get a confused or skeptical look in return.

My twin brother Scott and I have realized the following through extensive research into numerology and past-life regression: *everyone seems to have relationship karma and relationship cycles, even if they don't believe in the concepts.* Relationship karma is the result of one's actions in the past, both in this life and past lives, whether or not the current personality remembers or believes in past lives. Numerology doesn't determine relationship cycles; it only symbolizes them.

I don't expect you to believe these statements without any experience with numerology or past-life regression. Indeed, most of us make no effort to become aware of our relationship karma or cycles, let alone believe that we are affected by such things. This lack of awareness leads to expectations which create heartache in our love life and disharmony in other areas. In other words, our egos sometimes want something different than what actually is or what will be.

However, after reading this book, considering the information presented with an open mind, and then observing life with the information in mind, you may begin to perceive your life from a different perspective and, in the process, help yourself. For once you discover and release the root causes of personal problems and challenges (which most, if not all, of us have) and discover what potentials exist in the future, it becomes easier to perceive the self and others clearly, to go with the flow, and to navigate with confidence. Instead of spending time and energy trying to swim upstream, you'll be able to reach your goal of a happy love life.

Key Terms

God, Guides and Angels of the Light: some of the names used to describe the helpful energy that is available to us all.

Higher Self: Our higher consciousness or intuition.

Higher Self state or perspective: After moving through the death experience in a past-life regression, people often enter this state and have a heightened awareness about themselves, the life just explored, and their current life. This state can also be reached through meditation.

Karma: Your good and bad baggage from the recent and distant past. The theory that states that all actions, words, thoughts, and intent will return to you.

Karmic block: A problem in the present life that is the result of one's actions in the recent or distant past.

Karmic reason: The cause, which is often rooted in a past life. The spiritual reason.

The Light: What most people see after dying in this life or after perceiving a death experience during a past-life regression.

Predestined: Events or experiences planned by your Higher Self or soul prior to incarnating on Earth.

Relationship cycles: The patterns our love lives follow. These cycles can be determined by esoteric sciences such as numerology and astrology.

Root cause: Similar to karmic reason. The spiritual cause. The real reason. What first caused the issue or problem.

Root cause therapy: Used to discover and release the root cause of a problem or block. This process usually involves forgiving oneself and others involved after the root cause is identified.

Section I

What You Need To Know About Reincarnation, Karma, and Regression Therapy

The past doesn't matter
until you realize
it is interfering with your present.

1
What You Need To Know About Reincarnation, Karma, and Regression Therapy

Everyone knows at least one couple that seems to have the perfect relationship. They love spending time with each other, they always look happy together, they rarely argue, and they seem to have no relationship problems. Even after many years together, they seem to be compatible in many ways. Why do they have such a good relationship while others don't? Is it just a coincidence? From the perspective of reincarnation and karma, there is no such thing as coincidence; everything happens for a reason. More likely, they were destined to have an ideal relationship because of good relationship karma.

Throughout history, the belief in reincarnation and karma has been common. The concepts have been an integral part of Eastern religions including Taoism, Hinduism, and Buddhism, as well as the religions and beliefs of Egypt, India, and Greece. The Greek mathematician and philosopher Pythagoras taught that the soul survived after death of the body. The Greek philosophers Plato and Socrates believed in reincarnation. Other famous people who believed in reincarnation include Leonardo da Vinci, Edgar Allan Poe, Ralph Waldo Emerson, Henry David Thoreau, and Benjamin Franklin.

Reincarnation and karma work together. You can't have one without the other. Reincarnation is defined as rebirth, re-embodiment, or re-creation. In other words, our souls never die; they are born again and again into new physical bodies—but not just into any body. For each lifetime a soul chooses a vessel that is appropriate to the lessons and experiences needed to balance karma from experiences in prior incarnations. That body is chosen for its physical, emotional, and mental characteristics, its biological or adopted parents, location of birth, siblings, relatives, friends, lovers, economic situation, and for many other aspects that are important for the soul's growth.

The theories of reincarnation and karma state that everything you are today is a combination of what you have been in the recent and distant past. This applies even if your current personality doesn't believe in past lives. Many of your talents and abilities, especially those that come easy to you, may have been developed over lifetimes. Many of your fears and present day conflicts are the result of past-life, pre-birth, and childhood experiences (which themselves usually have past-life origins).

Our subconscious mind has memories of every event, thought, intent, word spoken, or action from every lifetime our souls have ever lived. When there is conflict in your life, the reasons can always be found within you. Unfortunately, that information is often so buried in our subconscious minds that we are not even aware of it until we have the courage to face the root causes. If you understand the cause of a problem or block and then release it, you'll be able to move in the direction you want and realize your dreams and goals.

Past-life regression can be considered "reverse hypnosis" because it helps wake us up from self-deceptions about ourselves and our lives. These self-deceptions (refusing to perceive ourselves, others, or situations as they truly are) cause much unnecessary pain and suffering. Past-life therapy can help us let go of illusions and see oneself and life more clearly so that we can live life fully, purposely, and harmoniously rather than as a victim of circumstances.

Past-life regression therapy is a less conventional approach compared to other more conservative therapies, but its techniques and principles are thousands of years old and have no harmful side effects. Often these processes are successful for those who have tried other methods without success.

Some might say that you should focus only on *now* because the past doesn't matter. It's true that the present is most important. However, all of us carry around baggage (karma) from the past that was never resolved. This baggage, which we often don't consciously remember, interferes with the present and the future. This applies even to those who don't believe in reincarnation or karma. *The laws of nature apply to all energy.* These laws don't care what your current personality believes or doesn't believe. We reincarnate to resolve karma and you have the choice of resolving it now or later. The past doesn't matter until you realize it is interfering with your present.

Our society is seemingly set up to keep us in denial about how we feel, who we really are, and our purpose for being here. We are programmed how to be/think/act/react. We can choose to wake up out of the deep slumber of this programming and make the most of our existence by beginning to question that which we have automatically accepted as fact. We can also choose to remain stuck in our fears and then, at the end of our lives, feel regret. Yes, you'll have the opportunity to come back and do it over again and again until you get it right, but wouldn't you rather get it right this time and not have to repeat your mistakes?

Reincarnation and Karmic Patterns

We choose, at the soul or spirit level, to reincarnate in this physical learning place to resolve or overcome all karma and fear which we have created for ourselves during current and past lifetimes, until we learn to love ourselves and everyone else *unconditionally*. Most everyone you know now you have known before, including lovers, partners, friends, enemies, bosses, coworkers, relatives, children, parents, and neighbors. The more significant a person is in your life, the stronger the connection. We often reincarnate in groups: families, companies, social circles, clubs, and so on. Indeed, certain patterns of incarnation characterize the journey of most souls as they work through all of their karma:

Male and Female: Each soul tends to reincarnate more often as one sex or the other. However, most have experienced life as both sexes. If masculinity, femininity, or being male or female are issues that cause stress in your life, there are reasons that relate back to experiences in your current life, a previous life, and often both.

Sexual Orientation: Experiencing life as a different sex than a soul is accustomed to may result in homosexuality or bisexuality. In addition, an attraction may continue when past-life male and female lovers return as the same sex. When we meet someone new, we are often attracted to or repelled by the connection we had with that person in the past.

Material Wealth: It is common to have had lifetimes on both sides of the track. The root cause of all prosperity issues can be traced back to childhood, previous lives, and usually both.

Physical Sensitivities: Someone with a weak digestive system may have had several lifetimes of gluttony. Someone with asthma may have died a heavy smoker in a past life. Someone born with a deformed leg may subconsciously feel guilty about accidentally running over someone's legs in a past life. Someone who died of alcoholism in a past life may be born into a family in which alcoholism is common, so they have a chance to finally learn to respect and love themselves enough to overcome the addiction.

Punishment: Nothing we experience in life is a punishment from a "judgmental God." We choose, on a soul level, all of our experiences out of love and compassion for others and ourselves. Sometimes past-life guilt may cause us to experience seemingly negative events in our current life. All of our experiences, including those that appear "negative," are opportunities for learning and growth. In fact, the "negative" experiences often provide us with the best opportunity for growth. We have the option of rising above what may seem like a punishment by finding the root cause and then forgiving and releasing the self and all involved.

Dislikes: Whatever you dislike in someone else is within you as well. Often this person is a mirror for what you are suppressing now or who you were and what you experienced in the recent or distant past. We are all teachers for each other. The next time someone irritates you, stop and ask yourself how they are a mirror for you. For example, if someone ignores you, what or who is it that you are not listening to? Could it be your intuition? If someone lies to you, how are you not being honest with yourself?

Past-life Clues

Your interests, likes, and dislikes, especially where there is no logical reason, can give you valuable clues about your past lives.

- Countries, states or cities that you like or dislike may indicate happy or unhappy experiences and lifetimes in those places.
- Groups—ethnic, race, religion, sexual orientation, or authority figures, for example—that you like or dislike may indicate positive or negative experiences with them in one or more past lives.
- Any phobias or fears you have may indicate traumatic experiences relating to that fear in one or more past lives.
- Anyone—lovers, friends, family, acquaintances, coworkers, neighbors, and so on—whom you immediately liked or disliked may indicate positive or negative experiences with that person in one or more past lives.
- Any natural, unlearned talents you have may indicate you developed that particular skill in one or more past lives.

Using Hypnotherapy (Guided Meditation)

Your beliefs and fears, conscious and subconscious, determine how your life unfolds. When subconscious beliefs and fears clash with present goals, the result is a problem, a phobia, or a block. One way to change what isn't working in your life is to discover, resolve, and release the *root* cause. This can be accomplished through hypnotherapy, or guided meditation as it is sometimes referred to.

Some therapists claim to use a "non-hypnotic" technique, perhaps because of the negative assumptions many have about hypnosis. However, if the client is led into a more relaxed state, he or she is in a state of mind that is similar to a hypnotic state. This state can be accomplished with flashing lights, with a series of words designed to focus the mind such as a countdown or a visualization, or with music.

When helping a client search for the root cause of a problem or block, I often begin by leading them through a simple relaxation process which may include gentle suggestions to breathe deeply, relax the body, and/or visualize pleasant scenes. After the person is more relaxed, I often have him or her focus on the emotions surrounding the problem or conflict and then allow those feelings to take him or her to the root cause. Once they begin to perceive related information, I help guide them to gain as much awareness as possible without asking questions or making statements that could lead them to make something up. For example, instead of asking, "How many children do you have in the lifetime you are perceiving?" I would say, "Tell me about your family."

A therapist who has a thorough understanding of metaphysics and regression can help lead you directly to the cause of any conflict, and then help you uncover, understand, resolve, and let go of it. You can also discover and release conflicts on your own through meditation (see chapter 14).

How do you know if the answers you receive through regression or meditation are correct? When you discover potential answers to current life problems in past-life therapy, you'll usually feel a definite sense of knowing and truth. This information is often accompanied by a deep emotional response. Sometimes you'll get additional confirmation during the days, weeks, months and even years following a regression through the experience of certain "coincidences."

It is important to realize that your subconscious mind isn't always on your side. Your customs, habits, and routines have been formed over many years in this life and past lives. Since taking the actions to reach your goals will create change, you may find yourself resisting. You may be consciously aware of how you could benefit from certain changes, and you may consciously want to change, but your subconscious mind can create countless excuses to stay the same. Beliefs about what is good and bad, whether they are reasonable or not, are stored in your subconscious mind. These beliefs can create fears, which can then influence your life in negative ways. *The more you resist actions that will positively influence your life, the more you may benefit from taking the action required.* If you really want to change, you'll ignore your inner critic and find the courage to overcome the fear and do what is best for you.

Hypnosis or guided meditation works under four conditions:

1. Just like anything else, you need to believe in it.
2. You have to want to change.
3. You must dissolve any subconscious blocks between you and your goal. For example, if you want to create more money but subconsciously you believe that "rich people are snobbish and mean," you'll never reach your goal. If somehow you do, you'll spend it or lose it.

4. You need to feel comfortable enough with the therapist in order to let go and allow yourself to be hypnotized. We have a natural tendency to attempt to control our situation and surroundings and defend ourselves. Consciously giving up the desire to do so and allowing yourself to relax during a session will encourage optimum results.

Why and How Hypnosis Works

How does hypnosis work? Our subconscious mind remembers everything that has ever happened to us. Often, experiences forgotten by the conscious mind remain in the subconscious mind as barriers that block goals and dreams. Since hypnosis acts as a bridge between the conscious, subconscious and superconscious minds, these barriers can be discovered and understood by the conscious mind, then resolved by dealing directly with the subconscious mind.

Suppose, for example, that when you were a child, your parents always commented that all wealthy people are rude and unhappy. As an adult, you know this is untrue. However, your subconscious mind, which received and retained this information, believes it is true. Even though you want to be wealthy, your subconscious mind will always sabotage your efforts to attain prosperity because you don't want to be rude or unhappy. Through hypnosis, you can discover, dissolve, and release this and any other false belief, fear, or block and reprogram the subconscious mind for success in all areas of life. Traumatic events can also be buried or suppressed in the subconscious mind. Hypnotherapy can uncover, resolve, and release these experiences as well, which in turn resolves the troublesome disorder resulting from them.

What is the difference between the conscious mind and the subconscious mind? The subconscious mind deals with repetitive activity such as breathing, digestion, and circulation. It is also where all your beliefs, fears and memories are stored, your version of a computer data bank. The conscious mind is your awareness of thoughts, images, sounds, and so on. You can relate these levels of the mind to those of a house. The basement is where we store things: the subconscious mind. The conscious level is the ground floor where we do most of our day-to-day living. And the upstairs deck, like an observatory of the night sky, is the superconsciousness, our link to all that is.

What is the difference between hypnosis and hypnotherapy? Hypnosis is the trance-like condition induced by a series of words designed to lead the person's body and mind into a deep state of relaxation. Hypnotherapy combines hypnosis with therapy or counseling. A qualified hypnotherapist uses training, experience, knowledge, intuition, and compassion to help the client effectively resolve their problem or achieve their goal.

Why is it so effective to access the subconscious mind through hypnosis or guided meditation? Your subconscious, not your conscious mind, controls your reality. To better illustrate this, think of your subconscious mind as you at age five. *In many ways, we are all still children who have merely learned to act like adults.* That child has many misconceptions and fears about life which are still affecting you. Most of your core beliefs were formed in your early childhood. These beliefs are based on information which may or may not be correct. Even though you may consciously have no fear, your subconscious mind may think differently. Until you uncover, face, and resolve past issues and fears, the fearful and misinformed child within you will run your life.

For example, if your subconscious mind associates smoking with maturity and confidence, it will be even harder for you to quit. If it associates being thin with sickness, your subconscious mind will do its best to retain extra weight. If it associates relationships with unhappiness, your subconscious mind will do its best to create conflict in a relationship, or keep you single, no matter how much you consciously want a compatible relationship.

What can hypnosis or guided meditation be used for? Hypnosis can be used for improving, letting go of, or attracting love relationships, shedding weight, smoking cessation, stress, phobias, fears, pain, career enhancement, self-esteem, creativity, discipline, self-confidence, concentration, sleep, attitude modification, motivation, sports performance, fitness, improving health, slowing the aging process, sexual enhancement, memory, learning, sales, public speaking, future progression, past/current life regression, and many other goals and dreams.

Additional information about hypnosis and guided meditation is available online at www.howisyourlovelife.com/clarifyinghypno.html.

2
Relationship Karma, Soul Mates, Twin Souls, and Destiny

We have all had "good" and "bad" relationships in past lifetimes, and many of us can say the same about our present life. But how do we unlock the relationship puzzle and achieve the love life of our dreams? The key lies in understanding our past experiences—our karma— and how those experiences continue to affect us, and our relationships, today.

What is "good" relationship karma? To define "good" relationship karma, I'll give a simplified example of "bad" relationship karma: A married man in seventeenth century France had numerous extramarital affairs that hurt his wife deeply. Now his soul has been reincarnated as a woman who is married to a man who has had several affairs. Not coincidentally, this man was the wife long ago in France. The woman now has "bad" relationship karma as the result of her actions as the male French philanderer of the past, specifically with the soul who is her husband now. What comes around really does go around. The soul who was the man in the past life didn't forgive himself; the soul who was the woman in the past life resented his actions. They reunited as husband and wife once again with the roles reversed. Will they play out the same drama? It depends on how they react to each other's actions. Reacting out of fear will create more karmic debt; reacting with love, acceptance, and forgiveness will allow one or both of them to move on.

Someone with good relationship karma may have acted in past-life relationships with integrity, love, and compassion rather than dishonesty, selfishness, jealousy, or greed.

Even though someone may currently have good relationship karma, this may not be the case for his or her entire life. One relationship may have been smooth sailing most of the way. Another may have been rocky the whole ride. *This is because we have different karma with each person we meet, and also because we all travel through relationship cycles.* For example, someone in her 20s may be in a cycle that attracts people with integrity issues. Between the ages of 32 and 44, she may be in a cycle that is favorable for heavy family responsibilities. In her late 40s, she may be in a cycle that is favorable for a long-term, compatible relationship. There are several ways to learn about your relationship cycles, including meditation, astrology, and numerology. A thorough numerology analysis will indicate and be symbolic of potential relationship cycles. Those who choose to be aware of their cycles will be able to prepare and react with love instead of fear (see chapter 17).

Is it possible to avoid negative situations resulting from your relationship karma? Ignoring or running away from problems doesn't work—karma will eventually find you. But when you become aware of and understand the karma of a relationship or a situation through meditation or regression, you'll be able to rise above or even avoid potential negative situations by forgiving and accepting yourself and all involved. *With awareness and understanding, it becomes far easier to react with love and compassion instead of fear.*

In addition to good relationship karma, some people have wonderful, harmonious relationships because their personality and behavior are more conducive to creating them. To begin with, they respect and love themselves enough to choose a partner who does the same. Before making a commitment, they most likely perceive their partner realistically instead of projecting onto him or her what they want or expect. As a result, they're able to make a sensible decision about whether or not they're a good match and there are fewer surprises later. They may even know they are compatible from the moment they meet or shortly after if they're in touch with their intuition. When problems do emerge, their ability to communicate effectively helps them to confront the issues reasonably instead of reacting with anger or by ignoring them and allowing them to get worse. *Most importantly, they realize it is often what you don't do that creates harmonious relationships: no expectations, no conditions, no projecting, no controlling. They let go and love each other unconditionally.*

Compatible and harmonious love relationships are not only for a select few. Regardless of your relationship karma, you can create a compatible and harmonious love relationship now by taking the right steps.

If you are involved in a relationship, discovering and dissolving the karma between you can greatly improve your bond. Why has it always been difficult for you to trust him? Why do you fight about money, sex, children, or in-laws so much? Why do you get angry when she gets attention from others?

You can significantly improve your relationship by finding the root or past-life causes of whatever is creating the most conflict or stress, forgiving yourself and/or your partner, and then releasing those causes (see chapter 14). *Even if your partner isn't interested in improving your relationship, the work you do by yourself will greatly impact the way you react to and perceive your partner, which will change how he or she perceives and reacts to you.*

If you are single, you can greatly improve your chances of becoming involved in a harmonious relationship by discovering and dissolving your relationship blocks and paying attention to your personal relationship cycles. You'll then be able to navigate your path with awareness, much like using a good road map for a long distance trip. You'll be aware of the most appropriate times to meet compatible people, the kind of people you may be attracting at certain times, and what kind of karma you may need to deal with at certain times. It can also be helpful to determine compatibility before getting too involved with someone new. This can be done through meditation, intuition, observation, numerology, astrology, or a combination of these. *Once you realize why you're together and the lessons meant to be learned, you can approach the relationship realistically.* If you have not perceived your partner or the relationship honestly, new awareness can sometimes be a rude awakening, but it may also help you avoid potentially disastrous situations in the future.

The Role of Romance

Whether you're single or involved, you'll be more successful in your love life by realizing that most relationships begin with romantic love. Unfortunately, this stage of a relationship can be misleading. Romantic love is passion and excitement. You see the good things and ignore the bad things. Similarities, no matter how insignificant, may seem like signs that you were meant for each other. Sometimes your feelings are so strong that it's difficult to see the person as they really are. You let the little things slide and focus on how good the person makes you feel.

In our society, we're bombarded with programming from movies, TV, magazines, and books that portrays relationships to be mainly about romantic love. Religions, parents, teachers, and peers insinuate that our relationships are supposed to stay in this phase. If they don't, then someone is blamed. These beliefs program us to perceive relationships unrealistically and set us up for disappointment.

Eventually, the romance fades and couples begin to perceive each other more realistically. Depending on the expectations for the relationship and each other, this can be a difficult phase. There can be blame, control, criticism, and other fear-related actions because the partners may not feel they're getting what they wanted and thought they had. This phase can progress until eventually things get so bad that the only seemingly logical answer is breaking up. Or they will "stuff" their feelings and suffer through the relationship.

Fortunately, these negative stages can be avoided if both partners are willing to approach the relationship with awareness about themselves, each other, and their relationship through various methods of consciousness raising. With greater awareness, we can perceive relationships realistically.

There will usually be both positive and negative karma between you and every person you become involved with throughout your life. Instead of expecting a perfect relationship, consider what you're meant to learn from each other. Consider what as a couple you're meant to resolve or accomplish. Consider how you can help each other. Consider if the relationship is for the highest good for both of you.

Soul Mates

I once knew a man who was waiting for his soul mate. He was convinced this woman would fit a certain description, including hair color and style, nationality, body type, and facial features. He even believed she had a specific name. His beliefs were based on dreams he had of this woman. He refused to get seriously involved with any woman who didn't fit this description, as he felt it would be "betraying" his soul mate. He was in his late thirties, and had been waiting for this perfect match since his early 20s.

After learning more about his situation, I felt he may have known someone who fit this description in a past life, and was probably deeply in love with her during that time and perhaps during other lifetimes as well. Yes, he may meet her again in this life, but I told him she may look quite different and have a different name. And even if she really exists, he may not reunite with her during this lifetime and may miss valuable experiences by avoiding other relationships. Furthermore, I sensed he was using this as an excuse to avoid intimacy and the possibility of abandonment, both of which he seemed to fear. Nevertheless, this example brings up an important question: Is there only one person who is best for each of us?

Many of us want to find our "soul mate," a term often used to imply that there is one perfect partner for each individual. Metaphysically defined, a soul mate is simply someone you have known in a prior existence. Each person may have hundreds or even thousands of soul mates. Edgar Cayce, one of the most famous psychics in the United States, stated many times that there isn't just one person out there who is perfect for you. He expressed in his readings that there are many love relationship possibilities for each person. Dissolving relationship karma and following love life cycles will increase the odds of becoming involved with one or more of these possible soul mates.

You may have a vision of your ideal mate. It consists of many factors, including fears, fantasies, past lives, childhood experiences, current life relationships, and more. It's good to have an idea of the characteristics and qualities that work for you in a relationship and partner, but should you wait for someone who fits an ultimate vision? If you hold out until you find someone who meets your requirements exactly and whom also finds you compatible, you may be single for a long time.

When you meet a soul mate, you may feel like you know the person but you can't quite place from where. Your souls knew each other in a different time and place, although your present personalities usually don't remember the details. You feel familiar to each other. You may have been lovers, siblings, relatives, friends, acquaintances, coworkers, or even enemies. You may instantly like or even love the person, or you may instantly dislike him or her. Subconscious memories or prior events and circumstances stimulate your emotions when coming in contact with each other. Most love relationship possibilities will seem familiar. Still, it's important to choose one that is compatible and a person with whom you have good relationship karma. If our current personalities and past-life karma never interfered, we would have countless perfect love relationship possibilities!

Soul mate relationships that develop into love relationships take many different forms, depending on the karmic reasons the couple has reunited again. *The present life interaction also depends on how much of their own baggage they've worked through, how much they take responsibility for themselves and their lives, and how aware and honest they are with themselves and others.*

There is always a reason for two souls reuniting. It may be due to unfinished business, such as one owing the other in some way. It may be in the form of a project they are to complete together, such as the birth of and caring for a child. Sometimes it's a test, to see if they can interact without hurting each other.

Some souls reunite simply for the purpose of enjoying each other again and have little or no negative karma to work through. They may have earned this relationship of harmony through many lifetimes of working through their conflicts. These are the kind of relationships sometimes portrayed in romance novels. Many of us fantasize about having these kinds of relationships, where there's little conflict and an excess of love, admiration, acceptance, and respect. Few of us, unfortunately, experience them. A harmonious relationship can be created, however, provided one or both partners are willing to take the necessary steps.

Twin Souls

A twin soul has been defined as a soul who was created at the same time as you and who may be your "other half." Based on my own research (or until I become aware of information that may change my mind), I feel this definition of twin souls is the result of earthbound thinking. We don't "pair off" with only one partner in the spirit world. Pairing off here on Earth and hoping for a lifetime relationship with the same partner often seems motivated by a fear of being alone and/or a fear of abandonment.

I propose a different definition of a twin soul: a soul mate with whom you have shared many lifetimes and, through those experiences, perfected the relationship. This soul is one of the most ideal soul mates for you—assuming you both get your current personalities and hang-ups out of the way.

In his book *Edgar Cayce on Soul Mates,* Kevin J. Todeschi suggests yet another definition: "The primary distinction between soul mates and twin souls is that soul mates are brought together as a means of assisting both people in soul growth and twin souls often come together in an effort to achieve a joint task or a united work." Cayce also indicated that twin souls are not always romantically involved and that there is more than one twin soul for each person.

Are Love Relationships Predestined?

We don't know for sure. You may have felt convinced you were meant to become involved with a certain partner after it happened. Metaphysical sciences such as numerology, when approached correctly, do indicate that certain events in our lives are predestined. Even if some, most, or all of our life is predestined, we always have a choice in how to react to it. This choice is called free will. If love relationships are predestined, information within these pages will help you repair or prepare for a relationship. You'll then be able to react to circumstances in ways that are beneficial for you and your potential or current partner. If relationships are not predestined, this information will help you create a compatible and harmonious love relationship or improve an existing relationship.

Section II

Exploring Love Lives Through Regression Therapy

3
"Why am I still single?"

First of all, being single isn't a bad thing. In fact, "single phases," whether they last a few weeks or many years, are important parts of your love life cycles. They allow you to get to know yourself, reflect on the past, and decide what you want for the future. They also let you concentrate on areas of life other than relationships.

On the other hand, if you are unhappily single or unhappily involved and feel you are ready to be happily involved but just can't seem to make it happen, there may be a block between you and your goal. These blocks are caused by experiences in a past life, before birth, in the current life, or all of the above. They may have been long forgotten by the conscious mind, but *they may be still affecting you due to your subconscious mind's reactions to the fears associated with them.* You are a product of your past and carry with you skills, talents, and baggage from all of your previous existences.

What baggage are you carrying around? When any area of your life isn't working, there is always a block, or root reason. The root reason isn't that you don't have time to look for a relationship or because you gravitate towards the wrong people. The root reason always lies within you; others in your life help to mirror it back. This root reason either began in a past life, developed sometime in your current life, or is a combination of both. It's up to you to love and respect yourself enough to find and resolve the root cause of whatever isn't working in your life so you can live the happy, successful, and fulfilling life you deserve.

Relationship Roadblocks

There are as many reasons for "bad" relationships—or for not having a relationship—as there are people. Here are some of the most common recurring themes:

Not taking action: Ideal partner possibilities usually don't come knocking at your door. Fortunately, there are many different ways to meet a potential love interest (see chapter 18).

"No time": Make a list of the priorities in your life. Then make a list of how you spend your time. If you eliminate the things in your life that really aren't serving you, such as watching a lot of TV or socializing with people who don't support your highest good, you'll have plenty of time to achieve your goals, including making time for a love relationship.

Fear of rejection: We all want to be accepted, but we've all experienced dating or relationship rejection in one way or another. It's important not to take such rejection too personally when it happens. There are many reasons people are rejected that have nothing to do with them: the person rejecting you is already involved, they may not be ready for dating or a relationship, they may have misinterpreted your words or actions, they may fear rejection from you, and a thousand other reasons. Think of it this way: each time you're rejected, you'll be one step closer to your ideal partner.

Settling: Are you settling for someone who is inappropriate for you just to have a partner in your life? A relationship is doomed when it's built on neediness; settling for the wrong person leaves no room for the right person. Are you questioning whether someone is right for you? If he or she was compatible, you probably wouldn't be questioning the relationship (although expecting perfection is unrealistic). It's impossible for one person to fulfill all of our needs, but don't settle for less if you feel you're worth something more. Does this person come close? If not and you *both* want to remain together, perhaps a *mutually agreed upon* unconventional relationship would be more appropriate. There are no laws that say your relationship has to be traditional (see chapter 13).

Trying to "make it work": Are you trying to "make it work" when deep down you know it's not meant to be? If the incompatibilities of your relationship outweigh the compatibilities, you ultimately will not be happy. In this case, you have two options: You can remain together, accept what you can't change, and change within yourself what you can, or you can end the relationship. Are you accepting less than total respect or love from your partner? Know you deserve better. Do you perceive breaking up or divorce as failure? *Not all relationships are meant to last forever.* Some are short and intense, and others are longer. How long a relationship lasts is irrelevant, even though much importance is placed on permanence in our society. When you have learned as much as you can from each other without sacrificing yourselves in the process, it may be time to move on.

Do you want it to last because you're afraid to change? People grow at different rates. Expecting to be compatible with the same person for 20 to 60 years while being the best you can be is ideal, but not usually realistic. Relationships in the past were more for economic and practical reasons; couples were expected to stay together forever, no matter what. Times have changed, thankfully. Fewer people are trying to fit the old relationship mold and are following their hearts and instincts about the kind of relationship and partner that is best for them. Today, separation or divorce is more accepted. Couples now are more likely to consider whether it's best for all involved to stay together when they and their situations change, and more of them are parting on good terms. Divorce doesn't have to cause unhappiness.

Unrealistic expectations: Know what works for you in a partner, but don't automatically discount new possibilities if they don't fit every one of your requirements. Sometimes the love of our life comes in completely different packaging than we expect. Try to overlook the little things you may not like such as a hairstyle, clothing or the car they drive by realizing that if and when you develop a love relationship, the little things may change and they won't matter as much. Lonely people often aren't preparing themselves or are requiring too much in a partner. Examine your requirements and prioritize for what really matters.

Selfishness: When sizing up a potential mate, do you focus on what they can do for you? If so, remember that a love relationship isn't the same as a business arrangement. Neediness and greediness will only sabotage them. The best love relationships are those in which both partners give and accept unconditionally.

Gold-diggers: If your main reason for seeking a relationship is to be supported financially, you won't be happy in love. You're sending a message to your subconscious mind and the universe that you are needy and dependent and can't make the money you want on your own.

Superiority complex: This disposition will hurt any kind of relationship. There are many ways to express this: ignoring, rolling the eyes, sneering, a condescending or patronizing attitude, and so on. We are all equal. Respect everyone as you would like to be respected.

Guilt: Have you ever unintentionally broken someone's heart? Perhaps you ended a relationship because it was the best thing for both of you, but the other person wouldn't let go and suffered. If so, it's time to forgive yourself. You did that person a favor and you served each other perfectly.

Fear of loneliness: If you fear being alone, you'll eventually have to deal with it. Discover the cause and release it or it will interfere with every relationship you have.

Dependency: Do you feel you need another person to make you happy? This is dependency. Don't look for your "other half"; you're already a whole person, whether you've realized it yet or not. Two half people create a dysfunctional mess. Two people who are happy with themselves and their lives, who have worked on their "issues" and are truly ready to share their life with the right person, naturally attract and create a healthy relationship.

Weak foundation: Use your time alone or in between relationships to heal and work on yourself. Learn to enjoy spending time with just you. Treat yourself with the love and respect that you would a partner. It's easier to build a healthy relationship when the foundations of both people are solid.

Desperation: Maybe you'll meet that special someone at the meeting today or at the club tonight or at the store tomorrow, but the harder you look the worse you'll feel. Each time you do meet someone, your eagerness (even though you mask it well) will either scare the person away or blind you to obvious and not-so-obvious incompatibilities. An important part of meeting the right person is giving up searching for Mr. or Ms. Right. Set yourself free by letting go of your neediness and desperation, prepare yourself for the relationship you want, and it will happen at the right time.

Lack of self-worth, self-love, self-esteem, and self-respect: If you keep attracting people who have been harmful to you, you need to love and respect yourself more so you can attract someone who will do the same. In short, you attract what you project. If you were abused as a child, you'll have a difficult time attracting and maintaining a healthy relationship until you've confronted and healed the damage that was done. Love yourself enough to heal the past and move on.

Taking action at the wrong time/ignoring your intuition: Just as the Earth has seasons, our lives follow cycles. Trying to force dating or a relationship when solitude and reflection are more appropriate will only cause conflict and stress. For more information about how to discover and follow your relationship cycles, see chapter 17. Also, pay attention to your intuition and you'll always do what's best for you. *Intuition can be severely clouded by foods that you are allergic or sensitive to (often the ones you crave) and drugs (including caffeine, nicotine and prescription drugs). Any substance that alters your mood will interfere with your perception, intuition and awareness.* Meditation can help you be more aware and stay open to guidance (see Chapter 14).

Not open to trusting others: Trusting yourself and others is essential for love and happiness. If trust is a problem in your life, identify the causes and take steps to overcome them. When you trust yourself you are better able to attract those who are trustworthy while recognizing those who aren't.

Trying to fill a void: Lonely, bored, tired of being by yourself, tired of waking up alone, tired of feeling empty inside? "If I only had a partner," you say to yourself, "everything would improve." Meanwhile, you fill the void with work, food, alcohol, drugs, or meaningless sex. The temporary fix fades quickly and leaves you feeling even emptier inside. Find out why you feel empty in the first place and take action to be complete on your own. Only when you feel complete by yourself will you have the foundation that is necessary for a compatible love relationship.

Fear of interference: How would your life change if you suddenly fell in love? Could your goals be so important to you that you have made a forgotten pact with yourself to never let anything or anyone interfere with them? Examine your fears and consider whether they are realistic. Consider the positive effects of an ideal relationship. There is always room in your life for the right relationship, one that would positively influence other areas of your life. The right loving relationship could actually help you become even more successful.

Fear of change: There is always a reason we resist change. Sometimes self-sabotage is our subconscious mind's way of resisting change. A change for the better is inevitable if you take the proper steps. Examine your fears and consider whether they are realistic. Resolution may be as simple as making it okay with yourself to move on and create a healthier and happier life. Or there may be hidden blocks in your subconscious mind. If you had what you wanted, would your life change in undesirable ways? Asking yourself in or out of meditation why you're resisting change is one way of discovering the cause. Going back to the cause of any hard-to-break habits and then releasing that cause through regression therapy or meditation can often make changing easier and in some cases effortless. Uncovering and releasing these blocks will set you free.

Fear of restriction: Some people subconsciously associate a monogamous, long-term relationship with a prison sentence. Relationships don't have to be stifling. Retaining your sense of individuality within a relationship can actually enhance a union.

False beliefs: "Relationships are hard work and they always result in a lot of pain." Consciously, you may not think this is true. However, if your parents had an unhappy relationship or if you have experienced a difficult one, you may subconsciously believe it to be true. You may be blocking a relationship due to past negative experiences that you don't consciously realize are still affecting you (see chapter 14).

Blaming: Were you hurt by a parent or a partner? Do yourself a favor: forgive and release this person and everyone else who has ever hurt you. Until you do so, you'll remain trapped. Forgiveness isn't about letting the person who hurt you off the hook. It is about releasing the anger and resentment that you harbor within so you can get on with your life.

Hanging on: Is there someone from your past that you're still obsessed with or in love with? Release the desire to be with that person. If it's meant to be, they will come back into your life when the time is right. Manipulating someone to be in your life will hurt you and them in the end.

Negativity: When meeting new people, positive first impressions will open doors for more possibilities; negative ones will close them. You can't control how another person responds to you, but you can control how you react.

Misperception of love: A healthy relationship stems from unconditional love, which is love given without any restrictions, given without any thought of benefit or reward. Although romance enhances a relationship at first, it's only an illusion. Romantic love is conditional love: "If you do this/say this, then I will love you." Controlling a loved one isn't love but possessiveness. Love is open, not closed.

Misperception of romance: In the beginning of a relationship, the romance and chemistry are exciting and intense. During this first stage of a relationship, it's easy to ignore danger signs. When the chemistry fades, what was overlooked becomes more obvious. Realize that chemistry can cloud perception. It's important to be realistic when getting to know someone. Evaluate the situation by the person's actions instead of their words.

Sex: This is an important part of a love relationship. Yet when a relationship is based on sex from the beginning, it may be more difficult for partners to perceive each other as they really are. That chemistry can distort perceptions and fuel illusions of what they want each other to be like. When a couple becomes physically intimate too soon, the relationship tends to center on the physical attraction rather than the friendship, because friendships take time. When the chemistry fades, there is no foundation remaining to support the relationship. When sex is introduced later, after spending non-sexual time together, the relationship may develop to be more solid.

Feelings of obligation: Do you feel obligated to your parents, peers, or society to be involved with someone? If being single in our society was more accepted and there were fewer pressures to be married, would you still want to be married or involved in a relationship? Decide what is best for you and let go of others' expectations. Its your life, so choose to experience a relationship on your terms and only when you are truly ready to share yourself with someone.

Outside resistance: As you begin to change and transform by dissolving whatever isn't working in your life, others may feel threatened because of their own unwillingness to change and will resist the new you. Try not to take it personally; they are doing the best they can. Just accept them as they are and, if necessary, let them go with love and compassion. You have served each other perfectly. You may have even planted a seed for them and someday they'll also decide to work on themselves. Conversely, as you become the best you can be, you'll draw new people into your life who are also being the best they can be, working toward their goals and following their dreams. Like attracts like.

"Why Am I Still Single?"

Most of us want to be involved in a compatible love relationship, but too often for reasons unknown to us we are either unhappily single or unhappily involved. Here are several examples of people who fit this description, and how past-life regression therapy turned their love life around.

NAME: Cecilia **SEX:** Female **AGE:** 39

DILEMMA: "I'm turning 40 in six months. I've never been in love and my love life is non-existent. It's depressing."

RELATIONSHIP HISTORY: Two-year relationship in her 20s which ended abruptly when her partner left her for someone else. She has been casually dating a man for three years, though it's more a like a friendship. There's not much chemistry or romantic attraction there for her. She says she isn't in love with him but hasn't told him this.

ASSETS: Caring, compassionate, intelligent, good communicator.

LIABILITIES: Poor diet, no exercise, not enough sleep, spends too much time at a job she doesn't enjoy, settles for and spends too much time with someone she isn't in love with instead of investing the time in herself to prepare for a compatible love relationship. Some may think that her lack of relationship experience is a liability. I have found this often to be irrelevant and sometimes an asset since many carry baggage from each relationship. What's more important is knowing yourself and developing effective communication skills. Furthermore, many mistakenly feel that a history of long-term relationships is an asset. *This may show stability, but it also may show fear of change, fear of being alone, or dependency issues.*

NOTES: Cecilia says that she has no time to look for a partner. She is shy and doesn't enjoy the singles scenes. She admits that she doesn't feel attractive and does little to look her best.

SESSIONS: Perceived a past life as a beautiful woman in the French Court. Men threw themselves at her, but she treated them poorly and abused the power gained from her looks. As a result, she feels subconscious guilt about her actions and has a subconscious fear of looking too pretty, which could encourage her to repeat her mistakes. I helped her dissolve the guilt through a forgiveness exercise and helped her make it okay with herself to look her best. During the session she also recalled experiences of rejection in her current life during high school. None of the boys she was interested in returned that interest so she rarely dated. She realized that her French Court lifetime experiences had set the stage for the rejection then and for the relationship betrayal in her 20s. I helped her forgive the man who left her, release the fear of abandonment, and move forward by seeing herself as a lovable, desirable, and worthwhile person. Lastly, I directed her to perceive a happy lifetime in which she was involved in a compatible relationship based on mutual trust, respect, and love. This was to remind Cecilia what a healthy relationship feels like. Her memories of this feeling and the visualization from the Love Life guided meditation recording (see chapter 14) would then be used to bring her closer to her goal.

RECOMMENDATIONS: Listen to Love Life guided meditation recording every night for at least six weeks for conscious and subconscious encouragement and reinforcement. Follow as many of the health recommendations from chapter 19 as feel right; listen to your intuition, not your inner critic, as the suggestions you resist may be the best ones for you. Spend more time on appearance, wardrobe, and exercise. Looking your best will make you more appealing to those to whom you are attracted. Find a more enjoyable job. Spend less time on current dating situation. Tell current partner you don't love him in case he doesn't realize this so he'll be free to find someone who does. When you feel ready, consider exploring options for meeting compatible partners. Pay attention to your love cycles (see chapter 17).

ACTION: Cecilia realized that since her love life was now a priority, she could make time for it and, more importantly, make time to invest in herself. She began exercising (yoga and walking) and eating healthier, and shed 20 pounds. She updated her hairstyle, make-up, and clothing and changed jobs, which gave her more free time and less stress. She stopped dating the man she didn't love, although they remained friends. Cecilia said she had considered making some of these changes in the past. She just never felt compelled to make an effort. *After the regression, she felt like a "weight" had been lifted off her and found it much easier to follow through with changes that would help her reach her goal of a compatible partner.*

RESULTS: The positive changes created a much more confident Cecelia. Now she feels like her life is falling into place and that she is "living on purpose" instead of just going through the motions. She joined a social group and a few months later, to her pleasant surprise, became involved with a man with whom she shares compatibility and chemistry.

NAME: Erin **SEX:** Female **AGE:** 42

DILEMMA: "I never meet anyone who even comes close to being right for me."

RELATIONSHIP HISTORY: Married at 23, divorced at 29. Married at 32, divorced at 36. Has dated occasionally during the last six years. None of the situations lasted longer than a few months.

ASSETS: Wealthy from two lucrative divorce settlements. In-shape from daily exercise. Makes the most of her appearance.

LIABILITIES: Abrasive personality, overly confident, has a superior attitude involving her wealth. Because she's financially well off, she'll only consider men who have more money than she does. After experiencing two husbands who were 20 and 23 years older than her, she will only date men who are her age or younger.

NOTES: I was upfront with Erin and told her that she isn't going to be happily involved with a compatible partner until she makes a conscious effort to become a nicer person. At first she took offense to my suggestion, but after the session she thanked me for being honest.

SESSIONS: I first helped Erin's heal her childhood abuse by guiding her through an exercise to forgive her father and grandfather for emotional and sexual abuse. Her father also had used his money to manipulate and control her, which she still resented. She had been through traditional counseling for the abuse, but had not completely understood the importance of forgiveness and how much the resentment was still affecting her. For the first time she was able to express forgiveness towards her father and grandfather. In past-life regression, Erin perceived herself as a woman in London during the early 1800s. She was deeply in love with her wealthy husband and seemed to have an ideal marriage until he left her for another woman. Since she was "beyond marrying age" and was left penniless, she was forced to find work as a maid. She deeply resented her ex-husband and the wealthy family she worked for who treated her poorly. She eventually died in her 50s, angry with everyone for her circumstances. I helped her forgive and release the man who left her (one of her ex-husbands in her present life) and the wealthy man she had worked for. In a Higher Self state, Erin broke down when she realized how her heart was still closed and how the importance of money had become magnified from those experiences. I helped her realize that she'll always have enough money and gave her suggestions to help her live in love instead of in fear. I then directed her to perceive a happy lifetime in which she was a loving and compassionate person, yet poor. I wanted to remind her that everyone is equal, no matter what their economic situation. She perceived a lifetime in Peru as a mother of five. They had no money and little food. Judging from her tears of joy and the way her face softened, they were a loving family that cared deeply for one another. Remembering this lifetime helped to cultivate a more caring Erin. Her abrasive nature seemed rooted in part from being hurt so much in her younger years and in the past life she perceived. Lastly, I directed her to perceive a happy lifetime in which she was involved in a compatible relationship based on trust, respect, and love. This was to remind Erin what it feels like to be involved in a healthy, loving relationship.

RECOMMENDATIONS: Do more forgiveness meditations to release everyone who has ever hurt you. Open up your age range and be less rigid with the money requirement. Listen to the Love Life recording every night for at least six weeks to help prepare you to be in the right state of mind for a compatible partner and to pay attention to your love cycles when meeting someone new.

ACTION: During Erin's follow up sessions, I noticed she seemed much more at peace, more relaxed, and even somewhat happy! She followed my advice and practiced the forgiveness meditation whenever she made time for it, usually a few times a week. She said she didn't realize how many people she was angry with. Erin said she felt she needed a break from dating for a while to get to know herself.

RESULTS: I spoke with Erin about two months after her last session. She said she still wasn't dating but felt good about her decision. She was reading many self-help/metaphysical books and had recently begun some charity work. I know Erin will be ready for the right relationship at the right time since she is making an effort to prepare. Defrosting her heart through regression therapy clearly changed her life.

NAME: Jon **SEX:** Male **AGE:** 48

DILEMMA: "I don't love my boyfriend but I can't leave him. I feel trapped."

RELATIONSHIP HISTORY: Current nine-year relationship. Seven-year relationship before that, five-year relationship before that, and a two-month break at the most in between each one.

ASSETS: Approachable, friendly, financially well off, attractive.

LIABILITIES: Doesn't like being alone. Feels his personal happiness is dependent on a relationship.

NOTES: This person isn't single. His case represents the common mistake of staying with a partner whom one doesn't love. This blocks the potential of forming a compatible, loving relationship with someone more appropriate.

SESSIONS: Through past-life regression Jon perceived himself as a female living in Switzerland in the 1700s. Her parents were strict, overprotective, and wouldn't allow her to marry. She had no friends and lived a lonely life until she died of an illness in her 40s. In another life, Jon perceived himself as a man who wasn't attracted to women, so he never married. Rather than dealing with his sexual orientation, he suppressed it. From the experiences of those two lifetimes, Jon subconsciously associates being alone with unhappiness, so in his current life he will do anything to avoid that. I helped Jon realize that he never really is alone and gave him suggestions to begin turning inward for his happiness. Next, Jon perceived himself in Spain during the early 1800s. He was a married male who had an affair. His wife found out and committed suicide (his wife then is his current boyfriend). Therefore, he feels terrible guilt when he even thinks of leaving his current partner. In a higher state, I led Jon through a forgiveness exercise and helped him to reconsider his current relationship and what was really best for him and his boyfriend. I gave Jon further suggestions while he was still in a meditative state that he would be able to communicate compassionately, honestly, and effectively with his partner about their relationship during the coming days and weeks.

RECOMMENDATIONS: Get to know yourself through daily meditation. Learn to enjoy spending time alone, perhaps through new or existing hobbies. The more you learn to enjoy your own company the better prepared you'll be for the right relationship. Talk to your partner and tell him how you feel. Pay attention to your love cycles when meeting someone new.

ACTION: Jon told his partner he didn't love him. His partner already knew. Jon began regular meditation.

RESULTS: Jon and his partner separated amicably. Jon resisted the urge to begin looking right away for another partner and instead traveled alone to Europe. He said the first couple of weeks were difficult. He eventually began to enjoy spending time alone, especially when he meditated daily, which helped him rise above any anxiety or loneliness.

NAME: Melissa **SEX:** Female **AGE:** 26

DILEMMA: "None of my relationships ever develop into anything." "Guys always treat me poorly."

RELATIONSHIP HISTORY: Several one- or two-month relationships.

ASSETS: Sweet-natured and considerate.

LIABILITIES: Overweight, lack of self-love, tries too hard, comes across as desperate.

NOTES: Melissa spends a lot of time going out to clubs hoping to meet the "right one."

SESSIONS: Discovered through questioning that Melissa's father never paid much attention to her or spent time with her. I led Melissa through a meditation that allowed her to tell her father how she felt and receive feedback from him. This triggered a big emotional release. She realized he just doesn't know how to express love and that, deep down, he really does love her. After realizing this, Melissa no longer felt the void she previously had felt. In past-life regression, she perceived herself as a female in New England during the late 1700s. Her anxiety and depression worsened as she grew older as she was never "taken" as a wife by any of the local men. She spent her life alone and unhappy. In the second life Melissa perceived, she was an accomplished concert violinist who took her work seriously. So seriously, in fact, that she had no time to date or form relationships. In addition, her rigid and demanding demeanor alienated anyone who tried to get close. Eventually she retired, but by then was "too old to marry," so she spent her remaining days unhappily alone. I helped Melissa release the fear of being alone from those two lifetimes. I also gave Melissa suggestions during her guided meditation session to begin looking inward through meditation for happiness and to stop spinning her wheels by seeking validation from others. Lastly, I directed her to perceive a happy lifetime in which she was involved in a healthy, compatible relationship based on trust, respect, and love.

RECOMMENDATIONS: Exercise and change diet. Follow as many of the chapter 19 health hints as feel right: listen to your intuition, not your inner critic, as the suggestions you resist the most may be the best for you. Respect yourself at all times. Expect respect from potential partners and reject men who give you anything less. Do special things for yourself to cultivate self-love: treat yourself as you would treat someone you are deeply in love with. An important part of meeting the right person is giving up searching for Mr. Right. Instead, know that you would like to have a compatible partner but stop hoping to meet that person every place you go. Set yourself free by letting go of your neediness and desperation. Prepare yourself for the relationship you want, and it will happen when the time is right. Pay attention to your love cycles.

ACTION: Melissa came back for two follow-up sessions to help shed her excess weight, and she began exercising. She told her father that she loved him and was happy to hear back the same.

RESULTS: Spoke to Melissa six months later and she had shed 30 pounds. She was enjoying the process of casually dating and getting to know several different men, but wasn't in any rush to settle down.

NAME: Jared **SEX:** Male **AGE:** 37

DILEMMA: "All the women I date turn out to be totally wrong for me." "I don't have time to look for a partner."

RELATIONSHIP HISTORY: Three-year relationship in college, two-year relationship in late 20s, three-year relationship in early 30s, just ended a one-year relationship.

ASSETS: Motivated, assertive, dynamic personality, in shape, attractive.

LIABILITIES: Workaholic. Perceives relationships as draining, requiring too much effort, and usually resulting in someone getting hurt.

NOTES: After speaking with Jared, I felt that he subconsciously developed relationships that wouldn't last. For some reason (to be discovered in past-life regression), he didn't really want one.

SESSIONS: In regression, Jared perceived himself as a young, attractive male in Italy during the early 1900s; many women competed for his attention. At the age of 16, he got a girl pregnant and was forced to drop out of medical school and work full time to support the girl and baby. He didn't love her. As a result of their religious upbringing and culture, they married and later had seven more children. He eventually found out that the girl got pregnant on purpose. She wanted to marry him, even though she knew he didn't want the same. Since divorce was unheard of, there wasn't much he could do and was never able to return to medical school. He spent the rest of his life working long, hard hours in an unfulfilling job to support his large family until dying of a heart attack in his late 40s.

In this life, Jared is subconsciously terrified that the responsibilities of marriage and children will interfere with his career and success. I helped Jared forgive and release his Italian partner and those experiences and then affirm that the right loving relationship could actually help him be even more successful. Next, Jared perceived himself as an artist in Russia during the mid-1500s. He was involved in a deeply satisfying love relationship and they were happy together until she died of an illness. He was devastated and never recovered. *As a result of that experience, Jared subconsciously believes that love relationships will always result in a lot of pain.* Jared lost his mother to cancer when he was 13, which further enforced this belief. I helped Jared release these experiences and, while in a higher state, realize that he was meant to experience the loss of a loved one for his growth. He realized during the session that love is forever and never dies, even if the person is no longer physically present. Lastly, I directed Jared to perceive a happy lifetime in which he was involved in a compatible relationship based on trust, respect, and love while he also had a fulfilling career. This was to remind Jared what it feels like to be in love and that you can have both a successful career and a successful love life. His memories of this feeling would then be used to help bridge the gap to his goal through visualization with the Love Life guided meditation recording.

RECOMMENDATIONS: Listen to Love Life recording every night for at least six weeks. I reminded Jared that relationships don't need to be stressful or result in unhappiness if one is realistic, honest, and communicates effectively. Decide what works best for you in a partner and a relationship and write a list of desired qualities in a partner (see chapter 15). Make a list of how you spend every moment of your day/week. Consider what could be streamlined, changed, or eliminated to make more time for a compatible love relationship. Consider how you might actually have more time with the right partner (sharing chores and other responsibilities if living together, no more time spent on fruitless dating, and so on). Make time for *quality* dating rather than *quantity* dating. Pay attention to your love cycles when meeting someone new.

ACTION: Reevaluated and then reorganized how he was spending his time. Decided what would and wouldn't work for him in a partner and began paying more attention to how compatible someone was before he became too involved.

RESULTS: Jared reviewed the qualities he wanted in a partner and used his list to create a well-written on-line personal ad with a good picture of himself. He carefully weeded out incompatible matches and occasionally met a possibility for coffee. Eventually Jared met Allison, and since he had set aside time for quality dating, he was able to enjoy his time with her. The last time I spoke with Jared he explained that he and Allison were seeing each other exclusively and were considering marriage. For the first time in his life, he could actually see himself being happily married.

NAME: Clara **SEX:** Female **AGE:** 52

DILEMMA: "I haven't dated in years." "I feel blocked."

RELATIONSHIP HISTORY: Husband of 25 years left her for another woman.

ASSETS: Stable career and finances, well dressed.

LIABILITIES: Negative and angry. Hanging on to past relationship. Overweight.

NOTES: Clara blames her ex-husband for her unhappiness. She resents the fact that their marriage "failed" and condemns him for "not respecting his commitment."

SESSIONS: In past-life regression, Clara perceived herself as a married male in England during the 1600s. He loved his wife but had frequent affairs. He eventually fell in love with another woman and left his wife for her. When Clara discovered that her spouse in that life was her current ex-husband, it suddenly made sense why she was so upset; she felt subconscious guilt for her past-life affair and for breaking up the marriage. Blaming her ex-husband was easier than taking responsibility for her situation. I helped Clara forgive herself and her ex-husband. Clara realized from a higher perspective that her relationship with her ex-husband was destined to end and that losing him to another woman was karmic. Instead of concentrating on what she lost, I helped Clara perceive the opportunity she now has: freedom to create a compatible love relationship with someone more appropriate. I also helped Clara release the bond with her ex-husband and to accept the outcome of her marriage.

RECOMMENDATIONS: Listen to Love Life recording every day for at least six weeks. Daily meditation and other forgiveness exercises in chapter 14. Exercise and change diet to look and feel better. Realize that caffeine can stimulate aggression and anger, sugar (all forms) can promote depression (especially if you are sensitive to it), and alcohol can cause both. Pay attention to your love cycles when meeting someone new.

ACTION: Clara began walking several times a week, eating less of the foods that didn't work for her and more of the foods that did, and meditating.

RESULTS: Clara now has a much more peaceful disposition. She met a man through friends whom she enjoys spending time with.

NAME: Lee **SEX:** Female **AGE:** 31

DILEMMA: "My relationships always start off intensely but never last."

RELATIONSHIP HISTORY: Many one- to six-month relationships
ASSETS: Fit, motivated in career

LIABILITIES: Misperception of love and romance. Often bases relationships on sex.

NOTES: Lee expects love relationships to be all passion and romance. When the sexual chemistry fades, she loses interest.

SESSIONS: In past-life regression, Lee perceived herself as a woman who worked in a saloon during the mid 1800s in the western United States. She had a tough and abrasive personality and wasn't shy about "bedding" many men. A love relationship was "not her style." I helped Lee rise above and let go of those memories and confirm that this approach to love doesn't work in our current society. Next, Lee perceived herself as the daughter of a monarch in Europe during the 1300s. She lived a pampered, privileged, and happy existence and had a long-term storybook romance with a compatible man. Lee realized that this relationship was a reward, the result of many lifetimes dissolving the conflicts between her and this man. Her subconscious mind still compared current relationships to this experience, which created unrealistic expectations that none of her current life relationships could live up to. I instructed Lee to focus on and remember the deep feelings of love she felt with this man. I also reminded her that no relationship is perfect, each one is different, and to accept potential partners as they are instead of how she wants them to be.

RECOMMENDATIONS: Write a list of qualities you want in a partner. Become friends with potential partners first, wait to have sex until you know each other well, and then decide if it's meant to go further. Pay attention to your love cycles when meeting someone new.

ACTION: Lee chose to take a break from dating. She said she was glad to release the need to fill her life with extreme "roller coaster ride" relationships.

RESULTS: Eventually a friendship with a coworker developed into a love relationship.

NAME: Jerry **SEX:** Male **AGE:** 35

DILEMMA: "I think I should be in a relationship but I don't really want one."

RELATIONSHIP HISTORY: Married high school sweetheart at 18, divorced at 27.

ASSETS: Compassionate, insightful, intelligent, good communicator

LIABILITIES: Spends most of his time alone, no social life.

NOTES: The above are listed as liabilities, and for someone who wants to meet potential partners, they would be. Jerry, on the other hand, doesn't perceive them as liabilities. He enjoys spending his time alone reading, researching, and writing. However, he wanted to make sure that nothing was blocking him from wanting a love relationship.

SESSIONS: Instead of accessing past lives, Jerry contacted and communicated with his Higher Self. He realized that he is meant to be alone now to get in touch with his inner guidance and complete a project he is working on. He will be more interested in a love relationship when the time is right. Until then, he is on the right path.

RECOMMENDATIONS: Continue on your path, meditate daily for guidance.

ACTION: Jerry continued meditating daily.

RESULTS: Jerry was happy about the confirmation and messages he received and felt even more motivated about his work.

4
Love or Lust at First Sight?

Fantasy love is much better than reality love. Never doing it is very exciting. The most exciting attractions are between two opposites that never meet.
— Andy Warhol (1928–1987)

Love at first sight. Or is it lust? Strangers lock eyes across a room. One or both feel an intense attraction and a strange familiarity. If one takes the initiative, they may talk and even exchange telephone numbers. If the feelings are mutual, they may date or develop a relationship. Whether the initial feelings were from a past-life love relationship, physical attraction, the projecting of desires and fantasies, or a combination of them all, the feelings were strong enough to cause them to want to explore the attraction further.

Sometimes love at first sight can't be validated; that perfect person steps onto a bus and disappears into the night, with nothing said or done, leaving the potential partners wondering what the relationship could have been like.

When you fall instantly for someone, how do you know if it's love at first sight, sexual attraction, an attempt by you to fill an emotional void, the fact that this person simply reminds you of someone else, or a combination of these? Sometimes we are so caught up in our feelings that we can't perceive the situation clearly.

The next time someone captures your interest, pay attention and you may be able to perceive the situation more realistically. What first caught your attention? What kept your attention? What were your first thoughts about him or her? On first sight, did you feel love, lust, relief, or all of the above? What thoughts were going through your mind? It is also important to examine how you were feeling during the weeks and months before the encounter. Had you been lonely or was a relationship the last thing on your mind? Were you on the rebound, or are you truly ready for another relationship? Being honest with yourself at all times will help you avoid disappointment and heartbreak.

One way to discover the potentials and pitfalls within a specific relationship is by becoming aware of the karma involved through past-life regression. Is this potential relationship for the highest good of you both? Find out by using the "Gain Awareness about a Potential/Existing Partnership" meditation in chapter 14.

As enticing as "love at first sight" can be, sometimes it isn't explored due to the circumstances. This was the case with Mandy, an attractive artist in her late 20s. She and her husband had recently moved to a new area. They had been happily married for four years. He worked different hours than she, so she joined a gym to stay in shape and kill time in the early evenings. One day, as she was walking past the glass-enclosed racquetball courts, she happened to lock eyes with a man playing on the court. She said she instantly felt connected to him and couldn't turn her eyes away. At first, she thought she knew him from somewhere, then realized that she didn't. Still, she had this overwhelming desire to talk to him and touch him. She knew that she had to maintain control. She was a happily married woman and intended to stay that way.

Mandy continued to occasionally see the man at the gym but usually made an effort to avoid eye contact. She found herself thinking of him during the day and frequently dreamed about him. Often while at the gym, she could feel him looking at her and she found it difficult to ignore her desire to approach and talk to him. She knew that if she did, it would lead to something they would both regret; she noticed he wore a wedding ring, too.

Finally, after about six months of this, Mandy felt she had to do something. A friend of hers who had used my services suggested she try past-life regression. She didn't know much about it, but at this point she was willing to try anything.

"I have to admit I feel pretty foolish about this whole thing," Mandy said to me at the beginning of her first session. "I'm not the type of person who develops obsessions with other men. This has never happened to me before. I just don't understand it. The more I resist the more I'm drawn to this person I don't even know."

"Considering my work with clients and their past lives, it doesn't sound foolish to me," I assured her. "In fact, I think it's quite common. From what you've told me so far, you may have a past-life connection with this man. We'll work together and find out."

"Do you really think that I may have known him in a past life?" Mandy seemed skeptical.

"It's a possibility. Even if we haven't lived past lives, the techniques I use will enable you to become more aware of the situation and release it, if you choose to."

I asked Mandy if she sensed that the man is attracted to her. "Oh, I know he is. At first I thought I was just imagining it, but after a while I knew it wasn't my imagination. He always tries to make eye contact with me. About a month ago, my husband and I were having dinner at a restaurant when in walked the man and a woman I assumed was his wife. When he walked past our table, we again locked eyes and at that moment I was certain he felt the same. I could feel the sadness he felt for not being able to pursue our seemingly unexplainable bond."

I then asked Mandy if she had discussed this with her husband. "No, I've said nothing of the man or of my consulting you. I usually tell my husband everything, but I just can't bring myself to tell him this." She paused. "Ever since we got married I've been afraid that something will come between my husband and I, especially something like this."

"Where do you think this fear comes from?" I asked.

"Well, my father left my mother for another woman when I was six years old. After I saw how unhappy my mother was, I promised myself that I would never let that happen to me. Marriage and monogamy are very important to me."

"How is your relationship with your father now?"

"Better than it used to be. I think I still have a lot of resentment towards him for leaving my mother. I don't discuss things I know he wouldn't want to hear about because I'm afraid he'll cut me off. He has a lot of money and helps me out financially. If he didn't, my husband and I wouldn't have been able to buy the house we did."

"So the house is more important than telling your father how you really feel?" I asked gently.

Mandy laughed. "Right now it is. I do plan to tell my father how I feel eventually. It's not time yet. Right now I just want to concentrate on my marriage." Mandy paused and seemed to suddenly be on the verge of tears. "This isn't supposed to happen! Marriage is supposed to be forever. I want to happily grow old with my husband. The crazy part is that I haven't even done anything wrong! But the emotions I feel about that man worry me. I shouldn't be feeling that way. Do you think I'm betraying my husband?"

"No, of course not," I responded. "Attraction to another is natural. Getting married doesn't make that suddenly disappear, and suppressing attraction will only intensify it. You've done nothing to violate your commitment and you're making an effort to maintain it. Are you ready to get started?" Mandy agreed so I explained more about the process of guided meditation and regression and answered her questions. When she seemed comfortable with all I had discussed, I led her through a relaxation meditation and into a regression. She was able to perceive images immediately so I began asking her questions.

Mandy saw herself as a 19-year-old female named Mary living in England in 1622. I asked about her love life and she told me about an unfulfilling marriage to a wealthy landowner. Despite having servants and living a life of leisure, she wasn't in love with her husband and was quite bored. I guided Mandy to move forward to an important event in that lifetime:

Therapist: What's happening?
Mandy: I'm watching him ride by on his horse and smiling at him.
Th: Who is it?
M: I think he's one of the king's men. I've seen him ride by often. He always looks at me. I like him.
Th: Move forward to an important event with this man.
M: (nervous) He shouldn't be doing this.
Th: What's he doing?
M: He stopped to talk with me. He is so handsome.

Through further questioning, I learn that he rode by often and he would stop and talk whenever her husband wasn't around. Her husband became aware of him, sensed her feelings towards the man, and warned her not to talk with him. Eventually she and the man ran off together, but her husband and his men found them soon after.

Th: What's happening now?
M: (crying softly) My husband stabbed him with a sword!
Th: Okay, rise above the emotion; view it all as an observer on the count of three. One, two, three. What's happening now?
M: (crying softly) My husband is telling me that I disgraced him and that I don't deserve to live.
Th: Move forward until something happens. One, two, three.
M: (pause) They stabbed me.

She died instantly so I led her through the death experience and into a Higher Self perspective. I began asking her overview questions about that lifetime:

Th: Why did you choose, on a soul level, to experience that lifetime?
M: To learn about commitment. I married for the wrong reasons then and didn't take my marriage seriously. I acted out of fear by marrying my husband for money instead of marrying someone for love.
Th: Do you know the man on the horse in your current lifetime?
M: Yes, it's the man at the gym.
Th: Do you know the man in your current life who was your husband then?
M: Yes, it's my father.
Th: What do you feel towards him at this time?
M: Even though I betrayed him during that time, I feel a lot of anger and resentment.
Th: Are you ready to let go of that?
M: (pause) I'm not sure if I can.
Th: It's important to realize that forgiveness is mainly for yourself. When you forgive someone, you're not letting him or her off the hook. They will eventually have to deal with their actions through the law of karma. Forgiving someone allows you to release the emotion within you which releases the negative symptoms caused by

that emotion. Are you ready to release those negative emotions within you?
M: Yes.

I led Mandy through a forgive and release exercise, brought her back to the post-death light, and then continued to question her:

Th: What else do you need to be aware of about the soul who is your father in this life?
M: (pause) I need to see him as a teacher instead of a bad person (pause). He is only a reflection of me—who I was and who I am, and he has helped me to learn my lessons.
Th: Was your current husband with you in the lifetime we just explored?
M: (pause) Yes, he was my brother in that life. We had a good relationship.
Th: Why have you encountered the man at the gym again?
M: To test my commitment to my marriage and to my husband.
Th: Who is testing you?
M: I am testing myself. I chose to experience it.
Th: What can you do about the man at the gym?
M: Now that I realize why I was so drawn to him, I can focus on why instead of my attraction to him (pause). I accept that he and I are not meant to be together at this time.
Th: What else can you learn about that life or your current life that will help you at this time?
M: (long pause) I realize that in that life it wouldn't have been wise to tell my husband that I didn't love him or of my attraction to the other man. In this life my marriage is based on love, so discussing things like this with my husband, if done with love and compassion, could actually reinforce our marriage. It's better to be honest and up-front, especially about sensitive issues such as this, rather than allow issues to worsen and come between us.

I concluded the regression and brought Mandy back to the present:

M: That sure explains not only my odd obsession with that man at the gym, but my anger towards my father.

Th: From what you perceived, how do you feel about commitment now?

M: (pause) Well, if that past life really happened, it's obvious why commitment has been so important to me. I still would like my bond with my husband to last forever. From what I saw, I think I have less fear about it now. If reincarnation is true, I suppose love does last forever whether you are physically together or not.

I gave Mandy meditations to help her continue to forgive and release the past on her own (see chapter 14).

Mandy reported a few weeks later that although she still saw the man at the gym occasionally, the bond between them no longer bothered her. She accepted it and allowed herself to rise above it. She also shared all of this with her husband. She said at first she was worried he would get angry or think she was "out of her mind" for exploring past-life regression. However, to her surprise, he actually appreciated her honesty and was open to what she had to say. Mandy feels her experience brought her and her husband closer together.

How Does This Relate To You?

- Have you ever been madly attracted to a stranger? There could be many explanations as to why. One reason may be that you have a past-life connection with this person. Mandy wasn't able to figure out her connection to the man on her own because past lives weren't part of her belief system. Even though her present life personality had not really believed in reincarnation, her soul may have experienced otherwise.
- You are far more than just your body and personality. Your subconscious mind has memories of everything that has ever happened to you in this life and in prior existences. As Mandy realized, these memories are constantly influencing how we react to events now, both positively and negatively.
- An understanding of the concepts of reincarnation and karma can, when practiced, allow you to live your life based more on love and less on fear. This understanding helped Mandy rise above her fears, which in turn improved her marriage and her self-esteem.

5
"Why do I keep attracting negative relationships?"

Deena, a 28-year-old office manager, came to me for help with relationship problems and abuse issues. The four relationships she had had during the last eight years were all difficult: two of the men were alcoholics, one she had to get a restraining order against, and one was mentally abusive and had several affairs. She felt that the mental and sexual abuse she endured from her father throughout her childhood and teen years had contributed to her negative relationship experiences. She wanted me to help her release the anger she felt toward her father and find out why she was experiencing such negative relationships.

Deena said she had memories of her father entering her bedroom late at night and sexually abusing her. She asked me to regress her to the occurrences of abuse in this life to help her uncover the details she felt she had blocked out. I told her current-life regression for sexual abuse is a controversial issue: Some feel this therapy can create false memories, or that if not used correctly can do more damage than good. For example, if a therapist gave a client a leading suggestion, such as, "Go back to a time in your childhood when you were sexually abused by your father," the client may respond to the assumption of abuse in that statement by creating situations in his or her mind that didn't really happen. *Alternatively, the option of past-life regression and root cause therapy offers a different approach: instead of operating in an atmosphere of blame, the karmic reasons for any possi-*

ble abuse are explored. This permits a person to take complete responsibility for all that happens and enables them to much more easily forgive, release, and rise above the experience. For instance, after explaining to a client how reincarnation and past-life regression therapy work, if I feel the person is ready to experience it, I may suggest the following after a guided meditation: "Go back to the lifetime where any sexual abuse you *may* have experienced in the current life originated; go back to the root cause." So, instead of concentrating on the abuse itself and falling into a victim mentality, he or she will become aware of what caused the conflict to begin with. Also, through the higher understanding achieved through hypnosis or guided meditation, they will be able to forgive themselves, anyone else involved with the experience, and release the emotions causing conflict in the current life.

Deena had been to a therapist who used a more traditional approach, but she felt it didn't help her. The therapist wanted to put her on an antidepressant because of the anger Deena felt towards her father. Deena refused. She said she has known people on antidepressants and said, "they become vegetables: no emotions." Deena said she wanted to face the causes of her problems, not bury them. She felt the therapist was a nice person, but she stopped seeing her as the therapy didn't seem to be going anywhere.

When I told Deena that I would like to use the process of past-life regression with her, she said she didn't believe in past lives because reincarnation wasn't in the Bible. I explained to her that reincarnation was taught by the early Christian leaders and may have been mentioned throughout the Bible before extensive editing for political reasons. Deena explained that her last boyfriend, who was mentally abusive and who had numerous affairs during their relationship, introduced her to the Bible. Apparently "he felt he could do anything he wanted, including hurting and using others, as long as he went to church and confessed his sins." I explained to her that I have found past-life regression to be extremely effective, even for problems that couldn't be solved through more traditional types of therapy. Furthermore, I told Deena that a belief in reincarnation isn't necessary for this therapy to be effective but that suspending any skepticism and acting as if she has lived before will improve results during and after the regression.

At this point I was still feeling a lot of resistance from Deena, so I asked her why. She said that she has a lot of fear about metaphysical subjects and didn't like to dabble in the dark side of spirituality. I explained how past-life regression has nothing to do with the "dark side" of spirituality and that the processes of past-life regression are completely safe when approached correctly. Even if it wasn't approached correctly, its about as dangerous as daydreaming. Furthermore, I explained to Deena that I make sure my clients feel safe and comfortable during their sessions by using techniques such as burning white candles, burning sage, calling in guides and angels of the Light, and visualizing white light for protection.

Though Deena's fears about anything related to metaphysics may not be related to her relationship issues, I felt that dissolving those fears would help her accept and benefit from past-life regression therapy. Therefore, I began the regression work with Deena by leading her through a relaxation exercise and into a lifetime that would explore her fear. She perceived herself as a 15-year-old female living in England in 1656. I asked her to perceive herself with the one person who was most important to her then:

Deena: That person is an older woman with long hair. She teaches me. She seems very wise.
Therapist: What does she teach you?
D: She has a lot of bottles of herbs and she heals people with them. She's a very caring person. She seems like a nurse or something.
Th: So she's teaching you how to use the herbs and heal people?
D: Yes, I like it. I enjoy it a lot. I'm working with the woman. I provide bottles of herbs and concoctions to people.
Th: Are you a healer?
D: Yes, but with herbs. It's the woman's place and I work with her. A lot of sick people come to us. I really like what I'm doing, working with the herbs. I love it.

What follows is an example of how one can gain intuitive awareness during a guided or solo meditation. This is common during a meditative state, when people are more receptive to thoughts. I was about to ask Deena about her love life in that life, but before I could get the words out she answered the question.

D: If you're asking if I'm married, no, I'm single.
Th: How old are you at this point?
D: Thirty-two.
Th: Have you ever dated or been involved with someone in this life we are exploring?
D: No, it's not that people don't like me. Most consider me different. Many respect me when they come to me, but most don't understand me.
Th: I understand. So you keep to yourself?
D: Yes, I spend most of my time studying the plants and herbs. I'm not involved with anyone. I'm more independent. There are a few who like me but I don't like them. I can see some negative qualities and I don't think they'd be good for me.

I asked Deena to move ahead to an important event:

D: Sarah, the healer woman, is in bed. I think she's dying. I'm talking to her.
Th: How do you feel about this?
D: I'm sad, but I feel really good for her. She's had a good life. She wants me to continue her work for her. She says I have a lot of talent.
Th: Good. Let's move forward again until something important happens.
D: There's a lot of controversy. People are mad.
Th: About what?
D: I think someone was sick and I couldn't help them, so they blamed me. It was incurable.
Th: They blamed you?
D: Yes. I felt bad that I couldn't help the person. It wasn't my fault.
Th: Move forward in that scene until something important happens.
D: Everyone is talking about me. I feel bad. I feel as if I should just leave. The village is coming down with some kind of illness and I'm not able to cure it. They're saying that I created it and they're blaming me for it.
Th: Keep moving forward and tell me what happens.

D: I'm seeing fire . . . they're burning my place. I'm angry about it. I was really good at what I was doing. The lady taught me well. I knew I should have left. I feel like I let her down.
Th: Keep moving forward and please tell me what happens.
D: They're dragging me away.
Th: Who's dragging you away?
D: The townspeople. They're angry and scared. They put me in a deep, dark hole. I'm just waiting. It's cold and it's dirty.
Th: Let's move forward in this scene until something happens. Tell me what's happening now.
D: (becomes visibly upset and begins to cry) They put me in a barrel and lit it on fire.

I quickly helped Deena rise above any pain and emotion and view the scenes only as an observer, and helped her to realize she is only remembering the experiences, not reliving them. I then led her through the death experience in that life. *Even though it may not seem beneficial to perceive such experiences, doing so will release the trauma and emotions trapped in the subconscious mind from the event.*

Th: Okay, you've now crossed over, you are now out of that body. Realize you are not that body and you are completely safe. Tell me what's happening please.
D: (tears) I still feel the emotions of betrayal.
Th: Is there one person in particular who led this persecution against you?
D: There are several men. I recognize one of them. It's one of my old boyfriends, the Bible guy.

I led Deena through a forgiveness exercise with all the townspeople who turned against her and persecuted her, focusing on forgiving the persecutor who is the ex-boyfriend in her current life. I also had her cut an imaginary link in her solar plexus which represented any remaining ties with her ex-boyfriend.

Deena's subconscious mind associated anything metaphysical with rejection, punishment, and death because of the experiences she had in that lifetime. Since releasing the experience and forgiving all involved, including herself, she no longer experiences any fear relating to metaphysical subjects.

During Deena's next session, now that she felt more comfortable with me and the idea of at least acting as if she had lived before, I guided her through a relaxation meditation and into a past life that would explain her current negative relationship experiences. Deena perceived herself as a 22-year-old female living in France during the 1600s. I asked Deena about her love life:

D: I'm not married . . . I'm going to be.
Th: Please describe him.
D: (doesn't sound interested in him) He has dark brown hair. About 25.
Th: Do you like him?
D: Not really.
Th: Are you in love with him?
D: No.
Th: Is it your choice to marry this man?
D: No, my parents decided. He was chosen for me.

Deena proceeded to perceive her grand wedding in that life and said she felt as if her "freedom is being taken away." After she observed the birth of a son in that life, no other significant events took place, so I guided her forward to the last day of her life in that lifetime:

D: I'm sick and I'm laying in bed. My son is kissing my hand. Th: How old are you now?
D: Sixty-five.
Th: On the count of three, please die or cross over, without pain and without emotion. One, two, three. Please tell me what you are perceiving.
D: I can still see my body laying in bed. My son is sad. I see a light.
Th: Please move toward the light until you meet someone or until something happens.
D: I see a bright, golden haze. There are people there, but they don't have physical shapes, mostly light.
Th: What happens next?

D: They're saying it's okay now.
Th: Please ask these people what you were meant to learn from that lifetime.
D: How important it is to respect people no matter who they are and whether or not they have money.
Th: Did you have a lot of money in that lifetime?
D: Yes, but I think I took advantage of it. I thought I was treating others with respect, but I wasn't. Some got their feelings hurt. I concentrated too much on the material world and there wasn't much love.

I took her through a forgiveness exercise to release the guilt from that lifetime and then asked her to keep moving forward:

D: (silent tears) Someone new is there. He's a knight—tall, with shoulder length hair.
Th: Who is this person?
D: I didn't respect my marriage vows. He is a man who I had an affair with during my marriage in that life. I fell deeply in love with him. I couldn't pursue him like I wanted, so I was unhappy.
Th: Please look into the knight's eyes and see if you recognize him as anyone you know in your current life.
D: (pause) Yes. Someone I was in love with in high school.
Th: Do you feel you still may be in love with him?
D: Yes, I am.
Th: How is that affecting your current love life?
D: (pause) I'm . . . in a way, saving myself for him, even though he's since been married.
Th: So by choosing relationships that won't work out, you'll always be available for him, even if he isn't available for you. Are you ready to let go and release this man?
D: I'm not sure I want to.
Th: Deena, releasing him now doesn't mean that you won't be together again. It means that you'll stop wasting energy on something that perhaps isn't meant to be right now. This block may be interfering with your love life. If you are meant to be with him again, it will happen. Are you ready to let go of him?

Deena agreed, so I led her through an exercise to help her release this man and to bring closure to the relationship which she felt never ended properly. I then continued questioning her about the lifetime she had just perceived (see chapter 14: "Express Unspoken Words" or "Forgive and Release" to do this on your own).

Th: What was the most important lesson you learned from that lifetime?
D: (pause) Money can't buy happiness.

To conclude this first session, I led Deena through a forgiveness meditation to help release anger against her father. Judging from her intense emotional release, the meditation seemed to be healing for her.

Deena and I both felt she had more relationship blocks to explore and release, so in her next session I again led her into a lifetime that would explain the root cause of her negative experiences with men in her current life. In this regression, Deena saw herself as a pirate who treated women poorly. Deena resisted seeing this incarnation at first because "he" wasn't a nice person. I encouraged her to explore the scenes and reminded her that we've all been "good" and "bad" and that remembering the bad will help her forgive herself and release blocks:

Th: Please tell me what you are perceiving.
D: Ships, like pirate ships. They are pirate ships. They're docking.
Th: Please find yourself in this vision.
D: I'm one of them. I'm male: tall, blue eyes, a little mustache, powerful build.
Th: What is the year?
D: (pause) 1790?
Th: What's happening in this scene?
D: The men are showing me some stock they got. They stole something from another ship. These guys are . . . they can be good, but they have bad intentions. I think I have authority here. I think I own the ship.
Th: Please tell me more about the ship.
D: It has little circular windows. It's very old-looking. There's a flag . . . it's white and red and has a symbol on it, like a cross.
Th: Move forward now to an important event.

D: They have women in some kind of room. I don't want to view this.

Th: Stay with the vision and tell me what you perceive.

D: (pause) The men treat these women like animals. They're being held against their will. They're raping them.

Th: Are you doing this?

D: (pause) Yes. I guess I'm sort of mean (becomes emotional).

Th: It's okay, that's not you now. On the count of three, perceive the most important person to you in that life. One, two, three.

D: I see a lady. Very beautiful. She has blondish hair.

Th: Who is this person?

D: Brittney? Brittney.

Th: Who is this person in relation to you?

D: She's my fiancée. I'm going to marry her.

Th: How old are you?

D: Twenty-seven. I'm a very . . . aggressive man. I'm like a typical man.

Th: You're perceiving this lifetime for a reason, so let's move forward to an important event in that lifetime that relates to your current life.

D: I'm taking in the fish. I married that woman. For some reason I don't really like her anymore . . . actually, I think I'm a cheater.

Th: Have you cheated on her a lot?

D: (pause) A little bit . . .

Th: It's okay, I won't judge you.

D: It's a lot. I've cheated on her a lot.

Th: Let's move forward to another important event on the count of three. One, two, three.

D: I see my ship. It's crashed. I think it was really windy. We hit some rocks, a lot of rocks. It's sinking.

Th: What are you doing?

D: I'm trying to get everyone out of the boat.

Th: Is it daytime or nighttime?

D: It's night. Most of the crew are in little boats. I'm trying to get out. Something came down on me . . . knocked me out. I'm trapped and panicking. All I'm thinking about is my wife and what I've done to her and how I've treated her.

Th: How do you feel about that?

D: I feel really guilty. I feel like I've been very bad this life. It's too late.

Th: Is anyone else still on the boat?
D: I think I got everyone out.
Th: So you thought of them first.
D: Yes, I felt like it was the right thing to do.
Th: So you weren't all bad.
D: No, but the way I treated women . . . The boat is sinking. I think I've died.

I assisted Deena in crossing over without pain and without emotion, and then led her into a Higher Self perspective. I then began questioning her about the experiences in that life and how they relate to her current life:

Th: Does the way you treated women then relate to your life now somehow?
D: I think so.
Th: In what way?
D: Two ways. I've always had problems with women, whether they be friends, acquaintances, or co-workers. I think my guilt from the way I treated women as a pirate has contributed to my current life conflicts with women. It's almost as if some women sense my guilt and then treat me accordingly without even realizing what they are doing.
Th: What is the other way the pirate life is affecting your current life?
D: Well, since I still had guilt from cheating on my wife and raping women, it caused me to attract negative experiences with men in this life. It's like I thought I deserved to be treated like that because I felt bad about treating others poorly in that lifetime.

I reminded Deena again that we've all been "bad" and "good" in past lives and how important it is to forgive yourself and everyone else. I then led her through a forgiveness exercise to help her let go of the guilt she felt from her actions then that were interfering with her life now.

Emotions and thoughts at the time of death, especially guilt and anger, are often carried forth into subsequent lifetimes. Deena's feelings of guilt about the way she treated her wife and other women in that life contributed to her negative experiences with men and women in her current life. However, remembering the root cause, forgiving herself, and releasing the feelings about those events finally set her free and ended her pattern of abusive relationships. After the session Deena and I both felt that her lifetime as a pirate was her main relationship block.

In Deena's final session, she wished to explore a past relationship that she called a "fatal attraction." Deena met Jeff a few years ago and they were involved for about six months. She ended the relationship because he was controlling, he used cocaine, and he pulled a gun on her. After she left, he stalked her for almost two years until finally she had to get a restraining order against him. She thought she was free of him but he recently tried to enter her life again. The situation caused her a lot of stress.

I led Deena through a relaxation meditation and then into a past life that would explain the root cause of the conflict. Deena perceived herself as a 17-year-old female house cook living in France during the early 1800s. At this point, she is telling me about a situation involving herself and her husband in that life. She is afraid of him due to his warrior appearance, strength, and attitude toward her:

D: There's a lot of hostility. My husband is slapping me a lot. He thinks I'm cheating on him.
Th: Did you cheat on him?
D: No, I didn't.
Th: On the count of three you'll have much more awareness about the situation. One, two, three. What else is happening?
D: I'm in a kitchen . . . stone floors.
Th: Is this your home?
D: Yes.
Th: Do you have children?
D: Yes. Three.
Th: What else is happening in this scene?
D: He's just yelling at me and slapping me. I think he's drunk . . . yeah, he's very drunk; he's wasted.
Th: Let's move forward now until something happens.

D: I'm slouched over and I'm crying. He stabbed me. There are stab wounds . . . blood dripping. I'm dying.
Th: On the count of three, please die or cross over without pain and without emotion. One, two, three. What are you perceiving?
D: (pause) (softly) Just white light.
Th: Is there anyone else there with you?
D: (pause) (softly) Yes, two people who feel like friends. We're dancing around in circles. I feel so peaceful.

I led Deena through the death process and into the Light so I could question her about the lifetime she had just perceived:

Th: I'd like to ask you some more questions about the lifetime we just explored. Please think about your husband in that life and tell me if he reminds you of anyone you know in your current life.
D: Yes, he's Jeff.
Th: What emotions do you feel about the man who was your husband then?
D: I feel like he betrayed me. I feel very angry.
Th: Please perceive that man in front of you. Know that you are completely safe and tell me when you can perceive him.
D: Yes, I see him.
Th: Please tell him either aloud or in your mind how you feel about what he did.
D: I think what you did was wrong. I feel hurt by how you treated me.
Th: How does he respond?
D: He's crying . . . and he's angry. I am worried about the children I left behind.
Th: Ask him why he's mad.
D: He's cheated on me many times.
Th: Do you think you could forgive him for the way he treated you and for ending your life in that incarnation?
D: (pause) Yes . . . I feel heavy.
Th: If you could give that heaviness an emotion, which would it be?
D: Anger.

Th: It's time to release the anger and forgive that man. Please look into his eyes and tell him that even though he hurt you a lot, you are ready to forgive and release him.
D: (breaks down, deep sobbing) I think he killed himself. The place is on fire. The kids died too.
Th: Rise above the emotion. It's not happening now. You're just remembering it and it's time to release it for good. Let go. Please perceive him in front of you again.
D: Okay.
Th: Tell him you forgive him for all he's done [Deena repeats this to him]. Please tell him you are releasing him with love and compassion and you wish him well [Deena repeats this to him].
D: (deep sobbing) I release you and all the hate I had towards you.
Th: Please also forgive yourself either for anything you may have done, intentionally or unintentionally, to hurt him or yourself. Forgive yourself and feel this now, please. Feel the release as you forgive yourself (pause). Now send him love and compassion: Picture light, any color that feels right, coming from your heart directed at him. This surrounds him and releases him. Wish him well and let him go now.
D: Yes . . . he's fading away now.
Th: Good. Watch him fade farther and farther way. Tell me when he's gone.
D: He's gone.
Th: I'd like you to again forgive yourself for anything you did that you feel guilty about consciously or subconsciously, in this life or in any other lifetimes. Feel compassion for yourself and make it okay to forgive yourself. You did the best you could and you'll do better in the future. Feel the forgiveness and compassion.
D: (silent tears)
Th: Good. I'd like you now to picture yourself as a young girl in this lifetime at about the age of two or three.
D: Okay.
Th: Please picture her walking into this room walking over to you, and crawling onto your lap.
D: Okay.
Th: Now look into her eyes and tell her how much you love her and that you'll always be there for her. Now listen for her response.

D: (smiles) She's hugging me.
Th: Excellent. Whenever you are upset, stressed, or angry about anything, you can picture yourself as this young girl and give her and yourself the love and compassion you need at that moment. Give her a hug and let her hug you (pause). Now ask her if she has any messages for you. Ask her if there's anything you need to be aware of right now.
D: She says it's going to be all right.

I concluded the session and brought Deena back to the present.

Jeff continued to leave her messages for a short time. Since Deena felt differently about him now—her anger toward him no longer was drawing him in—she was able to let him go in peace. He eventually left her alone.

Deena was able to stop her pattern of negative relationships in part from the awareness gained and forgiveness expressed through her regression sessions and in part from becoming more conscious of her choices. By listening to her inner guidance in and out of meditation, she was able to start avoiding relationship possibilities that were not for her highest good.

How Does This Relate To You?

- If you feel you may have been abused during your childhood but have no conscious memory of it, use caution if you decide to use current-life regression to uncover any potential memories. When not approached correctly, current-life regression can do more harm than good in situations like these. Consider past-life regression and root cause therapy as a different approach: instead of blaming, the root cause of any possible abuse is discovered and the reason you *chose*, on a soul level, to experience the abuse is explored. It may be difficult to believe anyone would actually choose to experience sexual abuse or any other negative experience, but when we realize our souls rather than our current personalities select certain events in our lives for our highest growth, the idea makes more sense. We only perceive these events as bad because of how our perceptions of life have been formed since birth. However, because of the difficult emotions involved in this type of inner work, it is recommended that you see advice and guidance from a trained professional.

- Past-life research indicates that most childhood events seem to be karmic, meaning there is usually a root cause resulting from experiences in one or more past lives. Therefore, it's beneficial to "go back to the root cause" in regression to discover if any current problems are rooted in childhood experiences or past lives. Your mind will lead you to the source event, whether it's in this life or a past life.
- Your subconscious mind influences your thoughts and behavior. For example, Deena's subconscious mind still associated anything metaphysical with rejection, punishment, and death because of her past-life experiences. If you feel fear or anger in relation to metaphysical subjects or anything else, past-life experiences may be part of the reason. By discovering the root cause, releasing the experience through meditation or regression, and then forgiving all involved, including yourself, you'll be able to rise above the fear or problem.
- Even though it may not seem beneficial to perceive traumatic experiences through past-life regression, doing so will release the trauma and emotions associated with the event that were previously causing conflicts and fears. You'll only perceive that which you are ready to see.
- We have all been "good" and "bad" in previous lifetimes. Uncovering and releasing the bad through regression will lead to forgiveness and healing.
- If you are still emotionally attached to someone from the past, it will complicate new opportunities in your present and future love life. For example, although Deena didn't consciously realize it, her feelings for the man she loved and lost in high school were strong enough to interfere with her current relationships. If she chose relationships that wouldn't last, she would always be available to her lost love in the future. Releasing old attachments will make you more available for future compatible relationships.
- Most of us have subconscious guilt from past lives. With Deena's example, her hidden guilt about cheating on a spouse

in a past life produced similar situations in her current life. From only the perspective of this life, Deena was a victim. From a perspective that includes the reality of reincarnation and karma, her past life actions affected her present life experiences. Releasing hidden guilt through forgiveness exercises allowed her to avoid similar situations in the future.

6
"My partner won't commit to me."

Jan, an attractive woman in her mid-40s, had read a great deal about reincarnation and felt that past-life regression could help her. She wanted to explore why Mark, the man with whom she had been involved for four years, wouldn't commit to her. He was also in his mid-40s and had never been married. Though Mark claimed to love her and said this was the closest he had come to marriage, he wouldn't marry her. Jan said that she was at a point where she needed Mark to commit or she needed to let him go. She hoped that past-life regression would shed some light on the karmic reasons for the relationship and whether or not she should set Mark free.

I led Jan through a relaxation induction and into a past life that would explain the reasons for her current relationship situation. Jan perceived herself as a young woman living in Europe in 1436. I guided her forward in that lifetime to when she was with the most important person to her in that life:

Jan: I'm standing outside a stone wall with a dark-haired man. We are not married . . . we plan to be. It's Mark.
Therapist: What else is happening in that scene?
J: He has to leave. I don't want him to go.
Th: Why does he have to leave?

J: Not a war, but . . . they're all going. He's telling me that when he comes back, we'll get married.
Th: Move forward to a time when you are with this man again.
J: We're getting married.
Th: How do you feel?
J: Very happy.
Th: What else is happening in that scene?
J: We're kneeling. He has such a smile on his face (smile). He keeps looking at me out of the corner of his eye, kind of grinning. My father is on the right. I don't see my mother. I don't think I have one. There's a lot of people around. My father is kissing me and hugging him.

I guided Jan forward to the next important event and she perceived herself giving birth to a girl. She was upset because her husband wasn't there. He seemed to be away a lot. I guided her ahead again:

Th: What's happening?
J: My father is here. We're both very sad. My husband was killed on one of those trips they were always on. (crying) I don't have his body yet. It's so sad.

Jan became upset so I guided her to rise above the emotion and view the scenes as an observer:

Th: Let's move forward again to another significant event in this lifetime.
J: My daughter is doing the same thing as me. She's marrying someone who's never there. I'm trying to talk her out of it. She won't listen.
Th: Once again, move forward to another significant event in that life.
J: Dying, dying, dying . . . another funeral. My daughter's husband died in battle.
Th: On the count of three, you'll move forward to one minute before your death in that life. One, two, three.
J: I'm in my big bed. My hair is all gray. I don't feel that bad. My daughters are there.

Th: On the count of three, you'll cross over without pain and without emotion. One, two, three.

I led Jan through the death process and into the Higher Self state so I could question her about the lifetime she had just perceived:

Th: Please tell me what you are perceiving.
J: It's beautiful. There is someone with me.
Th: Who is with you?
J: (pause) It's like a light . . . a guide, I think.
Th: Please reflect on why you chose to be with a man who would always be away. Concentrate on that and tell me what you perceive.
J: (tears) I was afraid. I was afraid to love, of getting too close. If they're always there it must really hurt when they leave.
Th: Is that fear still with you now?
J: Yes.
Th: Is that a valid fear?
J: No, I don't think so.
Th: What else do you need to be aware of about this experience and how it relates to your current life?
J: I thought that only Mark in this life had a problem committing. This is my fear too. I am the one who chose him; I chose someone who isn't available. I need to stop doing this to myself. I need to stop choosing people who are not available.
Th: Are you ready to let go of this fear?
J: Yes.
Th: Sometimes just the awareness will help resolve the problem. Let's do something else to help the process. Picture this fear as a thick tree trunk attached to your solar plexus area. Tell me when you can perceive it and describe it to me please.
J: It's a dark brown color, with lots of ridges. It's very thick. (laughs) It's a very old tree trunk.
Th: It's time to let go of this fear that is no longer serving you. When you are ready, take an appropriate instrument, cut the tree trunk, and set yourself free. Take your time and tell me when you're ready.
J: (pause) Okay, it's gone.
Th: How do you feel?
J: (pause) Lighter.

Next I guided Jan to a time in the future when she and Mark were happily involved and there was little or no conflict between them. I did this so Jan could perceive what it would be like if they resolved the issues between them.

J: I'm seeing a beach, we're walking on a beach. He looks so happy. I feel content.
Th: How far in the future is this?
J: I'm not sure. I just realized something.
Th: What did you realize?
J: I need to set Mark free. I need to let go so he can make his own decision. I now know what's best for me, and now he needs to be free to decide what's best for him.
Th: If you set him free, will he eventually come back to you?
J: That's what I'm feeling. I'm not sure if or when it will happen.
Th: If there is anything else that would help you at this time, please be aware of it at the count of three. One, two, three.
J: Mark is a mirror for me. If I let go of my fear of commitment, he will have no reason to reflect that back to me anymore.

I brought Jan back to the present.

In a higher state of awareness after her death experience in the past life, Jan realized that she is the one with a fear of commitment, and therefore she chose to get involved with Mark because subconsciously she realized he is unavailable. Jan's statement during the regression, "If they're always there, it will really hurt when they leave," sums up her hidden subconscious relationship block. With more awareness, she was able to take responsibility for her love life situation and rise above the fears associated with it.

I don't know how the relationship between Jan and Mark played out. Whatever happened, I do know Jan was more prepared after the regression to accept it and move on with her life.

More Examples

Beth, a 28-year-old computer analyst, had been involved with James for four years. She knew they were right for each other and she loved him deeply. However, Beth felt that James fell short of what she wanted in a partner and she wondered if she could find someone even more compatible. She admitted that she felt a lot of fear about committing to marriage, and had broken off two engagements prior to her current one. In past-life regression, Beth perceived herself in seventeenth-century Italy. She fell in love with and married a man who seemed perfect for her. However, shortly after the marriage, she found herself a prisoner within the walls of his castle and was forced to be a slave for his every need. She suffered many years of abuse until finally, angry and exhausted, escaping through death. From this experience, Beth now subconsciously perceived marriage as a terribly unhappy and brutal prison sentence. By becoming aware of the root cause, she was able to let go of the past which was still affecting her—even though she was consciously unaware of it—and allow herself to experience the love life she wanted.

Marty, a 42-year-old entrepreneur, was six weeks away from his wedding. He loved his fiancée and knew they were a great match. He couldn't think of any logical reason not to marry her. But he experienced such emotional turmoil when he thought of the commitment he was making that he was considering canceling the wedding. Through past-life regression, Marty discovered that the root cause of his fear of commitment was related to a life he experienced in the United States during the early 1900s. Coming from a wealthy family, he lived a life of freedom. However, at the age of 30 he was forced by his family to marry a woman he didn't like or love, and was unhappy the rest of his life. From this experience, Marty subconsciously perceived marriage as a loss of his personal freedom. By recognizing the root cause of his fears, he was able to release the past and allow himself to enjoy a more fulfilling love life.

Charlene, a 52-year-old writer, was married briefly in her 20s. She has been involved off and on since then, but often found reasons to end a relationship when she felt it getting too serious. She later regretted her actions, but continued repeating the same pattern. Through past-life regression, Charlene perceived herself as a monk in Tibet. She loved her life of peace and awareness through meditation. She became conscious during the regression of her fears that a relationship could take that state away from her and interfere with her work. By becoming aware of the root cause of her fear of commitment, Charlene was able to release it and consciously confirm that the right relationship could actually bring her more peace, awareness, and success.

How Does This Relate To You?

- You are a mirror for your partner—or who you want to be your partner—more than you may realize. As Jan summed up: "Mark is a mirror for me. If I let go of my fear of commitment, he will have no reason to reflect that back to me anymore." Accept and resolve a relationship problem within yourself and watch your life and relationship transform. If you're involved with someone who won't commit, instead of blaming that person, consider why, on some level, you chose them in the first place. Find out the root reasons you are choosing someone who isn't available for you. By taking responsibility for everything that happens to you, you'll set yourself free. Jan had the courage to take responsibility for her situation and search for answers that allowed her to solve her problem.
- As shown by these examples, fear of commitment is often a combination of fears: losing freedom, making the wrong decision, loss, success, even a subconscious belief that one doesn't deserve to be happy in love. Fear of commitment also interferes with other areas of life, such as friends, groups, exercise, diet, career, and finances. If you're breaking agreements with yourself or others, you have the option of finding the causes and releasing the fears associated with them.

7
Fear of Abandonment

Sidney, a 35-year-old high school teacher, was tired of his relationships ending poorly. He knew that he had a fear of abandonment, which caused him to either sacrifice his self-esteem by doing anything and everything to please a partner, or to cut off the relationship abruptly to avoid the pain of being dumped. He had been dating a woman for six months and felt their relationship could be long-term. He wanted to avoid repeating the same mistakes. Sidney came to me to find and dissolve the root cause of why he consistently sabotaged his relationships.

I led Sidney through a relaxation induction and into a different time and place where the root cause of his fear of abandonment originated. Sidney perceived himself as a 12-year-old male in the mid-1800s living with his mother. He and his mother were upset over the death of his father. I guided Sidney forward in that life to an important event:

Therapist: What's happening?
Sidney: I'm wearing my uniform and black boots, walking down the street. It's nighttime.
Th: Where are you?
S: I see cobblestone. Kentucky . . . no, it's not Kentucky, that's where I'm from. I'm somewhere else near Kentucky. (gasps) (moans) I just saw myself get shot in the stomach.

Th: Tell me what happens next.
S: I'm really stunned. I don't know what to do. There's no one else around. I just collapsed in a side alley, and I rose above my body. I see myself lying there.
Th: Do you have an awareness of who shot you?
S: I think . . . I think it was someone I knew. They didn't want me to know they were the one who did it. It wasn't part of battle.
Th: Are you ready to die?
S: No, I don't want to die. I was unhappy, though . . . I'm just flying right now. (peaceful expression)

I guided Sidney through the death process and into the Higher Self state so he could gain awareness about that life:

Th: Tell me what you're feeling.
S: Just . . . joy. It's all part of the plan. (tears)
Th: What did you accomplish through that life?
S: I needed to experience my father leaving . . . being killed (begins to cry) and being shot in the stomach. That was all necessary for this lifetime. I needed to experience the abandonment of someone I love leaving me. You get too close and they're going to leave anyway! (more tears)
Th: Now, you know that what you're remembering is in the past, right?
S: Yes.
Th: Those were lessons to be learned. Do you feel you learned those lessons?
S: (pause) I think so.
Th: If the lessons were learned, it's okay to let go of those feelings.

I led Sidney through a forgive and release exercise and into another life related to his current love life issues. He perceived himself in 1756 as a strong 60-year-old male who had just experienced a shipwreck. The only survivor out in the middle of nowhere, he lay dehydrated in the sun on some floating wood.

S: I'm in good shape, but not prepared for this.
Th: What country are you near?

S: I heard Jerusalem, but . . . I'm not in an ocean, it's like a huge lake. It's part of an ocean. Must have been a storm, because now it's bright sun, it's really hot. I'm sort of getting delirious, but I'm really confident and strong. I know I'm going to die . . . it doesn't really bother me. It's all right. I'm really hungry. (laughs)
Th: Tell me about the ship. What happened to the ship?
S: It was huge, three pillars, like a cargo ship. We just didn't see the storm coming. It was a large squall. The ship snapped in two.
Th: Why were you on the ship?
S: I was part of the crew. I feel really confident as this man. All man. (laughs)
Th: Look back over your lifetime and tell me what memories stand out. What's significant about this life?
S: I had a young daughter who is my sister in this lifetime. I saw my daughter at about age ten. My wife. (pause) I love her, but we weren't close for some reason. She didn't mind that I was always gone. (pause) I think I stopped feeling in that lifetime; no emotions.
Th: What caused that to happen?
S: (pause) Someone leaving, I think . . . when I was little.
Th: Tell me more about that.
S: I'm not seeing anything. I just know that someone left my life. I closed myself off.
Th: On the count of three, go back to that time in your childhood when someone left you. One, two, three.
S: I'm seeing some kind of church. I saw this priest. He's really "dark" . . . looks like fire in his eyes. I'm not sure why I'm there. I think I'm looking for someone. I'm a pretty tough boy. I don't think I had any parents. I lost both of them when I was very young. It didn't seem to phase me . . . at least, I don't think it did.
Th: Why are you in this church?
S: It's like I walked in and I wasn't supposed to be there. Oh . . . my parents were taken away. I was looking for them there, and that man had something to do with it. He knew that I knew.
Th: How do you feel?
S: Blank. Numb.

I guided Sidney forward to a significant event in that lifetime. He perceived himself getting married, yet felt little emotion about it.

S: I don't feel anything. It's like I'm blank all the time. Nothing fazes me. I'm sort of sleepwalking through life. I think I'm in a state of shock from losing my parents.
Th: What happened to your parents?
S: (pause) I think my parents were taken away for some reason. They were doing some kind of magic work and they were found out by . . . the church, I think . . . even though they weren't hurting anyone. And I became numb from loosing my parents.
Th: What country is this?
S: Yugoslavia. It's very different than here. I see a lot of lace. I didn't even taste food in that lifetime. I was that closed off.

I guided Sidney forward to few minutes before his death in that life. He again found himself floating on the wood after the shipwreck.

Th: What are you feeling?
S: I'm ready to leave. I knew as soon as I got in the boat that this was the end and . . . oh well.
Th: And you're okay with that?
S: Yes. I'm pretty brave. (laughs)
Th: Very well. On the count of three you'll release from that physical body and cross over. One, two, three. Release and tell me when you're there.
S: I'm there.
Th: What are you feeling now?
S: So much love for him/me.
Th: Now is your opportunity to look back and gain some insight. What was that life about?
S: Emotion, again. I needed to experience what it's like to close off emotionally, so I know what it's like to feel and love now. That's why I'm so sensitive now, like double the emotion. I still close it off.
Th: Now that you have this awareness and understanding from a higher perspective, do you think you can create more of a balance?
S: Yes. I'm seeing this bright star and this being comes from it. I believe it's my Higher Self.

Often those who believe in or are aware of the concept of a Higher Self, guides, or angels, and/or who meditate regularly, are able to access clear guidance from higher sources during a regression.

Th: Perhaps there's something you'd like to ask your Higher Self. If so, go ahead, take your time.
S: He's saying, "Sidney, you have no idea how much love is available to you" because I'm so closed off still. He's sending me energy which translates to the words "no fear, have no fear." (pause) He says to "be gentle with yourself." (pause) Now he's taking my hand and showing me my future. (pause) I'm seeing a baby in a crib. (pause) I don't feel anything, but I'm seeing this.
Th: Is this your future?
S: Yes. I'm in a totally different state of mind in the future, totally different! (laughs) It's very good.
Th: What is your state of mind?
S: Expressing so much love with everyone that I encounter . . . at the same time being so confident. (tears of joy)
Th: That's wonderful. Let these images be permanently imprinted on your mind.
S: My Higher Self is showing me a bunch of doors, with all these future probabilities, at the same time looking back to where I am right now and to the past and he's telling me, "See, there's no reason to fear, just let go of it." (crying softly). He just . . . totally accepts me. (pause) This is a very significant lifetime for me.

The overwhelming feeling of total acceptance and love from the Higher Self, guides, or angels of the Light is common when people come in contact with them.

Th: Are you ready to let go of the past?
S: Yes.
Th: Picture a cord in your mind, connecting you to the past and to your fear.
S: I can see the cord now.
Th: Okay, cut it in two. Let it all go and free yourself.
S: It's part of me, though. It's hard to cut. It's like a big trunk.
Th: Take an instrument . . .
S: My Higher Self just handed me a chainsaw. (laughs)
Th: Just let it go.
S: (Sighs)

Th: All those little things that got in your way were all about the past. They're just faded memories now (pause). Have you finished your dialogue with your Higher Self?
S: I can still see him. He said, "Don't take life so seriously. Just remember the lightness of spirit. It's what you make it. Be more gentle with yourself."
Th: Good advice. Are those his parting words?
S: Yes.

I concluded regression and brought Sidney back into the present. Sidney said afterwards he felt that the past-life scenes he perceived felt familiar and real, which is a frequent comment from those who are regressed. He also stated that the Higher Self session alone was enough to help him let go of his fear of abandonment. After experiencing this connection to what he called "the source," he realized he is never really alone. I recommended to Sidney that he continue his healing process with meditation forgiveness exercises and by reassuring himself that the past is over, mentally forgiving those who have left his life, and mentally acknowledging that no one ever leaves our lives permanently.

I heard from Sidney three weeks later. He said that he felt a renewed sense of enthusiasm for life and his love relationship. He found himself reacting differently to his girlfriend: more out of love instead of fear. She noticed the change, too. Four months later Sidney reported that his fear of abandonment was gone, as he no longer felt the need to constantly seek approval from his partner and hadn't considered breaking off the relationship since his regression sessions.

How Does This Relate To You?

- No matter how you consciously feel about something, if your subconscious mind feels differently, it will overpower and interfere with your goals. Remember that the subconscious mind is like a five-year-old child; it doesn't think like an adult. If someone abandoned you or hurt you in a previous relationship, until you forgive and release the original source of that pain, your subconscious mind will resent that person and perhaps even assume that all potential partners will behave the same way (even if you consciously know differently). Even though Sidney consciously realized that the past was over and that no one ever really leaves us permanently, the fear of abandonment from his consciously forgotten past-life experiences was still affecting his current life. His subconscious belief caused him to inadvertently select partners who repeated the pattern.

- How did Sidney know that his fear of abandonment was from a past life and not his present one? He did witness his father's devastation from his wife—Sidney's mother—divorcing him. Some would say that this childhood experience was the cause of his abandonment issues, which could be true. After root cause therapy, both Sidney and I felt that his mother leaving his father only added to his already existing fear of abandonment. Sidney's subconscious emotions and feelings where reinforced by his parent's divorce. Sidney also felt that he chose, on a soul level, to experience his parent's divorce so he would be more likely to confront his fears. Through past-life regression, he realized the root cause of his fear and that those experiences were necessary for his growth and learning.
- Why should you consider past-life regression therapy when you also can often find causes of the same problems in the current life? When only the current-life is explored to discover and release a cause of a problem, people seldom experience the rapid and positive results as they do when the root cause is discovered and released through past-life regression therapy.

8
Look Within For Love First

Perry, a 40-year-old entrepreneur, had been single for nine years and felt like he was "stuck" in his love life. None of his dating situations ever developed into relationships. He wanted to find out if there was anything from the past interfering with his present love life.

As I talked with Perry, I discovered that he used his work as an excuse to avoid dating, although he didn't realize he was doing it. He said that while he was successful, he often felt compelled to spend more time at work than he really needed to.

He turned out to be a good subject, though he had never experienced hypnosis, guided meditation, or past-life regression, and didn't meditate. He had not discounted the idea of reincarnation but said he had no reason to believe in it. As the result of his strict southern Baptist upbringing, he was somewhat skeptical about guided meditation and past-life regression, but was open-minded enough to temporarily suspend judgment.

He followed directions well and allowed himself to relax, which are both essential for a successful session. I guided Perry through a relaxation induction, into a different time and place that would explain the root cause for current love life problems, and began asking him questions. Perry perceived himself as an eight-year-old boy named Franz living in Switzerland in 1829. He had no parents and supported himself by working in a fabric factory. By age 19, he had worked his way up in the factory and was a manager. By age 29, he owned the factory. I guided Perry forward to when he was with someone he cared for deeply in that life:

Therapist: How do you feel?
Perry: (smiles) I'm really happy. She's so cheerful.
Th: Are you married to this person?
P: Yes. We've been married for a while now.
Th: Any children?
P: No.
Th: How do you feel about being in this relationship?
P: Very content. (smiles)
Th: Let's now move forward to an important decision you make during this time on the count of three. One, two, three.
P: I sold the factory.
Th: Are you still working?
P: No.
Th: How do you spend your time now?
P: With my wife.
Th: All right, let's move forward to an important event in that life time we are exploring. On the count of three. One, two, three.
P: She's not here anymore.
Th: Why?
P: She died.
Th: How do you feel?
P: Very sad.
Th: How did she die?
P: She was really sick. They just buried her. All the people who loved her are here. I'm very sad.

Through further questioning, Perry perceived that he gave up after his wife died and went into a deep depression. He didn't take care of himself or his home, and was moved into some kind of place for the mentally disturbed. Perry perceived no other significant events during that lifetime. I guided him forward to a few minutes before his death in that life:

P: I've been in this place a long time now and I feel like I'm ready to die.

Th: How old are you?

P: About 80.

Th: What is the year?

P: Almost 1900.

Th: How do you feel?

P: I'm so tired.

Th: On the count of three you'll die or cross over without pain and without emotion. 1, 2, 3. Please perceive the environment you find yourself in.

P: (smiles) My wife is there.

Th: Anyone else there with you?

P: (tears of joy) I don't need anyone else.

Th: What else are you perceiving around you?

P: She is the only place my attention is focused.

Th: I'd like to ask you some overview questions about the lifetime you just experienced. She may help you with these answers. What were you meant to learn or experience in that lifetime?

P: Loss.

Th: Anything else?

P: Work. I had to work very hard.

Th: What else?

P: I had to learn to look inside for love instead of outside.

Th: How does that lifetime relate to your current lifetime? How is it still affecting you?

P: It took me a while to find someone to love. I always felt like I had to get a lot done first. I had to succeed first. I had to show them I could do it.

Th: Is there anything else you were supposed to learn about love relationships in that life time?

P: How intense the bond can be between two people.

Th: Do you know that woman in your current life? Is she here once again?

P: No. I don't see her.

Th: Are those experiences from that lifetime still affecting you today?

P: I still feel driven to work and accomplish.

Th: Do you think it's possible to have your career enhanced by your love life?
P: Yes. I miss having support while I'm doing all this work.
Th: Do you have time for both?
P: Yes. I can make time.
Th: Is there any way you would change how you approach relationships based on what you just perceived?
P: I need to open myself up more. I need to stop putting up so many walls between others and myself.
Th: What else would you benefit from knowing about the lifetime you just experienced?
P: Perhaps that I have the ability to go on no matter what. To invest in myself instead of displacing all my love to another. Look inside for love first.
Th: Please perceive the woman who was your wife and tell me when you have.
P: Okay.
Th: Please ask her what else you could be aware of to help you in your current life.
P: Love myself more.
Th: What can you do to love yourself more?
P: Don't try to be so perfect.
Th: Accept yourself as you are?
P: Yes.

I concluded the regression and brought Perry back to the present. He said, "That was different. The thing that seemed so odd was the burst of emotion when I was so glad to see the woman who was my wife again." He dried his tears with a tissue. "I'm still not convinced, but it sure seemed like more than my imagination."

"It may have been symbolism your mind created to help you dissolve the fear of loss," I replied. "Even if it was only symbolism, it hardly matters. Do you now understand that loved ones who die aren't gone forever, just temporarily?"

"Yes, I can see how we will be together again with people we love."

How Does This Relate To You?

- It is important to look inside for love first. Invest in yourself first instead of displacing all your love to another.
- Your life doesn't end when a loved one moves on.
- You'll be together again with loved ones who have moved on.

Section III

Sexuality and Past Lives

9
Sexual Dysfunction

Twenty-nine-year-old Thomas sought my help for a problem that was causing him great stress: He was unable to maintain an erection with his present girlfriend and had never before experienced sexual dysfunction. They had known each other for six months, had been dating for five months, had been sexually active for four months, and were in love. I began the session by asking Thomas a few questions:

"Thomas, in cases of physical problems, I feel it's important to consider the spiritual causes as well as all potential physical causes, such as anything that is put on or into the body. Do you understand why I do that?

"Not really," he replied.

"I've found it's possible to trace the root cause of almost any problem back to an event in childhood or a past life, and often both. However, with physical problems, its also important to realize that everything you consume—all foods, liquids, drugs, medications, and so on—as well as products that are used on the body such as lotions, oils, and shampoos, will eventually influence your body's performance and how you feel. People aren't always in touch with their bodies and may not realize that something they are using is working against them, even if it isn't supposed to have side effects. Do you drink caffeine?"

Thomas laughed. "Yes, a lot."

"How much?"

"Well, I usually have about three cups of coffee in the morning, a couple sodas in the afternoon, and one or two cups of coffee in the evening. Caffeine doesn't really affect me; I can go right to sleep."

"Caffeine doesn't affect you because you're addicted to it. How do you feel when you don't have any caffeine for a day or two?"

Thomas laughed again. "Like hell!"

"Thomas, caffeine may not be a cause of this particular problem, but you may want to consider how you are treating your body. People who consume large amounts of caffeine over long periods develop serious problems. I know of a man who drank more than six cups of coffee a day for more than 30 years. He eventually developed kidney problems. When he finally stopped the caffeine, he had trouble staying awake during the day. His body was out of balance from being wired all the time. Eventually, he died of kidney failure."

Thomas's eyes widened.

"I don't mean to lecture you. I'm just trying to help you realize the importance of what you fuel your body with. Just because a product looks good in the commercials doesn't mean the company that makes it cares about your health or is even aware of what true health is. I noticed on your profile that you don't smoke, don't do drugs, and you rarely drink?"

"Yes, that's right."

"Have you had a physical lately?"

"Yes, three months ago. The doctor said I'm in good health."

"Are you taking any medications?"

"No."

"Any supplements?"

"Just Vitamin C. Even supplements can do that?" Thomas looked surprised.

"If your body can't digest or tolerate something in the supplements, yes. Have you ever experienced this problem with any women besides your current girlfriend?"

"No, just with Kristy."

"How many other woman have you had sex with?"

Thomas thought for a moment, "About 12."

"Is there anything different about this relationship compared to your other relationships?"

"As far as what?"

"Have you been in love with other women you've dated? Is this the closest you've come to marriage?"

"I've been in love with three others, and I was engaged to one of those, so this one isn't a threat, if that's what you mean."

"Yes, that's what I mean. Our subconscious minds sometimes perceive situations as threats and sabotages them to protect us. Did your sexual performance differ at all with those three you were in love with?"

"No, this is the only time I've ever experienced this."

"Have you tried anything else to fix this problem?" I inquired.

"No. My friends suggested I try Viagra™, but I prefer to keep it natural between my girlfriend and I."

"Okay. Are there any other factors that you're aware of, no matter how unrelated they may seem, that could be causing the sexual dysfunction?"

"No, that's why I'm here."

"Good. Lets do some exploring and look for the hidden root cause of this."

I explained to Thomas the basic principals of reincarnation and karma, why forgiveness almost always becomes an important part of this process, how guided meditation works, and what to expect with past-life regression. I also stressed the importance of pretending past lives are real, since Thomas had no experience with or knowledge of past-life regression. I led Thomas through a relaxation process and into a different time and different place that would help him to become aware of the root cause of his sexual dysfunction with Kristy, and then began asking him questions:

Thomas perceived himself as a 41-year-old troubled male living in Ireland in 1608. He spent most of his time painting and writing and was in love with his 17-year-old neighbor. The girl's parents were overly protective, so he rarely got to speak with her. One day he visits the girl when he knows her parents are away:

Thomas: I'm talking to her outside her front door. She's very nice. She invited me in. I'm attracted to her. She seems to be attracted to me too. (pause)

Therapist: What's happening now?
Thomas: We kiss. (pause) We are making love. (pause) No!
Th: What happened?
Thomas: Her parents came home early. No!
Th: What's happening?
Thomas: (upset) She's pretending that I attacked her. Her father is hitting me.
Th: Move forward until something important happens related to this. What's happening?
Thomas: They're preparing to hang me.
Th: Who is preparing to hang you?
Thomas: The townspeople.
Th: How do you feel about this?
Thomas: I feel like she betrayed me. I feel like no one believes me, which they don't. I wasn't hurting her! (tears) She initiated it!
Th: On the count of three, move forward until you're one minute before your death in the life we are exploring. One, two, three. What's happening?
Thomas: I can see her in the crowd. I know she feels sorry for what she did. I can see it in her eyes. I look at her with a blank look. They just put a hood over my head.
Th: On the count of three, cross over or die and tell me when you're there. One, two, three.
Thomas: (pause) I see my body hanging there, lifeless. I feel peaceful.
Th: What else is happening?
Thomas: A woman is coming towards me.
Th: Who is she?
Thomas: I think she's my mother in that life. She died when I was young.
Th: What is she saying or doing?
Thomas: She's smiling. It feels good to see her. (smiles) She said I did a good job.
Th: Do you know the female in your current life that accused you falsely of rape in that life?
Thomas: Yes, she's Kristy, my girlfriend now.
Th: Is there a reason you experienced that unfortunate situation in that lifetime?

Thomas: (pause) I'm not sure.
Th: Please mentally ask your mother if she can help you gain more understanding about the situation.
Thomas: (pause) She said as difficult as that was, it was necessary for my growth. I needed to experience betrayal. It also set me up for this lifetime to practice forgiveness.
Th: Good . . . do you forgive the girl and all involved with that situation?
Thomas: (pause) I understand why she did what she did, but I'm not sure that I forgive her.

I led Thomas through a forgiveness exercise to help him release the 400-year-old anger. More importantly, I helped Thomas let go of any guilt associated with what he was accused of and what actually happened. Before I brought him back to the present, I helped him affirm consciously that having sex with his current girlfriend wouldn't lead to being executed this time. Thomas seemed a little stunned after I brought him back to the present:

Th: How do you feel about what you just perceived?
Thomas: Man . . . I wonder what Kristy is going to think of all of this?
Th: Do you understand how your subconscious mind has been interfering with your sex life with Kristy?
Thomas: Yes.
Th: To put it simply, your subconscious mind perceived sex with Kristy as equaling shame, embarrassment, betrayal, and death. You have now discovered and released that block. Your subconscious mind will now feel differently about your interaction with Kristy and you'll naturally react differently to her.
Thomas: You know, I didn't like her father nor did he like me from the day we met. I wonder if her father then is her father now?
Th: It's possible. If he is, it would help you to mentally forgive him every time you think of him. Forgiving him during the regression and continuing to do so will reach him on some level and make your interaction more harmonious. Even if he's not the same soul who was her father then, if there are any negative emotions between you two, forgiveness and acceptance will only help.

I spoke to Thomas six weeks later and was happy to learn that he was no longer experiencing sexual dysfunction. He stated that the regression, along with some changes in his diet, had renewed his sex and love life.

What Does This Mean To You?

- Your body, mind and spirit are all connected. Problems sometimes have a physical, emotional and spiritual (past-life) cause. A spiritual cause will often have an emotional and/or physical affect. To become aware of a cause or to help discover and release any guilt or resentment that may be blocking your goals and happiness, see chapter 14.
- Your body really is your temple. Find and release the root cause instead of using bandage remedies. See Recommended Reading and chapter 19 for more information about true health.

10
"Have Past Lives Influenced My Sexual Orientation?"

There is no such thing as a homosexual or a heterosexual person. There are only homo- or heterosexual acts. Most people are a mixture of impulses if not practices.
— Gore Vidal (b. 1925)

In our society, males are expected to be attracted only to females, and females to males. However, since most souls have experienced both male and female bodies, we may have the ability and memory to be attracted to the same or both sexes. And while each of us can change sex over different lifetimes, our lovers can as well: two opposite-sex lovers in a past life may be the same sex in this life.

Daniel, a 43-year-old male, had perceived several past lives through regression sessions. He considered himself gay and was fascinated by how he had perceived himself in love with and sexually attracted to women in some of his past lives. He had never dated or had sex with women in his current life, and had been involved in a committed relationship with a male for seven years. He came to me wanting to explore any past-life reasons for his present life sexual orientation.

I guided Daniel through a meditation and into a lifetime that would explain the root cause of his current-life sexual orientation. He perceived himself as a 30-year-old woman named Raeina in 800 A.D. living near what is now called the Mediterranean Sea. Her responsibilities included the care of her young grandson since his mother was taken in a raid and his father never returned from looking for her. I guided Daniel forward to a proud moment in this lifetime:

Therapist: What's happening?
Daniel: The child is much bigger now. He's gotten an apprenticeship somewhere.
Th: What kind of work is he doing?
D: He's working with his hands.
Th: Let's move forward or backward now, no matter how unrelated it may seem, to an event or experience that will explain your current life sexuality.
D: (pause) The impression I get is anger with the grandchild for shaming us.
Th: How did he shame you?
D: With one of the other apprentices.
Th: How?
D: They were found together.
Th: I see. Is that unacceptable in your society?
D: Yes.
Th: How do you feel about this?
D: Anger and sorrow.
Th: Why do you feel sorrow?
D: (pause) He won't be allowed to live.
Th: Let's move forward to the time when they take his life.
D: Sorrow and rejection.
Th: Why do you feel rejection?
D: Shame is given to the entire family, and once a family has been shamed, no one will associate with them.
Th: I see. How was the boy put to death?
D: With a sword.
Th: Was he married?
D: No. He was so young.
Th: How old was he?
D: Fourteen.
Th: On the count of three you'll have much more awareness about this situation and how it relates to your current life. One, two, three.
D: I never forgave him for shaming us.

Daniel perceived no other significant events in that life so I guided him forward to the time of his death in that lifetime. He was killed in a raid on their village:

Th: How do you feel now?
D: Sad at the loss. Glad it's over.
Th: What happens next?
D: (pause) There are people welcoming me. I don't know them. They're glad to see me. (pause) My grandson has gone on. He won't be there to greet me.
Th: Where has he gone?
D: Back to live another life.
Th: I see. What else is happening in that scene?
D: My daughter. We're glad to see each other.
Th: Good. What else?
D: It's just a relief it's over, but I feel sorrow for what happened.
Th: Please see your grandson in front of you now.
D: I see a child, of about six years old.
Th: Is this your grandson?
D: Yes.
Th: He needs to understand your words, so please see an older version of your grandson in front of you.
D: Okay.
Th: Please tell him, either with my words or in your own words, that you forgive him for what happened and that you accept him as he is, no matter what.
D: I'm sorry I turned away and never said I loved you, because I do. I was just so hurt, and so ashamed, and so fearful for us both. I didn't want you to have to go through the rejection and the hurt.
Th: Notice his response please.
D: Just a hug. (crying softly)
Th: Good. Tell him you love and accept him no matter what.
D: I love you no matter what. You'll always be a part of me.
Th: What's his response?
D: He knows.
Th: If there's anything else he wants to say to you, please listen and perceive it now.
D: (pause) He said, "Just go and learn."

Th: Is there anything specifically that he wants you to learn?
D: To accept others no matter what.
Th: Good. How does that relate to your current sexuality?
D: By accepting my sexuality I learn to accept others, even if they are different. Accepting myself is harder than accepting others.
Th: Okay. Have you forgiven him and yourself for what happened?
D: Yes.
Th: Is there anything else you were supposed to learn from that lifetime? If so, you'll know it on the count of three. One, two, three.
D: (pause) Learn . . . to put my worth in myself and not have to depend on others who may reject me for things I don't have control over.
Th: Did you learn that?
D: (pause) No, I ran from it.
Th: Are you learning those same lessons in your current life?
D: Yes.
Th: If there's anything else to be aware of about that lifetime, you'll know it, and it will be clear on the count of three. One, two, three.
D: You decide for yourself what is right or wrong, and the judgment of others is irrelevant.

I guided Daniel forward to one more lifetime related to his current sexuality. He perceived himself as a young male soldier living in Germany in 1918. He describes how a fellow soldier has taken a liking to him:

Th: How do you feel as this soldier?
D: I'm furious at someone who told me he likes me in a way I don't want to be liked.
Th: Please tell me more about that. On the count of three it will become much more vivid. One, two, three.
D: He's in the same regiment as me and follows me like a sick puppy, even though I tell him not to, that I'm not interested. I hit him and tell him to stop.
Th: What's he doing?
D: Crying.
Th: How do you feel?

D: I'm furious. I've told him no and he persists. I slammed the door and left . . . I told him to leave me alone.

The soldier left the military soon after and went back home to find much of his neighborhood destroyed. He eventually took a job as a guard and remained single the rest of his life. He perceived no other significant events, so I guided him forward to the last day of his life in that lifetime:

Th: What's happening?
D: Bombs are falling everywhere.
Th: What's the year?
D: 1942.
Th: How do you feel?
D: Frightened. Everything is shaking and dusty. People are screaming.
Th: Please move forward until your death.
D: Direct hit. The whole building just blew up.

I guided Daniel into the Higher Self state and began asking him questions:

Th: How does the situation with the soldier who liked you relate to your current life sexual orientation?
D: I was suppressing my sexuality. I was attracted to him, too. I wouldn't allow myself to express it or even believe it.
Th: What were you meant to learn from that life?
D: (pause) I was a user. I had to learn not to use people. I spent that whole lifetime just taking whatever I wanted, wherever I could get it. I learned that it's important to consider how the other person feels.
Th: What else did you learn from that lifetime?
D: You don't always win just because you got what you wanted.
Th: Do you know the man now who was the soldier then?
D: I don't know.
Th: On the count of three, you'll know it, and it will become vivid to you. One, two, three.
D: Oh . . . an ex-lover of mine.

Th: How else has that lifetime influenced your current life?
D: I was just so mean. That lifetime made me more sensitive in this life.

I concluded the regression and brought Daniel back to the present.

Do we change sexual orientation through our lifetimes just as we change sex, careers, and social standing? If so, does this mean that only our current personalities and not our essential selves have a sexual orientation? Based on the information Daniel perceived, the answers to those questions would be seem to be yes. We experience most or all aspects of our lives, including sexual orientation, for growth and as the result of karma. Daniel is experiencing his current life as a gay male to learn more about accepting himself and others, and to learn about sensitivity. He struggled with his sexual orientation for several years in his teens in part because his strict religious upbringing implied that homosexuality is a sin. However, once he realized that those condemning homosexuality were struggling with their own sexuality and/or acceptance issues which had nothing to do with him, he was able to accept his sexual orientation. He now realizes that what others think of him doesn't matter.

Karmic Reasons for Sexual Orientation

As described in the above case history, one of the main karmic reasons of homosexuality or bisexuality is learning to accept the self and others unconditionally. According to the laws of karma and reincarnation, those who do not accept homosexuals, bisexuals, or anyone else who is different than themselves may eventually need to experience in a future life those very characteristics they condemned, to learn what it feels like to be treated with such contempt. Through this experience, they will have the opportunity to learn the importance of loving and accepting everyone, no matter how different, and in the process learn to love and accept themselves.

Such beliefs as "it just isn't right" or "it's a sin" allow some people to justify negative thoughts and behavior towards homosexuals and bisexuals. However, no matter how creative the justifications, the law of karma doesn't care what our current personality believes; all actions and words will eventually return to us. So, as with anything that is karmic, sexual orientation should not be seen as a punishment, but as an opportunity chosen by the soul for growth.

I have found through past-life regressions with clients that there seem to be various karmic reasons for non-heterosexuality. Many of these reasons have to do with acceptance and forgiveness issues. Sometimes there is more than one karmic reason for sexual orientation. The most common patterns are described in the following examples, but please note that, because everyone is unique, there are many variations and combinations of these patterns.

"Sex" is used here to denote biological orientation while "gender" is used to indicate the psychological aspect and the level of masculinity or femininity one projects.

Current life sex: Male
Current life gender: Masculine
Current life sexual orientation: Homosexual
Possible past-life experiences causing or contributing to sexual orientation:

- Many lifetimes as a male interacting mostly with males, primarily in military and religious institutions. This type of male often subconsciously perceives women as weak and/or inferior. He naturally feels more comfortable with and more attracted to other men. Sometimes this propensity is more obvious with gay men who place a lot of emphasis on masculinity or body mass. It also may be a reason some gay, "ultra-masculine" men are only attracted to other men who are the same.
- May have had one or more lifetimes in which he had negative, perhaps devastating experiences with women, often involving mistrust. If so, the person would benefit by uncovering those experiences and then releasing them by forgiving himself and all involved.
- May have hurt one or more women in previous lives, sometimes by rape. He carries subconscious guilt about those past events, which causes him to be unable to perform sexually with a woman now. Being gay this time will make it almost impossible for him to repeat his mistake.
- May have been abused by a woman in this life, which may have been caused by guilt felt about his actions towards women in past lives.

What he may need to learn from his current sex, gender and sexual orientation: Acceptance and forgiveness of self and others. May need to nurture and develop feminine side. Focusing on and getting in touch with the emotional and spiritual self could help accomplish this. Forming friendships with women and repairing or developing good relationships with his mother and any sisters may also help.
Challenge this lifetime: Respect and accept all humans, especially women and feminine or "emotional" men.
Best approach: See everyone as equal, including those who may not appear to be as strong emotionally or physically.

Current life sex: Male
Current life gender: Feminine
Current life sexual orientation: Homosexual
Possible past-life experiences causing or contributing to sexual orientation:

- Has been female many times in past lives, usually involved sexually and romantically with men and now he feels comfortable doing the same. Sex with women feels unnatural.
- Traumatic unresolved experiences as a female in past lives such as rape or abuse.
- Condemned homosexuals in past lives.

What he may need to learn from his current sex, gender and sexual orientation: If he condemned homosexuals in a past life, then acceptance and unconditional love of others and self, regardless of differences.
Challenge this lifetime: Rejection for being feminine and/or gay.
Best approach: Respect and love self and others unconditionally, especially those who condemn him for being gay or feminine. It would be best to actively find others who accept and love him unconditionally and to accept and release those who don't.

Current life sex: Female
Current life gender: Masculine
Current life sexual orientation: Homosexual
Possible past-life experiences causing or contributing to sexual orientation:

- May have lived more lifetimes as a male. Loving women rather than men feels more natural for her now.

- May have hurt women in past lives either emotionally or physically. May have been abused and mistreated by men in current life which was caused by her subconscious guilt from prior lives.

What she may need to learn from her current sex, gender and sexual orientation: To love and respect women.
Challenge this lifetime: To understand that the men who may have hurt her in this life or men she observes hurting other women are mirrors for the way she may have been in a past life.
Best approach: Forgive self for hurting anyone in the past, especially women. Forgive any men who have hurt her in this life.
Notes: Being treated by men in this life as she may have treated women in a past life can sometimes cause an aversion to men in general. This resentment needs to be addressed, since it's a mirror for her actions in past lives. This enforces the importance of forgiving and accepting the self and others.

Current life sex: Female
Current life gender: Feminine
Current life sexual orientation: Homosexual
Possible past-life experiences causing or contributing to sexual orientation:

- May have lived more lives as a female.
- Hurt physically or emotionally by men in the past.
- May subconsciously harbor feelings of distrust or uneasiness about men, so she is only attracted to females.

What she may need to learn from her current sex, gender and sexual orientation: Often acceptance and forgiveness.
Challenge this lifetime: Forgive anyone who ever hurt her in this life and in prior lives, especially men.
Best approach: Forgive and realize that men who have hurt her have given her an opportunity for growth.

Current life sex: Male, female
Current life gender: Masculine or feminine
Current life sexual orientation: Bisexual
Past-life experiences causing or contributing to sexual orientation:

- May have had lifetimes of loving men and lifetimes of loving women. Loving both now feels natural.

- May have had lifetimes in more sexually open cultures where bisexuality was accepted.
- Past-life lover is the same sex in current life.

What he or she may need to learn from current sex, gender and sexual orientation: Often acceptance. Sometimes they are learning (or have learned) that what we are attracted to most is a person's soul (and how we knew that soul in different lifetimes), not only their physical appearance or sex.

Challenge this lifetime: Rejection by heterosexuals and homosexuals.

Best approach: Accept others even if they don't accept him or her. Accept themselves even if they are different. Be true to themselves and their feelings. Be honest with those with whom they are involved with romantically and sexually.

Note: Bisexuals may be equally attracted to either sex or more attracted to one sex. They may be only sexually active with one sex.

In all cases, if sexual orientation has never been an issue and has never caused stress, it may not be karmic. The soul may have chosen that particular body and life for other reasons and the sexual orientation was simply part of the package deal.

Can Past-life Regression Effectively Alter Sexual Orientation?

Throughout history, sexuality has been the cause of much pleasure and pain. When sexuality has been expressed and accepted, it has helped us love and connect with each other. When sexuality has been suppressed or denied, it has at least caused personal turmoil and stress, and at worst caused murder and suicide. In the previous case history, Daniel learned to accept his sexual orientation and is quite comfortable living his life as he feels instead of as society expects him to. However, for many people who are attracted to the same or both sexes, their sexuality creates much stress. This isn't surprising when you consider how our society views sexual orientation. Those who are uncomfortable with their sexual orientation have gone to great lengths to try and escape their unwanted feelings, including extensive therapy and even marriage to a more socially acceptable partner. Ultimately, they find that denying or suppressing their feelings is neither effective nor even possible.

Some people have asked me if past-life regression and root cause therapy can help alter sexual orientation. They assume that since certain processes such as hypnosis or guided meditation and past-life regression can be used to find and repair the root cause of other conflicts, why can't the same be done for sexual orientation? While these tools have successfully been used to enhance sexual performance—increase sex drive, eliminate impotence, eliminate the inability to orgasm, and so on— *root cause and other similar therapies are unlikely to change a person's primary sexual orientation.* There are several reasons.

First, past-life regression research indicates that sexual orientation for each life is decided by a soul before choosing the body to be born into. If that orientation is part of the major lesson or theme for that lifetime, then the soul will choose appropriately. Our sexual orientation in each life thus depends on what our soul needs to experience for its highest growth. According to the theories of karma and reincarnation, our current personality has not "chosen" its true sexual orientation (the one it is truly more attracted to as opposed to the sex they say they're attracted to); it's a decision made by our soul before incarnating. Similarly, our soul has chosen the appropriate parents, body, environment, childhood experiences and more to better enable it to learn certain lessons through certain experiences. *Therefore, genes or environment, including childhood experiences and sexual abuse, are not the main causes of sexual orientation; they are only contributing factors.*

Still, even though hypnosis or guided meditation and past-life regression may not be able to transform a stereotypical gay male or lesbian female into a stereotypical straight male or female, these therapies can dissolve any fears that have *contributed* to sexual orientation which then might influence sexual orientation. For example, a gay male's extreme distrust of women may have contributed to his sexual orientation. If, through past-life regression, he were to find, forgive, and release the root cause, he may become more interested in forming relationships with women, which could lead to romantic/sexual expressions.

Second, as mentioned above, there are many contributing factors to sexual orientation, and so finding and releasing the spiritual root cause of homosexuality (why the soul chose to experience life as a homosexual) through past-life regression may not change or even influence the current life sexual orientation. There may also be physical, emotional, and mental reasons for the current life sexual orientation.

Third, our sexual orientation is the result of a combination of past lives (those from which we are currently drawing and from which we are experiencing karma). Also, there are many karmic reasons for homosexuality or bisexuality, both for those who are experiencing it *and* their family, friends and acquaintances. The most common is learning to accept the self and others. *Struggling against or trying to change such a fundamental part of the self may be missing the point.*

What about bisexuality? Some feel that since we have had many lives as both male and female, bisexuality may be our natural state. However, conditioning in our environment by peers, parents, and religion tells us to ignore same-sex feelings and act on opposite-sex feelings. Past-life regression may actually help dissolve fears about homosexuality for this reason.

Finally, and perhaps most importantly, *sexual orientation can't be treated as a fear-based problem (such as fear of flying or fear of heights) because sexual attraction isn't a fear-based problem.* In fact, sexual orientation isn't really a problem at all! What creates the conflict is society's intolerance of homosexuality and bisexuality. For that reason, only unconditional acceptance of self and others by all will lead to sexual orientation being irrelevant in our society.

11
Exploring Intimacy Issues and Sexual Orientation

Bill, a 36-year-old gay male, wanted to be in a committed relationship more than anything, but none of his relationships—"more than I care to remember"—ever lasted more than a few months. He said he was usually the one to break them up. He hoped I could help him discover and release any blocks that were causing this pattern and perhaps shed some light on any karmic reasons for his sexual orientation.

During the initial interview, I discovered that Bill had been sexually and mentally abused in his childhood by his father. He had experienced traditional therapy for these issues, which he felt had helped. But he was still unable to forgive his father and Bill realized that forgiveness is an important part of healing.

I also learned in the interview that most of Bill's relationships began with sex. Often when a relationship is based mainly on sex, there is less of a reason for the couple to stay together when the initial chemistry fades. However, when Bill developed a friendship first with someone he was attracted to, he found it difficult to then have sex with that person. Bill had not been able to overcome this through traditional therapy.

I spoke with Bill about what it would mean for him to be in a committed relationship. He seemed to have realistic expectations and said he felt ready to commit to someone compatible, but he still managed to sabotage any possibilities that came close.

I led Bill through a relaxation induction and then into a past life that would explain the root cause of his inability to remain in a love relationship. Bill perceived himself as Colin, an eight-year-old orphan. The year was 1894 and he lived in an orphanage next to a church in London. I asked Bill to move ahead to an important event in that lifetime:

Bill: Ooh . . . (grimaces) I don't like him.
Therapist: Who don't you like?
B: The priest. He's not nice.
Th: What's happening in the scene you're perceiving?
B: The priest is . . . having sex with me.
Th: Rise above your emotions and view the scene only as an observer. Has this happened before?
B: Yes. Often.

At age 13, Bill ran away from the orphanage. He was scared, yet excited to make it on his own. I learned through further questioning that Colin supported himself through prostitution. He would frequent a bar known for its older male patrons who were looking for younger boys for sex. He hated what he did, but didn't see any other way of surviving. Colin seemed tough and street smart on the outside, but lonely and sad on the inside:

Th: What are you doing?
B: I'm walking through the empty streets. It's Christmas Eve. I can see in the windows of houses. Everyone is with their family. I feel really alone. (silent tears)
Th: Let's move forward to another important event on the count of three. One, two, three.
B: I'm arguing with an older man.
Th: Who is this man?
B: A customer. He is the priest, the same person I saw raping me at the orphanage. I don't think he recognizes me. He won't pay me.
Th: Move forward until something happens.
B: He's calling me evil. (gasps) Ooh . . . he stabbed me with a knife. I think I died. I can see my body.

I took Bill through the death process and into the Higher Self state so I could question him about the lifetime he had just perceived:

Th: What were you supposed to learn from that life?
B: It was necessary for me to experience being abandoned by my mother.
Th: Why?
B: I had to learn to love myself even when no one else wanted me.
Th: Do you know the soul who was your mother then?
B: She is my mother now.
Th: Do you know why you were placed in the orphanage?
B: My mother then was only 13 when I was born. She didn't know the father.
Th: What are your feelings now towards the person who was your mother then?
B: I understand why she did what she did. I feel compassion for her.
Th: Do you now know the soul who was the priest?
B: He is my father now.
Th: What are your feelings towards the priest?

Bill answered that he felt a lot of anger, so I guided him through a forgiveness exercise to help release the negative feelings. I then continued questioning him about that life:

Th: What else where you supposed to learn during that lifetime?
B: Independence.
Th: Did you learn it?
B: It was meant to just be experienced, not necessarily learned.
Th: Before we end the session, is there anything else that you would benefit from knowing at this time?
B: (pause) I'm seeing the word forgiveness.
Th: And who does this relate to?
B: My father . . . other people, too. It's not easy for me to forgive.
Th: It will get easier through this process. Let's move into another lifetime that will explain the cause of your inability to maintain a love relationship in your current life. On the count of three, move

to a lifetime that will explain the cause. One, two, three. Please tell me what's happening.

Bill perceived himself as a single 19-year-old woman named Sylvia living in Salem, Massachusetts in the late 1700s. I guided him forward to an important event:

B: I'm seeing a black stagecoach pull up drawn by two large, shiny black horses. A man got out, dressed in all black and wearing a black top hat.
Th: Please look at the man and describe him.
B: He has a black beard and piercing blue eyes. They aren't friendly eyes.
Th: Follow this scene and tell me what's happening.
B: I am dining privately with this man. We are lovers. No one must know.

Through further questioning, I learned that this man was married and owned the town bank. Sylvia was his kept mistress. She eventually became pregnant by the man with the black beard and blue eyes. I questioned "her" about that:

Th: Have you told him yet?
B: No. I know he will not be happy.
Th: Okay, let's move forward to the time when you tell him.
B: Noooo! (holds both hands on his stomach)
Th: What's happening?
B: He's coming after me. He's beating me.
I guided "Silvia" above the pain and emotion.
Th: What's happening now?
B: I can see the body. I'm just laying there . . . I feel like I'm floating. I think I'm dead.

I guided Bill through the death process in that life and into the Higher Self state so I could help him gain awareness about that lifetime. Again, the man who murdered him in that life is his father in this life. He felt that his anger toward the man brought them together again. Obviously, they again failed to work things out harmoniously.

Bill went from the post-death Light right into anther life that turned out to be connected to the previous lifetimes. He perceived himself as a 10-year-old boy living in the southwestern United States in 1854. He didn't go to school. His mother had him working all day, every day, panning for gold. He was his mother's slave. I asked him to perceive his mother:

B: She has long black hair tied back in a bun, long skirt. She's not nice.
Th: How is your relationship with your mother?
B: We don't have a relationship, really. I just do what she says. I mainly work and give her my earnings.
Th: On the count of three, please move forward to a significant event. One, two, three. What's happening?
B: I'm on a horse. I'm leaving.
Th: How old are you now?
B: Fifteen.
Th: Tell me more, please.
B: I'm leaving home and my mother is very angry. She's yelling after me.
Th: How do you feel?
B: I feel nothing for her. It feels great to finally be free of her. I'm just casually riding away on my horse and not looking back.

He finally left his abusive mother after being her slave for the first part of his life. The rest of his short life was spent panning for gold and was relatively uneventful. I once again took him through his death and into the Light for post-death questioning. Bill told me that the woman who was his mother then is his father now.

I brought Bill back to the present and asked him for feedback about the session. He said, "Gosh, if my father was really that terrible in those lifetimes, no wonder I feel the way I do about him. My anger goes way back! I guess we've been together more than I realized."

"If reincarnation is true, you have," I said. "The sexual abuse this time wasn't the only cause of your anger, just part of the equation.

That's an example of why I feel it's so important to search past lives for the root cause of current life problems."

In all three lifetimes he perceived, Bill was the victim, and the soul who is now Bill's father was the persecutor. *When looking for the root cause of a current life problem in past lives, karma is always evident. In other words, there is always a connection between the events happening then and those happening now.*

For example, in the regressions Bill had experienced so far, he perceived events that could possibly explain his current life anger against his father and why he had trouble maintaining a relationship. However, he and I both felt that there was more he needed to understand that would further explain the karma between him and his father and his relationship problems. Why had the soul who is his father now felt the need to mistreat Bill over several lifetimes?

In a case such as this, sometimes the victim has never been the persecutor: The lesson could be one of learning self-respect and/or learning to love and accept unconditionally even a person who is cruel. Other times, if traced back far enough, the roles were reversed and the soul who was the victim then becomes the perpetrator, which in turn helps the soul who is the victim now balance karma. During the next session, I took Bill back to a lifetime that would further explain the current situation with his father and his inability to remain in a healthy, loving relationship:

Th: Please tell me what you're perceiving.

B: I'm standing in a room . . . stone floor and walls, dark, torches on the wall for light. I'm seeing a long wood dining table. Everything looks sort of medieval.

Th: Please describe yourself.

B: I'm male, dark hair, medium build. I don't like this guy.

Th: What year is it?

B: (pause) 472.

Th: What country are you in?

B: (pause) Italy, I think.

Th: Are you married?

B: Yes. It is for appearances. I don't love her.

Th: What do you mean, for appearances?

B: I am some kind of ruler. I had to take a wife.

Th: On the count of three, please move forward to a significant event in that life. One, two, three. What's happening?
B: I'm hitting him with some kind of long stick.
Th: Who are you hitting?
B: One of my servants.
Th: Why are you hitting him?
B: He did something wrong, as usual. He deserves it.
Th: Do you hit your servants often?
B: Not all of them. Mainly just this one.

Through further questioning, I learned that he routinely beat and sexually abused this servant—who is the same soul as his father now. Bill almost became physically ill when he perceived this sadistic, cruel man misusing his power by sexually abusing any males who were suspected of being homosexual. He believed that homosexuals were less than human, and therefore deserved the treatment he gave them. He was eventually murdered by two of his servants. No one missed him.

In the post-death questioning, Bill realized that he still subconsciously perceived gay men as less than human. Therefore, this made it difficult to love and accept himself as a gay man and next to impossible to love and accept any partners he had, especially after sex was introduced into the relationship. Discovering the root cause of his inability to remain in a relationship allowed Bill to forgive himself, which in turn released and dissolved the influence of those deep feelings.

Bill's lesson that time had to do with power. In this life, Bill resents and sometimes protests against those who mistreat homosexuals or abuse their power. These people are mirrors for Bill, reflections of how he was in the distant past. By accepting and forgiving (but not tolerating) anyone who mistreats homosexuals or abuses power, he would be accepting and forgiving himself. Furthermore, from being both the abuser and the abused, Bill now understands the importance of treating others with respect, no matter who they are and what they've done.

In the Higher Self state of mind, Bill felt that he had viewed the lifetimes necessary to resolve his relationship block. He also felt that he would now be free to create the love relationship he wanted. After

I helped Bill dissolve the guilt he was still holding onto from that previous lifetime as an abuser, I guided him back to the present:

B: Wow! (worried look on his face) I was a terrible person, wasn't I?
Th: Yes, you were. Don't worry, though; we've all been terrible in past lives.
B: No wonder my father doesn't like me! I don't blame him after what I saw. I guess I sort of deserve to be gay and abused by my father.
Th: Whether or not you deserved to be gay or treated like that isn't the point. That implies that someone else is deciding what happens to you which, in light of the laws of karma and reincarnation, is false. You choose, on a soul level, everything that happens to you. Negative experiences aren't punishments, just opportunities for growth and to love unconditionally ourselves and everyone else, even those who hurt us.
B: So I didn't deserve to be sexually abused in this life?
Th: No. Your soul chose the experience for learning and growth. Of course, if you look at the small picture, you're a victim. If you look at the big picture, it was part of your plan.
B: So I suppose my being gay is also part of the plan.
Th: From what you've perceived, yes, it seems that it has allowed you the opportunity accept and love all parts of yourself unconditionally, including your sexual orientation.
B: I can see how my disgust and mistreatment of gays then would be a hidden block for me now in relationships.
Th: Yes, and since you now know the cause, you can more easily overcome it by continuing to accept and forgive yourself and others.
B: After perceiving the "big picture" as you say, it almost feels like I should be grateful to have the opportunity to deal with my father—again.
Th: Yes, you and your father have decided, on some level, to reunite in order to work through the baggage you share.
B: So my job is to accept him and love him as he is, no matter what?
Th: Yes. No matter what. Know that he is serving you perfectly. However, that doesn't mean you need to tolerate any further disrespect. You always have the option of walking away. To react in a

negative way, though, would only create more negative karma for yourself.

B: What if I forgive, accept, and love him unconditionally, but he doesn't do the same with me? Will I have to come back with him again?

Th: If you "pass the test" this time you may not need to, although you may choose to in order to help him. On the other hand, you may be done with him, and some other soul who has similar karma will "stand in" for you with him until one or both of them get it right.

B: Boy, do I have more compassion for my father now.

Th: And more for yourself, too, I hope.

B: Absolutely.

Th: Do you understand why forgiveness is so important?

B: Yes. Forgiving others and myself felt like I was letting go of all the anger and guilt. I actually feel lighter from it.

Th: Yes, and that anger and guilt from the past is what creates negative situations in the present and interferes with what you want in life.

B: Like a relationship.

Th: Exactly.

Bill still expressed concern about seeing himself in a past life as such a bad person. I explained that most people, when regressed to enough prior lives, will see themselves as "bad" characters or doing "bad" things. Someone who was a murderer, torturer, or thief in a past life may be a saint in this life; they learned through their actions how important it is to respect and love others. *It doesn't matter what you did or what someone else did to you as long as you're willing to learn from your mistakes, forgive yourself and others, and take total responsibility for your actions in the current life. Forgiveness is essential to completely let go of the past and embrace the present and future.*

I gave Bill a forgiveness exercise to continue to forgive himself, his father, and anyone else in his life (see chapter 14) and some relationship recommendations (see chapter 15). Since Bill's subconscious blocks had been addressed and released, he was now ready to take conscious action that would further help him reach his relationship goals.

I heard from Bill three months later. He said he felt like a new person, especially in regard to his love life. He found himself approaching dating and relationships completely differently. He wasn't sure if he was attracting people who were different, or simply seeing people differently as a result of the past-life therapy and forgiveness work. Most likely both. Bill felt it was inevitable that he would reach and maintain his love life goals since he had chosen to and continues to make changes and improvements in himself.

How Does This Relate To You?

- When you search for the root cause for a current life problem in past lives, karma is always evident. In other words, everything you're experiencing now (effect) can be traced back to a past experience (cause), which either happened in this life or a previous life, and usually both. For example, Bill experienced difficulty in relationships now as a result of his childhood experiences and his past-life experiences.
- If you appear to be a victim now, it doesn't necessarily mean that you were the persecutor in a past life. Sometimes there are other root reasons for your "bad" experiences such as false guilt from accidentally hurting someone, or your soul choosing to be an example for others around you. However, role reversals—where the persecutor is reborn as the victim—do help balance karma.
- If you gain awareness about and take responsibility for what has happened to you, it will be easier to forgive and rise above any conflicts resulting from the experience. For example, before Bill's past-life regressions, he had a difficult time forgiving his father. However, once he became aware of the big picture it was far easier for him to do so. He no longer viewed himself as a victim. As the result of his new awareness, he was able to take responsibility for what happened to him. He realized that his father wasn't an enemy, but a teacher. He realized that forgiving his father was mainly for himself, to let go of the anger and resentment that was blocking his happiness.

Section IV

Dealing With Other Relationship Issues

12
How Do You Know When to Leave?

When two people decide to get a divorce, it isn't a sign that they "don't understand" one another, but a sign that they have, at last, begun to.
— Helen Rowland (1875–1950)

When a relationship ends, it's often called a "failed relationship." This implies that it was supposed to last forever, no matter what, and if it ends before one partner dies, there is something wrong with one or both of them. This belief is unreasonable yet surprisingly common. Not all relationships are meant to last forever—or even six months, for that matter. When people try to force a relationship to meet their expectations instead of allowing it to be what it's meant to be, the result will be unhappiness and stress.

The length of time a relationship lasts is irrelevant. What really matters is how we treat and react to our partners and what is learned and accomplished in the process, which is why we, on a soul level, choose the relationships that we do.

On the other hand, if staying together *is* for a couple's highest good, then confronting the problematic issues and working together to resolve conflict can often improve and save a relationship. Unfortunately, both partners aren't always interested in doing what is necessary to repair a relationship. Furthermore, if a couple spends more time in conflict than they do enjoying and loving each other, something went wrong: one or both of them didn't express their true selves in the beginning of the relationship, their expectations were or are too high, or they have grown in different directions.

To expect to be spiritually, physically, emotionally, and mentally compatible with the same person for an entire lifetime is usually unrealistic. This only becomes possible when both partners have obtained a high degree of awareness about themselves (especially before becoming involved in the relationship) and about each other, which in our society is rare. *Therefore, divorce is to be expected until couples know themselves on all levels, are honest about what works for them in a relationship, discover the reasons they were drawn together (again), and accept and love each other unconditionally.*

When looking at relationships with an understanding of karma and reincarnation, it becomes clear that there are many different reasons that couples come together (again). Therefore, forcing a relationship to conform to what society expects may be going against the karmic grain. Whether consciously understood or not, couples often reunite to continue where they left off in a past life. If the relationship ended poorly in the past, then it may be challenging and stressful. If the relationship ended happily in the past, then it will probably be more harmonious as they may have dissolved previous conflicts.

No matter how impossible it may seem now, we have the option of working things out this time. That doesn't always mean "together forever." It implies that as forgiveness, compassion, and unconditional love are practiced, negative karma is overcome and no additional negative karma is created.

Divorce or breaking up doesn't have to be the end of the world; it can be the beginning of a better life for each partner and even lead to a stronger friendship between them. When breaking up is the best option, a happy ending is possible and more beneficial for all involved. If this is the desired outcome, then both partners need to make an effort to end the relationship harmoniously.

The following case illustrates the typical way that society views breaking up and how forgiveness and awareness can make it a positive learning experience.

Gladys, a 52-year-old divorced woman, was brought to me by her daughter Lisa. Before the session, Lisa explained that her mother was depressed, angry and unhappy. Four years ago, Lisa's father had left her mother for a younger woman after 25 years of marriage. To make matters worse, the divorce turned into a battle over money which Gladys lost. After not working for 24 years, Gladys has been forced to support herself and save for her retirement. She felt that her whole life was ruined because of the divorce and she had no desire to go on. Lisa had metaphysical interests and understood how past-life regression therapy worked. She hoped that her mother could benefit from my services. Gladys, on the other hand, had no interest in anything metaphysical and considered reincarnation and karma "fantasy" and "wishful thinking." I explained to Lisa on the phone that I couldn't help her mother unless she was open-minded enough to temporarily suspend her skepticism. Lisa assured me that she could persuade her mother to allow the process to work for her.

I could feel Gladys' resistance as soon as she arrived at my office. It was obvious she didn't want to be there, so I asked what she hoped to accomplish by using my services.

"You mean what Lisa hopes I can accomplish," Gladys responded. "I'm not so sure about this."

"Mother," Lisa pleaded, "please try. You said you would." Lisa turned to me. "I am hoping that you can help my mother resolve her anger at my father for divorcing her and help her find some peace in her life. I know that the awareness she will find through what you do will help her, if she allows it to."

I looked at Gladys. "Yes, I can help you, if you let me. Tell me how you feel about your ex-husband."

"He's ruined my life."

"How has your life been ruined?" I asked.

"All the friends we had were 'our' friends; now they're mostly his friends. I have to worry about my financial future. Worst of all, who wants to marry an old woman like me?" Gladys appeared close to tears. "Marriage is supposed to be for a lifetime. If he had felt the same, we'd still be together."

I pressed the issue. "So what you're saying, Gladys, is that even if one or both people in a commitment aren't happy, they should stay together?"

"Yes, they need to make it work."

I considered her statement. "Yes, it's important to work out the conflicts if at all possible, but what if the relationship isn't meant to last a lifetime? What if two people just can't make it work, and by staying unhappily together would miss valuable learning experiences in other relationships? You seem to believe that the length of a marriage is more important than what is best for the two people involved."

Gladys looked irritated. "Him leaving me is best for him, not me. I wanted to work things out. My husband obviously didn't feel the same. He threw away our life together."

"You're angry with your ex-husband because he did what was best for him. Do you think that it could be what is best for you?" I asked.

"How?"

"Perhaps you needed to experience this breakup. Perhaps you need to be single now to have the time and energy to concentrate on some other area of your life. Perhaps if your husband hadn't left you, you wouldn't be available for a more compatible and satisfying relationship. Perhaps he did you a favor."

"I don't know about that." Gladys sat silently for a moment, then said, "What does reincarnation have to do with all of this, anyway?"

"More than you probably think," I said looking directly in her eyes. "For every action there is an equal reaction. That's called karma. Whatever you say, do, think, and intend will return to you, both the good and the bad."

Gladys looked angry. "You're saying that I deserved to have my husband leave me?!"

"It's not a question of whether or not you deserved it. That implies that there is a judging God, and I don't believe there is. We choose, on some level, our negative experiences to learn what we need to for our highest growth." I paused to allow her to absorb my statements.

"I chose to have my husband leave me for a younger woman?!" Gladys turned red with anger. "That's the most ridiculous thing I've ever heard!"

"Mother," Lisa said, "I think what Stephen means is that your *soul* chose to experience that."

"That's right, Lisa. Our current personalities don't want negative things to happen to us, but our souls know that sometimes the more difficult experiences will help us the most. Gladys, what do you feel happens to us when we die?"

Gladys pondered the question. "I'm not sure. My parents were very religious and they taught me that we go either to heaven or to hell. I do hope there is more than this waiting for me."

I began to have hope that I could get through to Gladys. "I do, too, otherwise life would seem rather pointless, especially the unpleasant things, like heartache."

"That's for sure," Gladys agreed.

"Gladys," I began, "if you look at life only in ways you can physically touch, it all seems rather meaningless. All this effort for what? However, if you look for and discover the root reasons for experiences, which often go way beyond what we are influenced from birth to believe, it all begins to make sense."

Gladys seemed to consider my statements. "How do you know that's the way it really works?"

"I don't, but reincarnation and karma are the only theories that make sense to me. And after all of the regressions and research I've done, I accept that we really do reincarnate, and I accept that everything I put out comes back to me. The more I apply these theories to life, the more they make sense to me."

Gladys crossed her arms. "Well, I'm not sure if I accept any of these ideas."

"You don't need to. In fact, if you automatically accepted these beliefs without applying them to your life, I would question whether you really understood them. You don't need to believe in reincarnation and karma for my processes to work for you. But you'll get far better results if you at least temporarily suspend your judgment and act *as if* you have lived before."

"Now that I'm here I may as well try it. What do you want me to do?"

I proceeded to explain the basic principals of reincarnation and karma, the importance of forgiveness in this process, how guided meditation works, and what to expect with past-life regression. I also stressed again the importance of acting as if she has lived before and pretending that past lives are real. After leading her through a relaxation process and into a past life that would give her more awareness about the reasons for her husband leaving her, I began asking her questions.

Gladys perceived herself as a 27-year-old woman living in Germany in 1668. She was wealthy and beautiful and used her beauty to manipulate and "take what I want without concern for others." She married for money, ignored her husband, and flirted and slept with whomever she pleased. At this point I asked her about her marriage:

Therapist: How does your husband feel about your affairs?
Gladys: He is upset by them, but never does anything about it. He's afraid he'll lose me if he does.
Th: Let's move forward to an important event in that life we are exploring, on the count of three. One, two, three.What's happening, please?
G: I'm leaving.
Th: Where are you going?
G: I'm leaving my husband to be with the man I love. We are very happy.
Th: What about your husband?
G: What about him? He can take care of himself.

The woman and her new lover were happy together for several years, until she left him, too, after meeting someone else. She continued this pattern until her mid-40s when she stopped taking care of herself and her beauty began to fade.

Gladys perceived no other significant awareness about that life related to her current life situation with her ex-husband, so I guided her into another. She perceived herself as a woman living in a primitive culture somewhere in Northern Africa. She felt they had no calendar system. At this point I asked her about her love life in that lifetime:

G: (pause) We don't get married like today. I do have a significant other.
Th: Please focus on this person. On the count of three, see this person in front of you. One, two, three.

G: I see a strong man, dark hair and eyes. I feel a lot of love for him.
Th: Do you have children?
G: Yes, three boys and one girl.
Th: Let's move forward to an important event on the count of three. One, two, three.
G: Ohhh . . . I feel very angry.
Th: Get in touch with that anger and tell me why you're feeling it.
G: I found out my partner is having an affair with another woman.
Th: What do you do about this?
G: Ohhh!
Th: What is happening?
G: (crying) I just stabbed him in the heart with a sharp blade.
Th: What happens next?
G: (crying) He's dead.

Gladys was banished from the community for the murder of her partner. She died alone and unhappy. I guided her through her death experience in that life and then to the Higher Self state to gain more awareness about what she perceived and how it relates to her current life:

Th: In the first lifetime you viewed as the beautiful woman in Germany, do you know the soul now who was your husband then?
G: Yes, he is my ex-husband now.
Th: What is the connection between your actions then and the events in your current life?
G: (pause) My ex-husband still had or has a lot of resentment against me for how I treated him. I don't blame him. I wasn't very nice to him. I stole from him and my actions made him look foolish to everyone.
Th: What else?
G: I still have guilt about how I treated him. That contributed to my husband divorcing me and leaving me with little money.
Th: How so?
G: (pause) I needed to experience him leaving me so I would realize what it felt like when I did the same to him.
Th: Is leaving a partner wrong?

G: (pause) No. The way in which it is done is the important part (pause). It's important to treat everyone with love and respect at all times, whether or not they do the same with you.
Th: Regarding the second lifetime you perceived where you killed your partner in a jealous rage, what were you meant to learn from that experience?
G: (pause) It was a test for me.
Th: How so?
G: Again, the man I was involved with is my ex-husband now (pause). That life was a test to see if I could react out of love instead of fear to my husband's infidelities. I obviously failed. That wasn't the first time we had been in that situation.
Th: Tell me more about that, please.
G: We have been together many times. Most of the time, our relationships ended because one of us treated the other poorly or had an affair.
Th: Will it happen again?
G: (pause) I have the opportunity now to break the cycle, at least for me. If I let go of the anger and forgive him, I can release myself from this pattern.
Th: Have you learned what you were supposed to learn from the experience of your husband leaving you?
G: If I react with anger, no, I have not. If I accept his actions and forgive him, yes I have.
Th: Are you ready to truly forgive and release your ex-husband?
G: Yes.

I led Gladys through a forgiveness exercise to help her let go of the anger and guilt she felt related to her ex-husband. Emotions were expressed and released, and the process was extremely healing for her. I had her converse with her ex-husband in her mind so that she could express her true feelings to him. By the end of that conversation, Gladys seemed at peace with both herself and her ex-husband. Even though he wasn't physically in her presence, this visualization process is powerful for both of them; the communication will reach the person on a subconscious level.

After gently bringing her back to the present, I gave Gladys time to adjust to what she perceived and then asked her what she thought about the experience:

G: I don't know if I believe it all, but it felt like I really was those women.
Th: You may have been. Like I told you earlier, it doesn't really matter if you actually lived those lives or not. The most important parts are forgiveness and acceptance. Even if your mind made it all up, the process still allowed you to take responsibility for what has happened to you, package the interfering emotions, and then release them.
G: If it is all true, I really do want to forgive my ex! I don't want to have to come back with him again!
Th: Even if we don't reincarnate, you still would benefit from forgiving him. You understand why that is important now, don't you?
G: Because it will only hurt me if I don't.
Th: That's right. Forgiving him is for you, not him. Do you realize what anger and resentment can do to someone?
G: No, what?
Th: Many feel that intense negative emotions can eventually manifest in the physical body as diseases like cancer. Of course, that would be the emotional or spiritual reason for the cancer, not the physical reason.
G: Well, all the more reason to forgive him!

If Gladys continues to express and feel forgiveness towards her ex-husband, she'll pass the test this time and also be able to move on with her life.

This case is yet another example of how our partners often mirror for us what we are suppressing or not accepting about ourselves, or what we expressed in the distant past in another time and place, and often both.

Gladys' anger towards her ex-husband was actually more about her own guilt for treating him the way she did in past lives. *Therefore, taking responsibility for what happens to you and forgiving others, no matter how much they have hurt you, will always be to your advantage.*

How Do You Know When to Leave?

In our society, we are programmed to believe and expect that all relationships should last a lifetime and that it is sad or bad when a relationship ends. In reality, each relationship is unique and none should be viewed with such rigid expectations. If you're unhappy in a relationship, how do you know when to leave? Are you meant to stay with your partner for some kind of karmic payback? Will you be incurring negative karma if you leave? Will you miss a valuable opportunity if you leave? Use the guidelines below to help decide if it's best to leave an unhappy relationship.

- If you're involved in an abusive relationship and your partner refuses to get help, especially if you or any children are in danger, get out as soon as you can.
- Consider discovering the karma between you both and the karmic reasons for the relationship (see chapter 14). Have you successfully worked through and overcome your karma with this individual, or at least expressed forgiveness and acceptance? If your partner was also willing to overcome the karma between you both—if it was necessary—have you helped him or her do this or played your part? If you haven't completed your karmic reasons for reuniting, you may not be ready to leave. If you have completed your end of the bargain and your partner refuses to do his or her part, it may be time for you to leave. Becoming aware of the spiritual/karmic reasons *why* you and your partner have (re)united will help you understand what is best for both of you. Such awareness can sometimes transform and greatly improve a relationship for both partners, or initiate a peaceful and joyous ending.
- Evaluate the pros and cons of the relationship from both sides.
- Evaluate the pros and cons of staying and leaving from both sides.
- Do you still love each other and want to stay together, yet your relationship seems restrictive? If so, perhaps honest communication and redefining your relationship is appropriate (see chapter 13).

After considering the above, if you do decide to leave and you do so with compassion, respect, forgiveness, and love and you don't neglect your responsibilities such as children and finances, leaving can be best for all involved.

The Peaceful Breakup

Breaking up in our society often means an unhappy ending which leaves one or both partners feeling angry, upset, or heartbroken. There are frequently fights over money, property, friends, and children. However, more couples are realizing that if they can't work things out and are better off apart, it's possible to end a marriage or relationship harmoniously and happily. Some even become better friends after the marriage or relationship is over. *Instead of perceiving divorce or breakup as a "failed marriage" or "failed relationship," they realize that not all relationships are meant to last a lifetime. They choose to perceive the ending as an opportunity for growth and a new beginning.*

How To Achieve The Peaceful Breakup

1. Consider that your relationship was most likely *meant* to be the way it was to help one or both of you learn and grow. It was most likely *not* meant to be only something you had wished, hoped, or expected it to be.

2. Consider that your unhappiness was caused by *your expectations* of the relationship or partner and not by the relationship itself or your partner.

3. Consider that it is impossible for marriage/commitment contracts/vows/your expectations to override karma. For example, if it's your karma to experience a partner cheating on you, you can't claim to be a victim ("he or she was supposed to be faithful").

4. Take responsibility for the situation; because of karma, there's no such thing as a victim.

5. No one is your enemy, only your teacher. He or she served you perfectly and has helped you learn what you needed to. You now have the opportunity to forgive and move on with your life.

6. Instead of blaming, focus on the lessons involved for you in the situation.

7. Release the desire to get even or see them pay for what they did. The law of karma states that all thoughts, words, actions, and

intent are eventually returned to sender. That includes how you react to your ex's actions.

8. Forgive, forgive, forgive. Every time you think of your ex, thank him or her for giving you the opportunity to love, learn and grow. Forgive them for everything they may have done; holding onto anger or resentment only hurts you. Forgive yourself as well.

9. Accept that they did the best they could.

10. Don't take your ex's actions personally. This only wastes energy and causes stress.

11. Detach from the situation as much as possible by accepting what is.

12. If necessary, allow each other time to release, forgive, and heal before attempting to interact.

13. If children are involved, never say anything negative about your ex in their presence. Stay neutral or don't say anything.

14. Meditate to help yourself relax and rise above the stress.

15. To avoid attracting incompatible partners or repeating the same mistakes, prepare for a more appropriate relationship by discovering and dissolving any relationship karma that could cause similar situations in your future relationships.

16. The past is over. Look forward to being in a better state of mind soon and, when you've healed and learned from this relationship, discovering a much more compatible, loving relationship.

Marrying to increase love is like gaming to become rich; alas, you only lose what little stock you had before.

— William Wycherley (1640–1716)

Reconsidering Commitment

We live in a society where marriage is expected. If a couple has been dating for a while and they appear to be a great match, their friends and family will ask, "When are you getting married?" as if it's the only logical next step. If a single person is approaching their 40s or 50s, their (usually married) friends and family will ask, "Don't you want to get married?" as if marriage is necessary for happiness. In the distant past, the contract of marriage was necessary for economic survival, but times have changed. Today couples usually get married because they believe they're in love and want to spend the rest of their lives together. However, nearly 50 percent of all marriages in the U.S. end in divorce, and staying together doesn't guarantee happiness. Are "till death do us part" vows and the traditional relationship expectations still a good idea?

Rather than just getting married or involved without a plan, perhaps a new kind of extended and improved commitment process, long before an actual ceremony, would be more appropriate for modern times. This process may also be used to transform and improve existing commitments.

Steps in the Commitment Process

1. First and perhaps most importantly, each couple who wants a formal commitment, whether heterosexual, homosexual or bisexual, would be encouraged to go through counseling together to determine what they each need in a love relationship, what they each can offer, and if they truly are a good match. This way there won't be grand illusions or expectations based on what a marriage or relationship is "supposed" to be like. They will be able to perceive each other clearly and make a rational decision about whether they are right for each other and for each of their relationship goals. At the end of counseling, they could then decide if they wish to proceed to the next step.

2. They would each be encouraged to discover their individual relationship karma and the karma between them through meditation, past-life regression, or through an experienced numerologist.

3. They would be encouraged to choose a mutual friend or advisor to help them navigate any rough periods during the union. This friend or advisor should be well-liked by both partners and be skilled at communication and negotiation.

4. They would be encouraged to design their own commitment contract. This process will help one or all partners to start realizing how compatible or incompatible they really are. If you think some of the following considerations are inappropriate, realize that if you don't discuss them now they may interfere with your commitment later and potentially cause separation or divorce.

This contract would include decisions about the following:

a. Children

- Do you really want kids or are you just being agreeable?
- How long will you wait to have kids (if you decide to).
- How many would you like to have?
- What form of birth control do you prefer?
- How will you handle childcare?
- What are your parenting techniques?
- What will the arrangements be for the children in case of separation or divorce? Who will pay for their schooling and other needs? These issues are much more complicated during a breakup. Plan ahead to share responsibility and do what is best for your children.

b. Money

- Will there be a prenuptial agreement? This is highly recommended no matter how much you're worth financially. You don't know for sure how your partner would react if their needs were not being met or if the commitment were to end.
- Will you have separate or joint savings, checking, and investment accounts?
- Make a budget and decide what percentage of both your incomes will go to savings, paying off debt, health care, auto expenses, rent or mortgage, insurance, wardrobe, entertainment, household expenses, food, furniture, utility bills, vacations, children, emergencies, miscellaneous, and so on. Take into consideration how you both have spent money in the past.
- Decide what you'll do if one or both of you are not sticking to the budget.
- What are your long-term goals or desires regarding money, and how do you plan to reach them?
- In case of separation or divorce, how will you decide who gets what?
- Consider wills in case something happens to one or both of you. This is especially important for those who choose to avoid a marriage license or for those who aren't allowed by law to obtain one.

c. Sex

- What are your sexual needs and desires? If you don't yet feel comfortable discussing this honestly with your partner, you aren't ready for a commitment.
- What will you do if one or both of you have sexual needs the other can't meet?
- What will you do if the sexual attraction for one or both of you wanes?

d. Monogamy

- What does it means to each of you?
- Be realistic: what will you do if one of you is attracted to someone else or has an affair?
- Have either of you had an affair in a previous relationship? If yes, you'll need to be able to discuss such situations and communicate about future situations before they create problems.

e. Relatives

- Where will you spend the holidays?
- What if one of you clashes with the other's relatives?
- What arrangements will you make for aging parents? Will they live with you?

f. Any other issues you feel are critical to a successful commitment.

5. They would be free to adjust this contract before and during the relationship as long as they both agreed upon any changes.

6. Instead of expecting the relationship to last a lifetime, they would analyze their commitment at pre-determined intervals and consider if the union was still for the highest good of both. In ancient Egypt, couples would agree on five- to ten-year unions. After that time they would either renew or dissolve the union, depending on how they both felt about their relationship at that point.

Monogamy is the Western custom of
one wife and hardly any mistresses.

— H.H. Munro (Saki)
(1870–1916)

13
Responsible, Mutually Agreed Upon Non-Monogamy as an Alternative to Dishonesty

It is the intent of the author to present responsible non-monogamy as an alternative to dishonesty. As explained below, there is a world of difference between cheating on a partner and having a mutually acceptable arrangement. Responsible non-monogamy is not appropriate for all relationships. Also, although responsible non-monogamy can help to avoid certain problems in relationships, it does not guarantee an ideal relationship. As long as we are imperfect humans, we will approach any relationship in a flawed manner: we may not be able to be 100 percent honest all the time with ourselves or loved ones, we may not always be able to share, and we may not always be able to like whom our partner is attracted to. However, responsible non-monogamy can allow us the freedom and opportunity to be more honest, more sharing, and more loving with ourselves and our partners. The more honest with and aware of ourselves we are, the fewer problems we'll have in any type of relationship.

Many people have perceived past-life recall of life on the lost continents of Atlantis and Lemuria. Some have described responsible non-monogamy as not only accepted, but as the custom during certain periods in these ancient yet spiritually and technologically advanced cultures. Inhabitants of Atlantis and Lemuria were raised to be more in touch with themselves and less dependent on others for happiness and love. Because of this, there seemed to be less jealousy and more honesty and unconditional love in relationships. While they sincerely respected their relationship commitments, they did not consider the love of someone else to "belong" to them.

We, of course, have been raised in a much different environment, so even responsible non-monogamy naturally feels foreign and even threatening to many of us. Still, when approached correctly, responsible non-monogamy can add a wonderful dimension to an already solid relationship *when it is practiced with caution as an alternative to dishonesty.*

Forms of non-monogamy have been accepted and even encouraged in many cultures since Lemuria and Atlantis, but in most societies during more recent times, monogamous relationships are expected, even when they're never discussed or mutually agreed to. Is everyone practicing what they preach? Accurate statistics on infidelity are difficult to determine as many people aren't willing to admit to an affair. Polls have shown that approximately half of all married men and a third of married women have been unfaithful to their partners.

Most people say and think they want a monogamous relationship, but perhaps only a small percentage of our population would truly be happy in such an arrangement over a long period of time. It's important to note that what actually destroys a relationship is dishonesty, not the actual act of sex outside the relationship. Therefore, perhaps more couples would remain together if they were completely honest with each other at all times and if they let go of their expectations for sexual exclusivity. Perhaps to those who have affairs, the illusion of monogamy is more important than being honest with themselves and their partner.

One possible explanation of why some people are more comfortable with non-monogamy is illustrated by the case of Carolyn and Mike.

Carolyn, a 38-year-old divorced attorney, had been interested in the subject of reincarnation for several years. She had never been regressed to a past life, but felt it was time for her to do some exploring. She had been dating Mike, a 39-year-old entrepreneur, exclusively for nine months. However, their different views about commitment and monogamy were causing conflict. She had always preferred more relaxed arrangements; he insisted that their relationship be closed and monogamous. Even though Carolyn preferred non-monogamy, she usually agreed to monogamy as long as she was in love and if her partner preferred it. With Mike, however, she felt an overwhelming desire to stray. Luckily for Mike, secret affairs were not her style, so she decided to discover the cause of why she felt these urges with him before they caused problems.

Carolyn appeared fiery, self-assured, intelligent, well-dressed, and looked younger than her 38 years. She seemed excited about the session and was ready to explore. Mike, also well-dressed and well-built, was supportive of Carolyn, but wasn't enthusiastic about the idea of past-life regression.

I began the session by asking Carolyn her definition of non-monogamy.

"A relationship to me is all about trust; not hiding anything," she replied. "Since our hormones don't stop working just because we get involved, repressing strong urges and attractions can create inner conflict and eventually may cause people to do things they'll regret. With responsible non-monogamy, it's discussed and shared instead of stuffed or hidden. It feels a lot safer to me and helps to strengthen the bond when it is all out on the table and there are no secrets."

"Mike, how do you feel about what Carolyn just said?" I asked.

Mike looked irritated. "I don't believe in it. I think the only thing it accomplishes is the eventual collapse of the relationship."

"You're right," added Carolyn, "but only if gratification is sought outside of the relationship in a way that doesn't respect all people involved. I'd like to clarify what I mean by responsible non-monogamy since most people have outrageous beliefs about it. That phrase to me implies completely honest, mutually agreed upon, ultra-safe, non-promiscuous, selective, and responsible sexual relations with someone other than your primary partner. In order for something like that to work, there needs to be specific rules, such as deciding what is allowed sexually and what isn't, whether or not people are allowed to be brought into the home, safe-sex issues, and others."

"You seem to have given this a lot of thought," I said.

"I've not only thought about it, I've experienced it. It can work if done correctly."

"If it's so beneficial, why did those open relationships you had end?" Mike challenged.

Carolyn looked Mike directly in his eyes. "Unlike your marriage, Mike, two of the three non-monogamous relationships I've had ended for reasons unrelated to non-monogamy. In the third, we began a responsible non-monogamous relationship after four years of a monogamous one. After he had several affairs I knew he wasn't the type to be monogamous, so we tried a responsible non-monogamous relationship. It's ironic that he broke up with me for the reason that he couldn't handle me seeing other people."

I asked Mike if his marriage had been open. "No, but part of the reason it ended was because I wasn't monogamous."

Carolyn looked at me. "See, that's a good example of how non-monogamy is blamed for destroying a relationship, when in fact it's because of dishonesty."

I addressed Carolyn. "Therapists who take a more traditional approach would search for reasons only in this life. Often, in situations such as this, they would consider fear of commitment or fear of intimacy issues, perhaps caused by childhood abuse. Do you think that's a possibility?"

Carolyn confidently responded, "No. In fact, I feel responsible monogamy strengthens a commitment for me and allows me to become more intimate with a partner because of more honesty. As for sexual abuse, yes, that did happen to me between the ages of seven and nine with a next-door neighbor. I'm familiar with how sexual abuse can affect children and adults, and I've gone through therapy for those experiences. While I don't feel they are negatively affecting me now, I feel they did affect me, especially during my marriage, before I got help in my mid-twenties. I don't feel that's an issue in this situation because of how I view a responsible non-monogamous relationship. To me, when it's done right, it can actually enhance a relationship."

"How so?" I asked.

"When I commit to someone, I totally commit. I'm naturally very loyal in personal relationships, sometimes to a fault. I like to share all of who I am with my partner: body, mind, and soul. At the same time, if I want to sleep with another woman or man I find attractive, I see it as only sex, not making love as I do with a partner. As long as no one is hurt and we play extremely safe, I see it as fun and harmless. When a partner has the same mindset or at least is accepting of mine, sex with others as a shared experience or one that is discussed openly breaks down those walls of mistrust and dissolves the fear of extramarital affairs. I actually trust my partner more in non-monogamous relationships because, let's face it, most think about straying and many act on it. I think it's pretty hypocritical that so many scoff at responsible non-monogamy, especially since the rate of extramarital affairs is so high."

"How can you say this enforces a commitment when there's always the risk in a non-monogamous relationship of one partner finding someone they're more compatible with or more attracted to?" Mike argued.

"Yes, that's a risk, but the same risk is present in monogamous relationships. You can tell attraction or compatibility without sleeping with a person. If the attraction is clearly more than just lust, it wouldn't be important to me like it would be if I was single, because of the way I commit. My relationship with you is deeply satisfying and I love you. If I wasn't in love with you or if the relationship wasn't satisfying to me, I wouldn't bother. I don't have relationships just to have them like some people. I tend to be quite independent and happy on my own. So what I'm trying to say is that commitment is important to me. Sex outside the relationship is just sex. I'm not the jealous or possessive type."

I wanted to allow enough time for Carolyn's regression so I asked Mike to wait outside. I then led her through a relaxation induction and into a past-life regression that would explain more about the monogamy issue between her and Mike. Carolyn was a good subject; she followed directions easily and seemed to trust the process.

She perceived herself as a 17-year-old female named Susan living in Wyoming during the early 1800s. She was in love with a 23-year-old man named Jack. They planned to marry soon. At this point I began to question her about her relationship:

Therapist: Do your parents approve?

Carolyn: Well, they like Jack, but everyone keeps telling me that he has a bad reputation with women.

Th: Please tell me more about that.

C: Some women have warned me that he isn't a one-woman man.

Th: How do you feel about that?

C: I don't care about Jack's past. The important thing is that we are in love. He would never do anything to hurt me. Besides, once we're married he'll settle down and he'll be all mine.

I instructed her to move forward to an important event:

C: (smiles) I feel so happy. We are getting married.
Th: Tell me about the wedding.
C: Just family and close friends.
Th: Let's move forward to another important event, on the count of three. One, two, three. Please tell me what you're perceiving.
C: I don't believe them.
Th: What and whom don't you believe?
C: My friends. They're telling me that Jack has a wandering eye. Actually, they say more wanders than his eyes. Jack wouldn't do that to me.
Th: Do you ask Jack about this?
C: No! I have a marriage to maintain and I'm not going to ruin it by accusing Jack of things he didn't do.
Th: All right, lets move forward again to an event that is connected to this one. On the count of three. One, two, three.
C: (crying) How could he do this to me?
Th: Who did what to you?
C: Jack. I came home early from visiting my parents and found him and some young woman in the barn! How could he do this?
Th: What did you say to Jack when you found him?
C: I just burst into tears and ran to the house.
Th: What did he do?
C: He ran after me and tried to talk to me. I wouldn't listen. He took some of his things and left. He's ruined my life! (visibly upset)
Th: On the count of three, move forward again to a significant event. One, two, three.
C: I'm older, about 50, and alone. I work at a supply store.
Th: How do you feel?
C: Very angry. Jack ruined my life. He violated my trust.
Th: Did you ever remarry?
C: No. I don't trust men. They're all the same.

I progressed Carolyn to the day of her death in that life. Since she and Jack had no children and she never remarried, she died alone and angry. She felt that Jack, because he was unfaithful, was responsible for her unhappiness. I guided Carolyn through the death process and into the Higher Self state:

Th: Please tell me what you're experiencing.
C: Peace. I feel relieved it's over.
Th: Do you perceive anyone there with you?
C: No. Just light.
Th: Please tell me the lessons you learned in that lifetime.
C: Humility.
Th: What else?
C: (pause) Well, I didn't believe in or trust myself, so I attracted a husband I couldn't trust.
Th: Were those part of your lessons to learn?
C: Yes.
Th: Do you feel you've learned those lessons?
C: Yes.
Th: Do you know Jack in your current life?
C: It's Mike.
Th: If you could go back and talk to "Susan," what would you say to her?
C: (pause) I'd tell her that love is open, not closed. Just because you get married doesn't guarantee your partner is "yours." It's not like owning a horse. You can't own a human being. I'd tell her to communicate with Jack and get him to talk to her about why he feels the need to wander.
Th: What else, from this perspective, can you become aware of about the lifetime you just perceived?
C: (said with a lot of compassion) She made herself so unhappy by holding on to the anger and resentment against Jack. She made her life much more difficult than she needed to.
Th: Is that life still affecting your current life?
C: Yes. It's why I have difficulty with Mike's expectation for me to be monogamous.
Th: Do you still feel anger towards Jack?
C: Yes, a little.

At this point, I led Carolyn through a forgiveness exercise to help her release the negative feelings, including her distrust of men. Forgiveness is an important part of regression therapy as resentment, anger, and guilt from past experiences cause physical and emotional problems in the present. In Carolyn's case, her subconscious anger at the past-life Jack was causing conflict between her and present-day Mike. *Even though she didn't consciously remember the events, the past was still affecting her present life.*

Th: How else is that life still affecting you?
C: I was miserable for the rest of my life because Jack didn't follow the marriage rules I expected him to. Even though I felt he violated my trust by cheating on me, it really wasn't there to begin with.
Th: How have your experiences in that life affected your current view of open relationships?
C: I reject monogamy because I don't want to waste another life feeling resentment or guilt just because a partner or myself is being human. If the love, trust, and communication is there, we don't have to follow someone else's rules, which could make us miserable.
Th: Is there anything else to be aware of about the experience that would help you?
C: Yes. Mike got divorced in this life because he had an extramarital affair. If he did it once, and doesn't become aware of and work on the reasons he did it, he may do it again.
Th: So what are your choices now?
C: Up until now he's insisted on monogamy, so I can stay with him, be monogamous, and hope he is too. Or considering his track record, I can tell him to either dissolve his straying issues through therapy, consider responsible non-monogamy, or leave.

At this point, I gave Carolyn suggestions to help her become completely aware of her options and the consequences of her actions regarding this situation. I also suggested that she will know the best path for herself regarding this situation in the coming days and weeks.

When the regression ended, Carolyn seemed happy about what she received. "That fits. All of it."

"Any further insight or comments about what you experienced?" I asked.

"Now I know why I've always said that true love isn't about ownership; it's unconditional. I think Susan felt that marriage was about ownership."

"Your view of an ideal love relationship is certainly different in this life, isn't it?"

Carolyn sat up in the recliner. "Yes. Many don't agree with my views, and it seems it's mainly because they are afraid of losing their partner, being alone, or having to start all over again. Perhaps since I've already experienced that and lived with it for so long, I realize it doesn't have to be like that. Gosh, if you really look at the rules of marriage and the monogamous expectations without the communication that go along with them, they seem so outdated and dysfunctional now, don't they?"

"In that light, yes."

Carolyn laughed. "I doubt Mike is going to accept any of this. I wish he would be more open to exploring his desire to stray. It may prevent him from sabotaging future relationships. That's okay; I have the awareness I came for and it's helped me. I now will have to make a decision."

I spoke with Carolyn two months later. She had encouraged Mike to explore his reasons for failing to be monogamous in the past. He refused. A few weeks after her regression, Carolyn told Mike that she felt the relationship was no longer serving their highest good. She feels that their relationship was an experience that each one needed before moving on to future relationships.

What is your first emotional response to the topic of non-monogamy?

Is it anger or disgust? The need to blame or condemn? Maybe your response is curiosity. If so, let's examine the possible reasons behind your feelings:

- Is it due to **conditioning** from how society views non-monogamy? Considering the number of people who participate in extramarital affairs, the often harsh and critical opinions most have about responsible and honest non-monogamy seem hypocritical. *This may be due in part because our society still views* *sex as "bad" or "sinful."* If non-monogamy was accepted in our society, think how differently things would be. You could ignore the opinions of others and choose what works best for you and your partner. You could act out of love instead of fear. As long as you're respecting all involved and not hurting anyone, it is only your business what you do behind closed doors. Let go of the guilt and express, not repress, your sexual self.

- Do you have **misperceptions** about non-monogamy? When the subject is mentioned, many people imagine wild, unsafe sex with as many partners as one can find. Such behavior, especially during these times, is dangerous and irresponsible. Responsible non-monogamy involves complete honesty, safer sex, and respecting everyone involved with and affected by the actions. When someone is involved in a responsible non-monogamous relationship it doesn't mean they are unable to commit, sleeping around, cheating, or risking sexually transmitted diseases (STDs). In fact, those who choose responsible non-monogamy find that this approach can actually strengthen an existing commitment. Non-monogamy doesn't mean sexual addiction or compulsion. Seek help if you feel you may have a problem with this. *Realize that lying and cheating, not actual sexual contact, are the damaging aspects of extramarital sex.* As Carolyn mentioned above, the illusion of monogamy in our society is often more important than honesty to those who are having the affair. Responsible, mutually agreed upon non-monogamy allows people to express their desire to be intimate with more than one person and maintain their primary partner commitment by respecting and being honest with all involved, including themselves.
- Have you ever been **rejected by a lover** who left you for another? If so, realize that non-monogamy works best when practiced by two or more people who first have a strong bond consisting of love, trust, communication, and friendship. If you feel the need to keep a partner on a leash so they won't stray, you may want to question if the relationship is meant to be and why you chose such a mate; remember that it's not your right to demand that anyone be who you want them to be. When both people are honest with themselves and each other, there

are no surprises or victims. Sex between them involves their love for one another; sex with others may be seen as just sex. Even if sex with another is more than sex, they honor their commitment with their partner first and foremost. Furthermore, they choose to be together because they truly love each other, not out of loneliness or pressure from family, peers, or society to be married or involved. Since their bond is important to them and they keep communication lines open, there is no fear about losing their partner to another. If conflicts arise regarding non-monogamy, they discuss them and adapt, just as they do with other issues relating to their union.

Through observing thousands of couples, I have noticed that when someone's personality is more compatible with non-monogamy but he or she refuses to acknowledge or accept this part of themselves, they may attract and become involved with a partner who will express it for them. Non-monogamy is usually not discussed between partners; this can create problems later when a couple is forced to confront it. If you want monogamy but have attracted cheaters, you need to discover why. You may be suppressing a desire to have more freedom in relationships. If so, you don't need to be non-monogamous. But discovering and releasing why you reject the concept and then accepting the concept may help to stop the pattern of cheating partners. It will also help to discuss the concept openly with your current or future partners.

When non-monogamy doesn't work:

- When both or all partners don't understand that compatible and harmonious love relationships flourish when love is open (unconditional) and not closed (conditional).
- When one, both, or all partners don't know themselves.
- When one partner doesn't really want a non-monogamous relationship, even though he or she may agree to it.
- When one, both, or all partners aren't or can't be honest about what they do and don't feel comfortable regarding their non-monogamous rules and guidelines.
- When non-monogamy is used as an excuse to exit a relationship.

- When one, both, or all partners don't consider their primary relationship a priority when seeing others.
- When a relationship hasn't yet developed into a solid commitment between two (or more) people.
- When a relationship isn't equal.
- When those involved aren't best or at least good friends.
- When one, both, or all partners have issues with jealousy or fears of abandonment.
- When those involved don't share enough compatibility.

Spiritual reasons people want or reject non-monogamy

Just as some of us have only one or two close friends and others have many close friends; some people truly feel sexually content with one partner their whole lives and some don't. Many factors can influence the desire for or the rejection of non-monogamy. They are often linked to subconscious fears, resentment, and guilt, or else a successful history of such unions.

- Souls who had positive experiences with non-monogamy in ancient cultures where it was accepted may have a more difficult time adjusting to our present society's expectations of strict monogamy.
- On the other hand, those who had happy monogamous relationships in past lives may seek the same in their current life.
- Negative experiences with irresponsible non-monogamy in past lives, such as abandonment by a lover or guilt from cheating will cause negative reactions to non-monogamy or monogamy in the current life.

We're all different. Instead of expecting everyone to be monogamous, perhaps monogamy and non-monogamy should be openly considered as preferences in relationships, just like personal interests and whether or not someone wants to have children. This way, monogamy isn't assumed or expected and those who demand it will be more likely to find someone who wants the same. If someone is adamantly opposed to non-monogamy of any form, he or she may have unresolved issues related to this area that may interfere in any relationship.

Are you better off in a non-monogamous relationship?

More couples today are realizing that, while they still want a strong commitment with each other, the old traditional version of relationships where one person is supposed to meet all of your needs for life is outdated and unrealistic. They feel that traditional monogamy is one type of a loving relationship, but not the only type. These couples find that discussing and being honest about attractions to others and why they feel the need to stray is a healthier approach and part of creating and maintaining a truly compatible bond.

It's important to consider why you want a non-monogamous relationship. If you're involved, ask yourself if your commitment with your partner is still worth it. If it isn't, consider why that is and if the relationship is salvageable. Communicate with your partner to make sure he or she truly feels and wants the same, or your expectations and actions will cause you both unhappiness.

If you're single and feel you may be happier in a responsible non-monogamous relationship, consider sharing this section of this book with those you date. Discuss the issue and consider his or her views.

When considering monogamy or non-monogamy in a new or existing relationship, realize that everyone has their own relationship needs. This is the result of their environment, including their role models such as parents, grandparents, and so on, their religious or spiritual beliefs, and their relationship and sexual history. All of these factors, along with the dynamics of the current relationship, will influence how a person feels about non-monogamy. From the beginning of your relationship, be honest with yourself and your partner about what does and doesn't work for you.

If relationship longevity is your goal, recognize that couples who stay together the longest tend to be adaptive, flexible, and original. The more you're willing to alter your expectations, the greater your chances of developing a lasting compatible and harmonious love relationship.

Ask yourself the following questions to determine if a non-traditional relationship is for you:

- Do you tend to be independent rather than dependent?

- Do you prefer to communicate and be up front about everything with a partner, even if it may cause one or both of you stress or uncomfortable feelings initially?
- Do you prefer to confront potential problem areas instead of ignoring them?
- Have you strayed before without telling your partner?
- Do you perceive your relationship with your partner as a priority and sex with someone other than your partner as just sex?
- Is it easy for you to separate sex and love?
- Are you able to love more than one person?
- Do you occasionally feel the need for sexual variety and at the same time place great importance on a commitment with a partner?
- Do you accept that it's normal to feel sexual attraction to others even after you become involved with someone?
- Do you feel that an agreement to have responsible sexual relations (with guidelines) with others, based on trust and communication between you and your partner, could actually enhance your sex life with your partner?
- Would being honest with your partner about your attractions to others make you feel more secure with your relationship, especially if you knew you would be accepted by your partner no matter what?
- Are you comfortable with the idea of your partner having sex with someone else with your consent?

If you answered yes to most of these, you may find that an honest, mutually agreed upon, and responsible non-monogamous relationship is ideal for you.

Non-monogamous relationship rules and guidelines

Non-monogamous relationships fail not because they are open, but as the result of a lack of communication: either two (or more) people didn't create or follow rules and guidelines they each felt comfortable with and agreed upon ahead of time, or one or both (or all) of them couldn't be or simply weren't honest about their sexual and emotional needs. Possible rules that may be included in a non-monogamous love relationship agreement are as follows:

- Safe sex only, and what exactly this means to both partners.

- Whether certain sexual acts or acts of affection aren't permitted, and define them.
- Sex with others permitted but not discussed.
- Sex with others only together as a shared experience.
- Sex with others only together and only with other couples.
- Sex with others only when alone.
- Sex with others alone or together as a couple.
- Sex only with mutual friends or acquaintances.
- Sex only with the opposite sex.
- Sex only with the same sex.
- Sex with others only while on vacation.
- Sex with others only when one partner is out of town.
- Sex with others only on previously agreed-on special occasions.
- Sex with others as long as it is safe and involving consenting adults.

There are many different types of non-monogamous relationships:

- A couple may adapt and change their non-monogamous relationship over time as their needs and wants change. Again, everything is out in the open in a responsible non-monogamous relationship.
- A couple may have an agreement to be non-monogamous, but remain monogamous most of the time.
- A couple may have an agreement to be non-monogamous and exercise this often.
- One partner may be non-monogamous and one may be monogamous.
- One or both partners may be non-monogamous with the same sex, the opposite sex, or both.
- One or both partners may have long-term relationships outside their primary relationship.
- One or both partners may have short-term relationships outside their primary relationship.
- Both partners may share a third, fourth, or more sexual and/or love relationship within their primary relationship.
- Three or more people may have a non-monogamous group relationship.

Be safe!

When you're responsible, respectful, honest, and safe, there's nothing left that's bad about sex! Enjoy sex and do so responsibly. Whether you're single, involved in a monogamous relationship, or involved in a non-monogamous relationship, always practice safer sex. It's important to practice safer sex in monogamous relationships unless you're 100 percent certain your partner is monogamous or practicing only safer sex with others. If you don't discuss it, don't assume it (see "The Two Rarely Talked About Risks of Sexual Contact" in chapter 19).

What Does This Mean To You?

- You must decide for yourself whether or not responsible non-monogamy is best for you. If you both agree to be monogamous, remember that we are only human. You can sweep the issue under the rug and hope that you both are strong enough to remain monogamous. Or you can you can help avoid the possibility of *irresponsible* non-monogamy (and the pain and heartache that accompanies it) by discussing these issues with your partner throughout your relationship before they become problems.
- Whether you agree to non-monogamy in any form or not, the sources listed in Recommended Reading will help you understand the advantages and disadvantages of non-traditional relationship styles, how to deal with jealousy, and how to be more honest and compassionate in any type of relationship.

Section V

Discover, Forgive, Release

14
Meditation and Past Life Self-Regression

To see, to hear, means nothing. To recognize (or not to recognize) means everything. Between what I do recognize and what I don't recognize there stands myself. And what I don't recognize I shall continue not to recognize.
— André Breton (1896–1966)

Meditation is the process of becoming calm, focused, and centered through deep breathing, relaxing the body, and emptying the mind of thoughts and worries. The goal of mediation is to be in the moment. It is a useful technique to rise above stress and become more aware of your body, your surroundings, and your inner guidance. When you're centered from meditation, you instinctively know how to help yourself.

Meditation can also be used to discover the cause of a problem or the answer to a question. All our answers are within us, but they are not often obvious because of the many distractions in our busy lives. Like hypnosis and guided meditation, solo meditation allows us to access the subconscious and superconscious.

Regression is the process of accessing memories of the past which are stored in your subconscious mind. Past life self-regression is the process of guiding your mind to access information from the past for fun or awareness. This process is easier when you are centered and relaxed, so it's best to meditate just before a regression.

You'll have fun exploring on your own and your results will improve with discipline and practice. A properly trained regression therapist can also help you become aware of answers to questions and the causes of problems. See "How To Find a Competent Past-life Regression Therapist" at the end of this chapter for more information.

Read "Meditation and Regression Preparation" below before using any of the scripts. Have a good friend read you a script or record it to help lead yourself through the process. You can also order pre-recorded CD versions of the following meditations and regressions. See the order form in the back of the book, or order from www.howisyourlovelife.com and view up-to-date product listings and descriptions.

Never use a meditation, guided meditation, hypnosis, regression or progression recording in a moving vehicle or at any time when you need to remain completely awake and alert.

Meditation and Regression Preparation

Experience more productive and successful sessions by following these suggestions:

- Read chapter one, "What You Need to Know About Reincarnation, Karma and Regression Therapy," before attempting to use any of the following scripts.
- Learn and practice meditation before attempting regression. Improving concentration through meditation will lead to more successful regressions.
- You'll perceive what you're ready for. If you view something traumatic, you decided on some level that it was time to face it rather than continuing to avoid it. Accept whatever comes up. Be willing to accept, even if only temporarily, that we have all been "good" and "bad" in past lives. Most of us have incarnated again and again to work through karma. It's okay if you perceive yourself as a "bad" person in a past-life regression or as someone who's being abused in some way as long as you forgive yourself and others for anything that happened, learn from your mistakes, and avoid repeating those mistakes. Don't take the actions of others personally. See them as helpers who assisted in what you chose, on a soul level, to learn about and grow from.
- Realize forgiveness of the self and others is a key part of regression when it's used to solve problems. When you or

someone else has acted negatively in a past life, and if you're having a difficult time forgiving them, focus on the reasons for those negative actions. *With awareness comes understanding; with understanding comes acceptance and forgiveness.*

- Understand that your subconscious mind has a memory of all your experiences, both in this life and in past lives. You have the ability, through practice and perseverance, to access these memories.
- Don't expect a miracle cure in one or two sessions for a conflict that may have formed over many lifetimes. Let go of your expectations and be open to what you receive. Although answers can be discovered and some problems solved in one or two sessions, this isn't always the case. Past-life regression does work, but you must be willing to go deep enough to find the root cause of a conflict. Some processes require many sessions to be completed. It's helpful to think of meditation and past-life regression as part of an ongoing journey toward enlightenment. It will be more successful when that journey also includes reflection on or work with whatever emerges during each session. Remembering a single past life which seems to explain the cause of a current life problem may sometimes be enough, but *it's necessary to follow through by taking responsibility for your life, forgiving yourself and anyone involved, and by taking appropriate actions that will help to solve the problem or reach the goal.*
- Past-life regression compliments other forms of therapy, especially after you've found and released the root cause of the problem.
- You'll most likely feel as if you're making up some or most past-life recall. This is normal, for even those who have experienced many regressions. It can happen because information we receive from the subconscious mind has to be interpreted by our conscious mind, just as we interpret information we receive through our eyes from books and through our ears from the radio. This interpretation—made up of images, thoughts, smells, or sounds—may seem like make-believe since we can't validate the information we're receiving and/or we have been conditioned to believe that past lives are just our imagination.

In spite of this, during the days, weeks, months, and years after a regression session, most people learn information or experience coincidences that seem to validate what they perceived during a regression.

- Don't expect to black out. Relaxing so deeply during mediation or regression that you don't remember what happened is unusual. If you do black out or fall asleep, you'll awaken shortly afterward, depending on how tired you were, just like you do from a nap.
- You'll be able to return to the present easily on your own by counting from one to five. Counting from one to five is not necessary, but it helps the process.
- Accept responsibility for yourself and your life. A victim mentality will block awareness. When you perceive through meditation and regression that past-life events have contributed to present life situations, it will be easier to accept that life really is fair.
- You must sincerely want to improve your life in order for the process of regression and meditation to successfully help you find answers and solve problems. If there are hidden benefits for you to hold onto a problem or conflict, your subconscious mind will not allow the process to help you reach and maintain your goal. Make a decision to improve your situation and then consider everything that would change in your life if you reached your goal. If, after honest self-appraisal, the goal is still important to you, accept the changes that would come with reaching it.
- Don't expect that what you perceive during meditation and regression will be like watching a movie. The images you see or sense may only be fragments. However, they'll become more clear as you make an effort to accept what comes and to suspend any doubt while doing so. Some people only hear information, some only feel it, some just know it, and others perceive in a combination of these methods. You'll perceive more as you relax and trust the process.
- Don't try to control it or make it happen; just let go and accept what you perceive.

- If you're naturally skeptical or religious, you may have difficulty allowing the process to work. Try to suspend your beliefs and temporarily *act as if* past lives are real, otherwise your doubt will cloud or block awareness.
- Be willing to accept, even if only temporarily, the law of karma and science which states that for every action there is an equal and opposite reaction. This means that everything you have done, said, thought, and intended in your past has contributed to your present life. You have the option of improving your present circumstances by finding and releasing the past cause.

Meditation Instruction

Step by Step Guide to Finding Answers and Gaining Awareness

Everything you need to know is within you. You'll find answers to your questions by following the simple steps below.

1. **Write out your question.** Be specific. Writing out your question not only clarifies what you want to know, it sends a clear message to your mind and the universe that you're asking for help. If you don't have a specific question, ask what you would most benefit from being aware of at this time.

2. **Write out a conscious, "logical" answer.** This helps get your left-brain out of the way and makes room for right-brain intuitive guidance to enter your consciousness. This more logical answer will often be different from the one you receive in meditation; the answer you "think" will not usually be as ideal as the answer you "know" or "feel."

3. **Center yourself and then meditate.**

a. If you're alone and you feel comfortable doing so, explain the situation and state the question out loud. This helps you clarify what you're seeking.

b. Ask for protection and guidance from God, your guides and angels of the Light, and/or from your Higher Self and be grateful for their help in advance. Repeat the following, or something similar, either out loud or to yourself: "God, guides and angels of the Light and Higher Self, please allow me to gain the awareness I need through this meditation and through my dreams and insight. Assist me to forgive and release myself and everyone else so that I can lead a more productive and happy life. Please make your guidance clear and concise so that I may easily receive, understand, and interpret it."

c. Mentally surround yourself with white light. Imagine yourself protected and being cleansed of all stress and worry. Feel the light repairing and restoring you on every level: physical, emotional, mental, and spiritual. Take a moment to bask in this light. Imagine a gentle wave of relaxation washing over you. Cut any unnecessary ties between you and anyone you have interacted with recently.

d. Close your eyes, breath in deeply through your nose, and bring the air to the pit of your stomach. Exhale slowly through your mouth. Mentally relax your body, beginning with your feet and working your way up to your scalp.

e. Now that you're ready, there are many ways to meditate. Three methods are described below. Notice that with each one, there is a focus point. This will help you reach a deeper state.

- **Method 1:** Breathe in to the slow count of five, hold to the slow count of five, breathe out through your mouth to the slow count of five, then pause to the slow count of five. Repeat. Concentrate on the rhythm of your breathing.
- **Method 2:** Count in your mind from one to one hundred. Breathe deeply, and on each exhale picture the number in your mind. Feel yourself going deeper and deeper with the count of each number.
- **Method 3:** If you prefer to keep your eyes open or if you fall asleep easily, focus your attention and your eyes, slightly closed, on the flame of a candle. As you do so, keep your mind in the present by either visualizing yourself within the flame, counting, closing your eyes and visualizing the flame as vividly as possible, or a combination of these.

f. Since you're focusing on breathing and counting or visualizing, your mind is occupied, which allows you to get out of your own way. If thoughts and worries of the day should enter, dismiss them for the time being. Visualize them as clouds crossing effortlessly across the sky.

g. After about 10 to 20 minutes, more or less, depending upon your ability to focus, you'll feel more relaxed and it will be easier to focus and remain open for guidance and answers. You may feel your mind expanding to fill the entire room, a slight floating sensation, or a wave of peace and calmness. This is our natural state, when we're able to access our subconscious and superconscious minds where all our answers reside.

h. Focus on your question. Try asking your question or stating your intent out loud if you have trouble focusing. *Trust the impressions that enter your mind, no matter how unrelated they may seem.* Everyone "receives" differently. You may see vivid pictures or fleeting glimpses. Images may come as symbols—what does the symbol mean to you? You may see words. You might hear, feel, or simply "know" the answer. You'll know if it's correct when it feels right. Follow all the images you receive. Ask out loud or to yourself, "What does this mean?" or say "It will become more clear on the count of three. One, two, three." Don't answer "I don't know." This will close the door to your awareness. It's impossible to ask a question if you don't, on some level, already know the answer. Keep asking in and out of meditation until you get an answer or are guided to another image. With intent, you'll become aware of the answer at the right time.

i. Give thanks again to God, your guides and angels of the Light, or your Higher Self for their guidance and *for the discipline to meditate every day.*

j. When you feel you're finished, count yourself up from one to five telling yourself that you'll be wide awake and feeling good on the count of five.

k. Write about your experience and any answers you receive.

4. Be patient. You may not receive answers right away, but stay confident and believe that you will eventually. When you receive the answer to your question you'll know. It may be in the form of a dream, an announcer's words on the radio, or an article you find in a magazine. Sometimes it may feel like the message was specifically meant for you.

5. Practice. If you have a hard time turning off your racing mind, don't worry. It will get easier with practice. The more you meditate, the more you'll want to do it and the more you'll get out of it. Eventually you'll wonder how you ever survived without it!

6. Meditation can also come in the form of writing, drawing, painting, running, walking or biking, any repetitive activity that occupies your mind and body so your higher consciousness (Higher Self) can shine through.

7. **No excuses!** Everyone's favorite excuse for not meditating is not having enough time. When you make time to meditate, especially first thing in the morning, your day will seem easier and less stressful. You'll react to everything in a more relaxed way, with calm and detachment, intuitively navigating through your day. Making time to meditate in the morning will actually make you more productive, which will give you more time to concentrate on what is really important to you. You can also meditate before bed. By relaxing and emptying your mind of all the day's activity, you'll sleep better and may dream more vividly.

8. **Expanding your awareness through meditation makes the following become more obvious:**

- Messages, symbols, and signs: The answers to our questions can be found anywhere: overheard words within a conversation; a TV program that you just happen to turn to; a billboard on the freeway. Ask for assistance, then trust and follow your intuition. Remain open for guidance and realize *there are no coincidences.*
- Dreams: Which is more real, our waking or dreaming state? Ask for answers before going to sleep. Be specific about what you want to know and be grateful in advance for clear concise guidance.
- Astrology, numerology, tarot, or palm readings: These metaphysical sciences can be much more accurate than they may seem from the general newspaper or magazine horoscopes and articles. Studying on your own or receiving an in-depth reading from someone who truly knows their craft can confirm your intuition and give you helpful guidance and insight (see chapter 17).

Trigger Questions

Ask the Right Questions to Discover the Cause of Conflicts

The following questions can be used in conjunction with meditation, past-life regression, or intuitive readings. After each question or statement, ask who, when, where, why, or how for more clarification. Also, inquire about any of the following that may be interfering: fears, baggage from past-life traumas, baggage from unresolved childhood issues, false beliefs, a lack of self love/worth/respect, guilt, anger, or resentment.

Love and Relationships

- What is blocking me from being happily involved with a compatible partner?
- Am I currently learning any karmic lessons about love and relationships? How can I resolve these issues and move on?
- What will be with my love life?
- Is there a future love I am predestined to meet? What is the time frame? What might this person look like?
- What could I stop or start doing now to help create a compatible, loving relationship in the future?
- Have _____ and I lived past lives together? Were they harmonious experiences or did we come together again to resolve unfinished business? What main issues are we working out? What can I do to help myself/_______ in this situation?

Sexuality

- What is blocking me from completely enjoying and experiencing my sexual self?
- Why can't I enjoy sex with_________?

Health

- What could I do to feel and be healthier?
- What is blocking me from achieving my ideal body shape and weight goals?
- Are there any potential health problems I need to be aware of?
- Which chakras (energy centers of the body) need attention or repairing?

First chakra: red. Located in the upper thigh area. Corresponds to the adrenals, spinal column, kidneys; physical senses; manifesting; initiating instead of just reacting; trying new things; becoming sensitive to other's feelings; living in the present moment; how you create.

Second chakra: orange. Located in the area below navel and above upper thighs. Corresponds to the gonads, reproductive system; how you relate to people; creativity; sexual expression.

Third chakra: yellow. Located in the area above navel and below heart. Corresponds to the pancreas, stomach, liver, gall bladder, nervous system; ego and power center; self confidence; ambition; being your own authority; using power effectively; learning to link the soul-self with the ego.

Fourth chakra: pink/green. Located in the heart area. Corresponds to the thymus, heart, blood, circulatory system; love; trust; faith; self belief; attachment/detachment; the need to feel secure, validated, and loved; going inward to fill the gap instead of turning to others; trusting the universe and yourself; self-esteem; the ability to allow love in.

Fifth chakra: sky blue. Located in the throat area. Corresponds to the thyroid, bronchial and vocal apparatus, lungs, alimentary canal; expression of self through voice and mind; ideals, philosophy, psychology; the ability to focus on the present instead of the past or future.

Sixth chakra: indigo. Located in the third eye area. Corresponds to the pituitary, lower brain, left eye, ears, nose, nervous system; intuition; visions; symbols; psychic abilities; awareness of your guides; ability to think abstractly.

Seventh chakra: violet. Located in the top of head area. Corresponds to the pineal, upper brain, right eye; ability to receive light; connection to your Higher Self; astral travel; imagination.

Prosperity and Career Success

- What do I most need to know at this time regarding my finances?
- What will be with my financial situation/career if I continue on the same path)?
- What is blocking me from achieving my prosperity and career goals?
- What kind of career would I feel most fulfilled and happiest with?

General

- What do I most need to know at this time?
- Which past life is affecting my current reality the most?

Challenges to Successful Meditations or Regressions

- Laziness. While meditation and past-life regression can become, through practice, as easy as watching TV, it takes patience and perseverance to reach this stage. By following directions and through discipline and preparation, you'll gain far more than from any TV program. Turn off the TV and transform your life.
- Rigid views about the way things are supposed to be. This often becomes more true as we get older. An openness to the possibility of new ideas and viewpoints will help. A realization that age has little to do with spiritual awareness also helps.
- Failure to trust the process. If you need to, suspend all skepticism and pretend you believe. Make it okay with yourself to feel like you're making up whatever you perceive. If you feel strong emotions during a regression, it may indicate a higher possibility of validity.
- No specific goal in mind. Even if the goal is simply to experience a happy past life or what you would most benefit from perceiving at this time, it's important to give the mind some direction.
- Uncomfortable with the person assisting the regression or with disclosing private information during the process. Find someone with whom you feel relaxed and who accepts and loves you unconditionally, or try the process alone with a recording.
- Reason for using meditation or past-life regression isn't clear enough. What do you really want to know? Is that the real problem? Do you really want to reach the goal? What would happen if you did reach your goal? Would you like it?
- Can't focus long enough to perceive anything of value. The discipline of daily meditation will help.
- Closed off to the truth. You must be willing to consider whatever comes up, even if it's unpleasant. It's helpful to remember that you aren't reliving whatever you perceive, only recalling and observing it. There is no danger of getting stuck in the past.
- Trying to avoid responsibility for current life situations. You must accept that only you are responsible for your life situations and that there are no victims.

- Violent past-life death. Once you explore and release this experience, you'll usually be able to more easily explore other past lives. It's sometimes helpful to explore these situations from a detached viewpoint by telling yourself to perceive any traumatic events as an observer and to rise above any uncomfortable emotions.
- Fear of losing control. This may be the result of a death in a past life from drowning, drugs, alcohol, or anesthesia, or from being manipulated or controlled in either the current or a past life. You may have better results by using past life self-regression recordings on your own.
- Out of touch with emotions or body. The discipline of daily meditation will help you get in touch with yourself and your true feelings.
- Addictions to or use of drugs or alcohol. Recreational drugs can block meditation and prevent regression insight and awareness, even if the drug was last used weeks or even months earlier. Some prescription drugs, especially if they are mood altering, can also block awareness. Use of recreational drugs and alcohol may also allow spiritual parasites to cloud insight, intuition, and awareness.
- Food allergies or intolerances can have the same affect as drugs.
- Lack of interest in or fear of awareness. Ironically, these can be remedied by finding the root cause of them through regression therapy.
- Awareness through past-life regression about a particular conflict may not be appropriate now. If not, keep asking for help and you'll know what needs to be done at the right time.

"What if I've followed the advice above and I still can't seem to focus well or go very deep in meditation or past life self-regression?"

- Try meditating on an empty stomach or at a different time of day.
- Try it after a hot bath or shower.
- Try it after exercise.
- Try it after sex or instead of sex when in the mood.

- Try relaxing music. Experiment with different kinds to test which works best for you.
- Try no music.
- Try aromatherapy. Open a window when burning incense or candles indoors to vent any toxic fumes. Try rubbing a dab of a pure scented oil on the back of your hands or on your neck. The scent will relax you and help you focus.
- Try meditating with someone you love or with a group of friends. The combined energy will help you go deeper.
- You may be sensitive to something you're eating or drinking. Pick a day and eat lightly, perhaps about half of what you usually do. Consume what you know will be easy to digest, such as lightly steamed vegetables. You should be able to focus more easily provided you feel lighter and more alert.
- Avoid sugar, including fruit sugar if you have sugar sensitivities.
- Watch the caffeine. Don't go without it if you know you'll have withdrawal symptoms, but don't overdo it either.
- Certain supplements, herbs, and medications, especially if they affect your mood, may be disagreeing with your system and causing you to be scattered. Ask your doctor or health professional for alternative recommendations or if you can do without them for a while.
- Try deep breathing *rapidly* in and out through your mouth or nose for at least five minutes. Ten is better.
- Roll your closed eyes up to your third eye area, between and just above your eyes. Keep them focused there at a comfortable position without straining them.
- Close your eyes, breathe gently, and fantasize about your dreams and goals. What would your life be like if your dreams came true? These fantasies will help you become relaxed and may allow you to focus more.
- Patience and practice. Sooner or later something will click.
- Ask for help. If you keep asking God or your guides or angels of the Light how you can be more successful with meditation or past life self-regression, you'll eventually become aware of effective ways to go deeper and focus better. You'll be a pro in no time!

• If you're still having trouble perceiving anything, jump start the process by using your imagination. Tell yourself you'll perceive the first image, thought, or feeling, in response to any of the questions or instructions in the script, on the count of three. Then count one, two, three and provide a picture or thought from your imagination or memory. Continue this process until other (past-life) images that feel more related to the issue you are exploring start filtering into your mind.

• If you have trouble perceiving past-life information, begin with small steps. First try a regression back to an event which took place a few years ago in your current life. Then, after you're successful with this, try an event 10 years ago. Keep going back until you feel you're ready for a simple past-life review, such as a lifetime where you were happy. After success with that, you should be ready to view a lifetime that will explain how you knew someone in your current life or reveal the cause of a problem.

• If you have tried everything and you still can't seem to have successful meditations or past life self-regressions, there may be two other reasons: First, your expectations may be interfering. You may be expecting to see something when you might be more successful perceiving in a different way, such as sound or feeling. Try not to think during the process. Stay open and try visualizing white light around you. Second, you may be blocked emotionally, mentally, or spiritually. Keep asking for help, continue practicing while utilizing the white light, and stay open for clues.

Forgive and Release Meditation

Resentment and guilt about experiences from the past block your energy and interferes with your goals. Forgive and release yourself and anyone who has ever hurt you with the following meditation. This meditation is different than a regression in that you will be consciously creating scenes in your mind that will be symbolic of letting go and forgiving. It can be used for forgiving yourself or others for current-life situations or after a past life self-regression. Have a good friend read you the script, create a meditation recording from the script, or order the pre-recorded CD version. Read "Meditation and Regression Preparation" at the beginning of this chapter before using this exercise.

If you still have difficulty forgiving yourself or someone else after this exercise, meditate and regress back to the scene that caused the guilt or resentment and focus on why you or the other person behaved the way they did. With awareness comes compassion and with compassion comes acceptance and forgiveness. Also, consider perceiving life in a different way. We are all actors on this stage called Earth. We play our roles and interact with other characters, easily or with difficulty, in order to carry out the story. However, when the curtain falls after the last act, we take off our masks, go backstage, and become who we really are again. Those who we had conflict with on stage may be our good friends backstage. They helped us play our role, and we helped them play theirs. "Backstage" we are grateful for the chance to "act" and for the opportunity to play out our dramas with all the characters, even the "negative" ones.

This exercise will help you to release negative emotions between you and another person and can be used for any kind of relationship. It will enable you to love and accept people as they are. Releasing someone doesn't mean you're releasing him or her from your life, but if you continue to interact with them, the anger and resentment from the past will no longer interfere with that relationship.

(Begin)

Never use this meditation recording in a moving vehicle or at any time when you need to be completely awake. Also, know that you can return to the present easily on your own by counting from one to five. When doing so, you'll immediately feel relaxed and be wide awake. Please begin by finding a place where you can relax and won't be disturbed.

Sit or lie down and take a few deep breaths, in through your nose to the pit of your stomach and then exhale through your mouth. As you exhale, feel your body letting go of all the stress from the day. Now close your eyes and take another deep breath. Continue breathing throughout this meditation. Relax and let go. Feel your body relaxing with each breath that you take. Feel your legs relaxing . . . (pause) and your arms relaxing . . . (pause). And as you take another deep breath, feel your stomach area relaxing . . . just let go of all the tension and stress . . . (pause). Now feel your neck and back relaxing . . . just melting into the chair, bed, or floor . . . (pause). This wonderful relaxing feeling is now moving into your face and scalp . . . feel all the tension dissolving away . . . (pause). It is now time to ask for protection and guidance. Please repeat after me, either out loud, or to yourself: "God, guides and angels of the Light, and Higher Self, please allow me to gain the awareness I need through this meditation and through my dreams and insight. Please assist me to forgive and release myself and everyone else so that I can lead a more productive and happy life. Please make your guidance clear and concise so that I may easily receive, understand, and interpret it. I thank you and am grateful for your assistance."

Take another deep breath, and as you exhale that breath visualize a bright white light of protection surrounding you (pause). Now visualize this bright white light filling and illuminating your entire body. Feel it cleanse away anything you don't need anymore. Feel it repairing and restoring you on every level: physical, emotional, mental, and spiritual. Take a moment to bask in this light (pause).

I am now going to count from nine to one. With each count, feel your body relaxing and letting go even more. Nine . . . eight . . . seven . . . six . . . five . . . four . . . three . . . two . . . one . . . Good.

As you take another deep breath, please find yourself outside, standing on a platform of a train station. Notice the wooden planks and the old-fashioned steam-engine train. You can hear the sounds of the train and feel the crisp, fresh air (pause).

As you look at this train, you know that it's a special train. This train will help you release negative emotions between you and anyone in your life, including those within yourself.

In the distance, you see someone walking toward you. This is someone you know, someone with whom you have unfinished business. This person may have hurt you; you may have hurt them. You feel safe, secure, and confident. It's time to resolve and release all the negative emotions between yourself and this person. See that person in front of you now (pause). Express to this person how you feel about them and their actions towards you in the past. Tell them exactly how you feel. Don't hold back. You may do this out loud or to yourself. Express as much emotion as you wish. So go ahead now and tell this person how you're feeling about the situation between you two, and how hurt you have felt by anything he or she has done or said (pause for one minute).

Now listen to their response. What does he or she say to you? Feel how he or she feels (pause for one minute).

How do you react? (pause for one minute)

You now realize that this person hasn't really been an enemy, but instead a teacher helping you to learn your lessons. It's now time to forgive this person and thank them for what they have helped you learn. This forgiveness is for your benefit so you can release the negative emotions. If you don't forgive them, you'll remain trapped in the negative emotion (pause). Go ahead, look them in the eyes, tell them that you forgive them and release them for good. *Feel* the forgiveness (pause).

Now listen to their response. What do they say to you? (pause)

How do you react? (pause)

You suddenly become aware that there is a lot of baggage on the platform next to you and this person. These old suitcases contain all the miscommunication, resentment, anger, guilt, and fear that have been between the two of you (pause). A porter walks up and asks if he may take the bags. You're happy to get rid of them, so you say, "Yes, thank you." You watch the porter load the suitcases onto the train. Just let it all go. It doesn't matter any more. You feel a huge sense of relief, as if a heavy burden has been lifted from your shoulders. Notice how good it feels to be free of all those old emotions. Forgive and release (pause).

It is time to say goodbye to the person who hurt you. They are getting on the train now (pause). You again tell this person that you forgive them and you wish them well and they say the same to you (pause). Listen to their parting words through the open train window as the train begins to pull away.

You watch as the train fades in the distance (pause).

The anger and resentment are gone. It no longer matters. Let it go completely (pause).

It's now time to forgive yourself. It's time to let go of all the guilt. The past doesn't matter anymore. Let go of it all. Tell yourself that you forgive and release yourself for anything you feel guilty about. Release it, and be free (pause).

As you turn to walk away from the train tracks, a friendly porter walks up and says that he has a message for you. Listen to his insightful words carefully (pause).

It's time to come back to the present, to this room. Know that if you interact with this person again you'll be able to do so calmly and with compassion. You've now forgiven and released them completely. On the count of five you'll be wide awake, feeling refreshed and peaceful. One: you're starting to come back; two: begin to be aware of your body and surroundings; three: focus your attention on the present; four: on the next count you'll be wide awake and feeling refreshed; five: open your eyes and feel wide awake.

Relationship Meditations

Steps to Gain Awareness About Another

The following exercise is to be used as a tool of compassion and love, never to overstep boundaries or to pry. It can be used for any type of relationship to help understand another's feelings and perceptions. Use the information gained to help, never to hurt. Respect this person: they are entitled to their own thoughts and feelings. Try to accept the answers you receive. It isn't your right to expect anyone to feel the way you want them to. Read "Meditation and Regression Preparation" at the beginning of this chapter before using this exercise.

1. Close your eyes, breath deeply, and relax your entire body and mind.
2. Visualize a bright white light of protection and guidance around and within you. Ask God, guides and angels of the Light, and/or your Higher Self for assistance.
3. Concentrate on the person about whom you would like to become more aware.
4. As you're concentrating on that person, consider what it would feel like to be that person. Put yourself in their shoes.
5. Ask this person the following questions and pause for a response:
    - How do you (the other person) feel about him/her (yourself) or the situation?
    - Do you feel a/the relationship with him/her (yourself) is for your highest good? Why or why not?
    - What do you need in a relationship?
    - What do you need from this relationship?

- Who do you love?
- What do you fear?
- What is your biggest worry?
- To feel loved, what do you need?

6. Send peace and love to this person.

7. Now disconnect completely from this person and come completely back into your own energy. Visualize a bright white light of protection surrounding and cleansing you and this other person and separating your energy from theirs.

8. Other ways to gain more awareness about how someone feels about you.

- Instead of focusing on the person in meditation, focus on the situation.
- Before going to sleep, ask God, your guides and angels of the Light and/or your Higher Self for guidance and information through dreams.
- Ask the person directly. However, most people find it difficult to be completely honest in such situations. For example, if he or she isn't physically attracted to you, they may not tell you the truth out of a fear of hurting your feelings.

Gain Awareness about a Potential or Existing Partnership

The following exercise is to be used as a tool of compassion and love, never to overstep your boundaries or to pry. Use the information gained to help, never to hurt. Read "Meditation and Regression Preparation" at the beginning of this chapter before attempting to use this exercise.

1. Close your eyes, breathe deeply, and relax your entire body and mind.

2. Visualize a bright white light of protection and guidance around and within you. Ask God, guides and angels of the Light and/or your Higher Self for assistance.

3. Concentrate on the other person.

4. Ask out loud or to yourself: "During the next few days or weeks, help me to perceive everything I need to know to decide if this relationship is for the highest good for us both."

5. If, after the few days or weeks, you decide to end or no longer pursue the relationship, follow steps one through three and then

say: "Thank you for all that I have learned from you. I now wish you the best and release you to go your own way."

Express Unspoken Words

Express your true feelings to someone you didn't have the opportunity or courage to. Use this meditation just before sleep at night.

1. Surround yourself with white light.

2. Thank God, your guides and angels of the Light, and/or your Higher Self for guidance and protection.

3. Visualize the person to whom you wish to give a message as clearly as you can. Picture a pink ray of light connecting your heart chakra with theirs.

4. Tell this person, with compassion, what you want to say ("I feel the need to tell you . . ."). This is spiritual communication, not physical, so the other person can be anywhere and still receive your message on a subconscious level.

5. Complete the message with the following: "I surround you in white light and I thank (or forgive) you." If forgiveness is appropriate, it's important to feel the forgiveness and release the person. Holding onto resentment will hurt you. Let them go in peace.

6. *Important:* After the meditation, disconnect completely from this person. Visualize the pink ray of light dissolving and come completely back into your own energy. Visualize a bright white light of protection surrounding and cleansing you and this other person and separating your energy from theirs.

Forgive and Release While You Sleep

Resentment and guilt about experiences from the past blocks your energy and interferes with your goals. Forgive and release yourself or anyone who has ever hurt you with the following meditation. Use this meditation exercise just before falling asleep.

1. Close your eyes, breathe deeply, and feel your body and mind relaxing.

2. Take another deep breath, and as you exhale visualize a bright white light surrounding you (pause). Now visualize this white light entering the top of your head and filling your body with its brilliance. Feel the light cleansing away anything you don't need anymore. Feel

it repairing and restoring you on every level: physical, emotional, mental, and spiritual. Take a moment to bask in this light.

3. Ask for protection, guidance, and assistance in forgiving by repeating the following out loud or to yourself: "God, guides and angels of the Light, and/or Higher Self, please allow me to gain the awareness I need through this meditation and through my dreams and daily insight. Please assist me to forgive and release myself and ____________ (and everyone else) so that I can lead a more productive and happy life. Please make your guidance clear and concise so that I may easily understand, interpret, and receive it. I thank you and am grateful for your assistance."

4. Concentrate on the other person(s) involved or yourself if the forgiveness is for you. Send yourself and/or the other person(s) a white light of forgiveness. Feel the forgiveness and mean it. Tell yourself that you and/or they did the best you/they could at the time and that the past no longer matters. Consider what you learned from the experience and how this has helped you grow.

5. Count yourself down into a relaxed state from ten to one. With each number feel your body relaxing and letting go, breathing gently and deeply as you do so. Repeat this countdown until you drift into a peaceful sleep.

Love Potion Meditation Script For Singles

For optimum results, record this meditation and listen to it every night for six weeks or more as you fall asleep. Or, listen to the recording all night on an endless loop. This meditation is available on CD. See the order form in the back of the book.

This meditation consists of suggestions for your conscious and subconscious minds. It is best used in conjunction with regression therapy (finding the root cause), either with a qualified therapist or by discovering and dissolving blocks on your own using the "Past Life Self-Regression" exercise.

(Begin)

Never use this meditation recording in a moving vehicle or at any time when you need to be completely awake. Also, know that you can return to the present easily on your own by counting from one to five. When doing so, you'll immediately feel relaxed and be wide awake.

Please begin by taking a deep breath in through your nose . . . now release the breath slowly through your mouth . . . and begin to feel your body relaxing . . . let go of all of your concerns and worries . . . just for the moment . . . take another deep breath in through your nose . . . and release the breath slowly through your mouth . . . repeat this process throughout this session. Breathing deeply will help you to relax and let go of your body and conscious mind so your subconscious mind can accept all the suggestions.

If any outside thoughts should enter your mind, allow them to float by like clouds in the sky. Now is your time to relax and let go.

In order for this to be even more effective, we are going to ask for help from God, your guides and angels of the Light and/or your Higher Self. They are happy to help you when you ask. Please repeat the following words either out loud or to yourself and feel the gratitude: "I now call out to God, my guides and angels of the Light, and my Higher Self. I am grateful for your assistance along my path to a compatible love relationship. Thank you in advance for helping me and guiding me to be in the right place at the right time and to do the right things so that I may reach my compatible love relationship goal. Thank you for your assistance in my dreams and my awakened state. Please make your help and guidance clear, concise, and obvious. Thank you for helping me to love and accept myself. Thank you for the discipline to do what I need to do to reach my love relationship goals. Thank you in advance for your love and assistance."

Take another deep breath . . . and release . . . Now imagine that your feet and legs are relaxing . . . feel your feet and legs relaxing . . . they are feeling heavier and heavier with each word I speak . . . good . . . Now imagine your stomach is relaxing . . . and as you imagine this, it does relax and you can feel the tension being released from your stomach . . . just melting away . . . good . . . Now feel your arms and chest relaxing . . . all the tension is being released from your arms and chest . . . just let go . . . let go . . . take another deep breath, please . . .

Feel your neck and shoulders relaxing . . . your neck and shoulders are relaxing . . . now your eyes and jaw are relaxing . . . Allow your eyes and jaw to feel relaxed and comfortable . . . relaxed and comfortable . . . letting go more and more with each word I speak, going into deeper and deeper levels of relaxation.

Now feel your scalp relaxing . . . Notice now that your entire body is more relaxed. Please focus on this relaxed feeling as I count backwards from seven to one. With each number that I count, feel your body relaxing and letting go even more . . . seven . . . deeper . . . deeper . . . deeper . . . six . . . down . . . down . . . down . . . five . . . deeper . . . deeper . . . deeper . . . four . . . down . . . down . . .down . . . three . . . deeper . . . deeper . . . deeper . . . two . . . down . . . down . . . down . . . one . . . good . . . Now take a deep breath please and as you release it, go 10 times deeper . . .

One more time . . . this time really let go and allow the process to work for you . . . seven . . . deeper . . . deeper . . . deeper . . . six . . . down . . . down . . . down . . . five . . . deeper . . . deeper . . . deeper . . . four . . . down . . . down. . .down . . . three . . . deeper . . . deeper . . . deeper . . . two . . . down . . . down . . . down . . . one . . . Now take a deep breath please and as you release it, go 20 times deeper . . .

As you continue to breathe at a comfortable pace, please imagine, as vividly as you can, a bright white light of protection and guidance surrounding your body . . . Imagine this light cleansing you and dissolving away any fears you may have . . . You have access to this protective, white light whenever you choose. All you need to do is imagine it surrounding you.

It is now time for forgiveness. It is time for you to forgive any past partners for *everything* they have ever done or said that hurt you. Remember that forgiveness isn't about letting someone off the hook. Everyone will eventually have to deal with his or her actions due to the law of karma. Forgiveness is about releasing resentment from within you so it will no longer interfere with your current or future love life. You ultimately forgive someone *for yourself.* Imagine in your mind any partners who have hurt you. Feel the forgiveness and compassion for them when you tell them you forgive them. Make sure to notice their reaction. Take a few moments now to do this (pause for one or two minutes).

And finally, it is time to forgive yourself for everything you have ever done to hurt any past partners. Mentally forgive yourself and feel the forgiveness. You did the best you could, you have suffered enough, and you'll do better in the future . . . Let go of any guilt. Take a few moments to do this now (pause).

Take another deep breath, and as you release that breath, repeat the following positive statements. They will be accepted as fact by your conscious and subconscious minds:

- I am becoming aware of any hidden reasons I am avoiding a compatible relationship.
- I am now choosing to learn and grow through joy instead of sorrow and struggle.
- Every day my discipline is increasing so that I can prepare myself on all levels for a loving and compatible relationship.
- I now realize there is plenty of time and room in my life for the right person.
- I am becoming aware of and dissolving any blocks between myself and a loving and compatible relationship.
- My subconscious mind is assisting me in being in the right place at the right time to meet compatible love relationship possibilities.
- I am taking healthy chances now with those I would like to meet by making eye contact and smiling, then, if it feels right, by approaching and talking casually.
- I now realize that rejection is part of life. If it happens, I easily dismiss it and know that the person who rejected me wasn't right for me and actually did me a favor. I'll be one step closer to the person who *is* right for me.
- I realize that it is to my benefit to be flexible in love matters, so I give each possibility a chance.
- I have the self-discipline to listen to this recording every day. I choose a time and listen to this recording every day at that time.

I would now like you to repeat the following statements, either to yourself or out loud:

- My heart now opens to accept the love I deserve.
- I am now letting go of the past and anyone who ever hurt me.
- I now forgive myself and everyone else.
- I am now ready to love another unconditionally.
- I take action to meet the people I want to meet.
- I am drawn to those who are compatible, and I avoid those who are not.

- I am friendly and people are drawn to me.
- I am self-confident and self-assured.
- Each day I improve what I can and accept what I can't change.
- I love and accept myself.
- I now accept the love I deserve.

It is now time for creative visualization. Visualizing is powerful because your subconscious mind perceives what you imagine as real. The more you do this, the more likely your subconscious mind will set up situations that will lead to your goals. I am going to pause, and I would like you to imagine what it would feel like to be involved with a compatible partner. . . (pause for one or two minutes).

Now, I would like you to imagine what you and your ideal partner would do together, where you would go together, and again, how it would feel to be involved in this compatible love relationship (pause for one or two minutes).

Now I will give you a special tool to use whenever you're in a situation where you come in contact with a potential love possibility. All you have to do is take a deep breath and say the word "relax." Any time you say or hear this word, you'll instantly feel a boost of self-confidence. You'll have the confidence to be yourself. You'll be friendly, happy, charismatic, outgoing, and approachable. This word, "relax," is a reminder that helps you to achieve your goal of a loving compatible relationship. This tool helps you do what you need to do to experience the love relationship you want. Every time you hear or say this word, "relax," it will become more helpful for you.

I will now give you a suggestion: every time you listen to this recording you'll let go and relax even more deeply than the time before and the suggestions will become even more powerful and real for you.

If you're using this recording at bedtime or throughout the night, ignore the awakening suggestions and sleep deeply and peacefully until it is time to wake up. You'll awaken refreshed and feel ready to start a new day.

[If you choose to listen to this recording on an endless loop throughout the night, don't record this next paragraph.]

On the count of five, you'll be wide awake, feeling relaxed and self-confident. One: coming back up . . . two: feeling happy and well rested . . . three: feeling excited about your life . . . four: on the next count you'll be wide awake . . . five: wide awake . . . Open your eyes and feel good.

Love Potion Meditation Script For Involved Individuals Or Couples

For optimum results, record this meditation and listen to it every night for six weeks or more as you fall asleep. Or, listen to the recording all night on an endless loop. This meditation is available on CD. See the order form in the back of the book.

This meditation consists of suggestions for your conscious and subconscious minds. It is best used in conjunction with regression therapy (finding the root cause), either with a qualified therapist or by discovering and dissolving blocks on your own using the "Past Life Self-Regression" exercise.

(Begin)

Never use this meditation recording in a moving vehicle or at any time when you need to be completely awake. Also, know that you can return to the present easily on your own by counting from one to five. When doing so, you'll immediately feel relaxed and be wide awake.

Please begin by taking a deep breath in through your nose . . . now release the breath slowly through your mouth . . . and begin to feel your body relaxing . . . Let go of all of your concerns and worries. . .. just for the moment . . . Take another deep breath in through your nose . . . and release the breath slowly through your mouth . . . Repeat this process throughout this session. Breathing deeply will help you to relax and let go of your body and conscious mind so your subconscious mind can accept all the suggestions.

If any outside thoughts should enter your mind, allow them to float by like clouds in the sky. Now is your time to relax and let go.

In order for this to be even more effective, we are going to ask for help from God, your guides and angels of the Light, and/or your Higher Self. They are happy to help you when you ask. Please repeat the following words either out loud or to yourself and feel the gratitude: "I now call out to God my guides and angels of the Light, and my Higher Self. I am grateful for your assistance along my path to a compatible love relationship. Thank you in advance for helping me and guiding me to do the right things so that I may reach my love relationship goals. Thank you for your assistance in my dreams and my awakened state. Please make your help and guidance clear, concise, and obvious. Thank you for helping me to love and accept myself. Thank you for the discipline to do what I need to do to reach my love relationship goals. Thank you in advance for your love and assistance."

Take another deep breath . . . and release . . . Now imagine that your feet and legs are relaxing . . . feel your feet and legs relaxing . . . they are feeling heavier and heavier with each word I speak . . . good . . . Now imagine your stomach is relaxing . . . and as you imagine this, it does relax and you can feel the tension being released from your stomach . . . just melting away . . . good . . . Now feel your arms and chest relaxing . . . All the tension is being released from your arms and chest . . . just let go . . . let go . . . Take another deep breath, please . . .

Feel your neck and shoulders relaxing . . . your neck and shoulders are relaxing . . . now your eyes and jaw are relaxing . . . Allow your eyes and jaw to feel relaxed and comfortable . . . relaxed and comfortable . . . Letting go more and more with each word I speak, going into deeper and deeper levels of relaxation . . .

Now feel your scalp relaxing . . . Notice now that your entire body is more relaxed. Please focus on this relaxed feeling as I count backwards from seven to one. With each number that I count, feel your body relaxing and letting go even more . . . seven . . . deeper . . . deeper . . . deeper . . . six . . . down . . . down . . . down . . . five . . . deeper . . . deeper . . . deeper . . . four . . . down . . . down . . .down . . . three . . . deeper . . . deeper . . . deeper . . . two . . . down . . . down . . . down . . . one . . . good . . . now take a deep breath, please, and as you release it, go 10 times deeper . . .

One more time . . . this time really let go and allow the process to work for you . . . seven . . . deeper . . . deeper . . . deeper . . . six . . . down . . . down . . . down . . . five . . . deeper . . . deeper . . . deeper . . . four . . . down . . . down. . .down . . . three . . . deeper . . . deeper . . . deeper . . . two . . . down . . . down . . . down . . . one . . . Now take a deep breath, please, and as you release it, go 20 times deeper . . .

As you continue to breathe at a comfortable pace, please imagine, as vividly as you can, a bright white light of protection and guidance surrounding your body . . . Imagine this light cleansing you and dissolving away any fears you may have . . . You have access to this protective, white light whenever you choose. All you need to do is imagine it surrounding you.

Take another deep breath, and as you release that breath, repeat the following positive statements. They will be accepted as fact by your conscious and subconscious minds:

- I deserve a loving and compatible relationship.
- I make quality time to spend with my partner.
- I accept my partner unconditionally as they are.
- I give unconditional love to my partner.
- I am becoming aware of and dissolving any blocks within myself that are interfering with the loving relationship I deserve.
- I am now choosing to learn and grow through joy instead of sorrow and struggle.
- Whenever I find myself becoming angry with my partner, I stop, take a deep breath, and calmly discuss the situation.
- I discuss my needs, I'm open to my partner's needs, and we create solutions together.
- I tune into and listen to my partner and what is being communicated verbally and non-verbally.
- I stop blaming my partner and start taking responsibility for myself and my situation.
- I have the self-discipline to listen to this recording every day. I choose a time and listen to this recording every day at that time.

I would now like you to repeat the following statements either to yourself or out loud:

- I am now letting go of the past and releasing anyone who ever hurt me.
- I now forgive myself and everyone else.
- I am now ready to love my partner unconditionally.
- I avoid judging my partner and accept them as they are.

- I now express love and compassion to my lover in creative ways.
- I now drop my expectations of my partner and love them for who they are.
- I now love and support my lover in every way I can.
- Whenever I find myself becoming angry with my partner, I stop, take a deep breath, and calmly discuss the situation instead.
- I appreciate my partner's opinions, even if I don't agree.
- I love and accept myself.

It is now time for creative visualization. Visualizing is powerful because your subconscious mind perceives what you imagine as real. Your subconscious mind will help create situations that match your visions. I am going to pause, and I would like you to imagine yourself harmoniously interacting with your partner (pause for one or two minutes).

Now I would like you to imagine your partner in front of you. Picture your partner in front of you and tell your partner that you love him or her. Notice their reaction.

Now tell your partner you realize that no one is perfect, and that you accept him or her as they are. Notice their reaction.

And now, most importantly, I would like you to forgive your current partner for *everything* they have ever done or said that hurt you. Remember that forgiveness isn't about letting someone off the hook. Everyone will eventually have to deal with his or her actions due to the law of karma. Forgiveness is about releasing resentment from within you so it will no longer interfere with your current or future love life. You ultimately forgive someone *for yourself.* Imagine your partner in your mind. Feel the forgiveness and compassion for them when you tell them you forgive them and accept them as they are. Notice their reaction. Take a few moments now to do this (pause for one or two minutes).

And finally, it is time to forgive yourself for everything you have ever done to hurt your partner. Mentally forgive yourself and feel the forgiveness. You did the best you could, you have suffered enough, and you'll do better in the future. Let go of any guilt. Take a few moments to do this now (pause).

Now I will give you a special tool to use whenever you're in a situation where you need help with your love relationship. All you have to do is take a deep breath and say the word, "compassion." Any time you say or hear this word you feel love and compassion for yourself and for your partner and realize you're both doing the best you can. This word, "compassion," reminds you of the love you have for your partner. It reminds you to accept your partner as they are and to love them unconditionally; that means with *no* expectations of anything in return. Every time you hear this word, "compassion," it will become more helpful for you. You believe this works for you, and it does.

I will now give you a suggestion: every time you listen to this recording you'll let go and relax even more deeply than the time before, and the suggestions will become even more powerful and real for you.

If you're using this recording at bedtime or throughout the night, ignore the awakening suggestions and sleep deeply and peacefully until it is time to wake up. You'll awaken refreshed and feel excited about a new day.

[If you choose to listen to this recording throughout the night on an endless loop, don't record the following paragraph.]

On the count of five, you'll be wide awake, feeling relaxed and self-confident. One: coming back up . . . two: feeling happy and well rested . . . three: feeling excited about your life . . . four: on the next count you'll be wide awake . . . five: wide awake . . . Open your eyes and feel good.

Past Life Self-Regression

Use this exercise for discovering and dissolving the root cause of a problem or for fun to explore different lifetimes you may have lived.

1. Read "Meditation and Regression Preparation" in the beginning of this chapter before using this exercise.

2. Read over the following instructions and then use the meditation instruction steps A through G (see pages 165–167) above to lead into the past life.

3. Have a friend lead you through the meditation and regression or create a recording to help lead you through the process.

- Never use the recording in a moving vehicle or at any time when you need to be completely awake.
- Speak slowly and clearly and pause frequently to allow time to explore and reflect.
- When you reach step E in the meditation instruction above, use one of the methods listed or use a count down relaxation method. For example, count slowly from 10 backwards to one. Feel your body relaxing more and more deeply with each number. Use this count down as many times as it takes you to completely let go and relax.

4. Make sure you formulate a question or statement ahead of time for step H that will most effectively lead you to the root cause or where the situation began. Otherwise you may gain awareness but not fully understand the karma. For example, if you have conflict with someone, the question "Why do we fight so much?" may not take you to the *root* of the conflict. Instead you may perceive the little reasons but not why it began. "Why am I so mad at him/her?" is also too general. It may uncover some answers for you, but perhaps not those that will help you become fully aware of the situation and why you both are together again. *A more effective statement* would be "Please allow me to perceive information about where, when, and why the conflict between _______ and I first began. Please help me to completely understand that conflict and the karma between _______ and I and how I/we can resolve it and make our interactions more harmonious."

- If you're interested in finding the root cause of a fear, such as a fear of commitment, intimacy, or abandonment, examine what bothers you most about the issue before you begin the regression meditation. Concentrate on your feelings and choose words that describe your feelings. They may give you clues about the root cause. An effective regression question/statement to find the cause of a fear could be "Please allow me to perceive awareness about where, when, and why my fear of _______ *first* began. Please help me to completely understand my fear of _______ and I and how I/we can resolve it."
- If you don't have anything specific that you want to explore, try a general statement: "Please allow me to perceive the life-

time(s) that would help me the most at this time to remember" or "Please allow me to perceive what would help me the most at this time." If you wish to use past life self-regression for fun or for reasons besides searching for the cause of something, see "Past-life Regression Options" for other ideas.

5. There are many ways to access a past life. Some methods are as follows. Remember that your visions don't need to be clear for them to be effective.

- Focus on the emotions you feel about an issue, conflict, or problem. Allow these feelings to take you back to an event that will explain the root cause.
- Visualize yourself walking down a long hallway with doors on both sides. Each door is a past life. Choose the door that you intuitively feel will lead you to the answers you are seeking. On the count of three, open the door and walk through. Allow the impressions of a different time and different place to enter your mind easily and vividly.
- Visualize yourself walking down a stairway. At the bottom of the stairway is a beautiful door. Behind this door are the answers that you seek. On the count of three, open the door, walk through it, and enter the past life that relates to the reasons for your regression.
- Visualize yourself taking an elevator down to the lower floors of a beautiful building. The elevator stops at the appropriate floor for you. You walk out of the elevator and into a beautifully decorated room. In this room, you sit down in a chair and look up at a screen on the wall. On the count of three, images will begin to appear on this screen that relate to the reasons for your regression. At the count of three, you find yourself becoming part of these scenes.
- The most direct: On the count of three, you begin to see vivid images of the past life that relates to the reasons for your regression.

6. *You are always safe in a past-life regression.* Your mind will not show you anything that you aren't ready to see. The "worst" or scariest or saddest regressions, which can be unpleasant to experience, are usually the most effective! In other words, perceiving a negative situation allows one to face it, forgive it, and release it.

Otherwise, you'll continue to waste energy carrying emotional baggage (subconscious guilt, anger, or resentment) and will continue to create or attract negative situations that mirror the past. If you perceive a negative situation, realize that you're remembering it, not reliving it. If you choose to, tell yourself to rise above the emotions and view the scene as an observer. *You can choose to be in control and end the regression at any time simply by opening your eyes.*

7. We access information from past lives through our intuitive right brain or through our Higher Self, but if you're doing the regression yourself, you'll need to switch to your left brain to think of the questions you want to ask yourself during the regression. An easier method is to record your questions and then play them back during the regression. Have your finger on the play button and hit play for each question as it comes up and then hit pause. You can also write down your questions and have a friend read them to you. Some questions you may want to explore are location, time period, names, appearance, career, family, spouse, children, friends, love interests, lessons learned, issues that cause a lot of stress, important events, attitudes, and beliefs (see "Trigger Questions" on page 168). Don't ask leading questions during the regression such as "How beautiful is my wife?" or "How wealthy am I?" Instead, ask to perceive your love interest or economic situation. When using regression to find the root cause of a problem, you may need to ask direct statements during the regression such as, "Please move forward or backward to the event that first caused the conflict with _______."

8. Once you're perceiving a past life, you'll most likely encounter situations that you'll want to know more about. One way to help yourself become more aware of the answers to your questions during a regression is to tell yourself the following: "On the count of three, I'll perceive why/who/what/where/when/how [pick one]. One, two, three." Let your mind go blank and allow the answer to enter your mind. Explore each past life as if it is the present. You'll perceive more if you act as if you're there.

9. You most likely will encounter situations where forgiveness is in order, of either yourself or others. Forgive the best you can during the session and then if you feel the need, use the forgiveness exercise in this chapter after you've finished your session.

10. When you have explored the life as much as you want to, move forward (on the count of three) to the time of your death (make sure to specify "in the lifetime I am exploring"!) and view it as an observer, rising above any unpleasant emotion.

11. After the death experience in the past life, review the lifetime(s) perceived:

- Ask if anyone you knew then is in your life now.
- Ask what you were meant to learn from the experiences.
- Ask what karma you incurred and how that life is effecting your current life.
- Ask how you can release any resentment and guilt (in addition to using the forgiveness exercise in this section).
- Ask anything else you would like to know about what you explored.

12. You may need to occasionally pause and count yourself down again to deepen the trance. Simply count slowly from ten to one and feel your body relaxing more and more with each number. The more relaxed you are, the better your results will be. Tell yourself that with each number you become increasingly relaxed, and that by the time you reach one you'll begin to see the images more vividly and will have more awareness about what you're perceiving.

13. When you feel you're finished, count yourself up from one to five and tell yourself you'll be wide awake on the count of five. As noted above, you can return to the present any time during the regression. Counting from one to five helps the process but isn't necessary.

Past Life Self-Regression Options

Lifetime that your Higher Self feels you would most benefit from at this time.

Lifetime that relates to current problem/situation (back to root cause).

First lifetime (on Earth or elsewhere).

Most recent lifetime.

Lifetime when you knew________ (specific person).

Lifetime where you were an expert at something (good when desiring a new and successful career direction).

Lifetime when you developed an existing current-life talent/ability/skill.

Lifetime where you were involved in a happy and harmonious love relationship (good for improving current love life).
Lifetime where you were in extremely good health (good for improving health in current life).
Lifetime where you were financially responsible and disciplined (good for improving personal money management skills).
Lifetime in which you where incredibly self-confident/compassionate/powerful.
Lifetime when feelings of lack/poverty began.
Lifetime when need for control originated.
Lifetime when fear of _______ began.
Lifetime when your dislike of ________ began.
Lifetime when you were happiest/healthiest/poorest/wealthiest/famous, and so on.
Lifetime that took place in Atlantis.
Lifetime that took place on a different planet/dimension.
Lifetime that took place during a certain era.
Lifetime where certain physical symptoms originated.

Couples Past Life Self-Regression

Find out the details of a previous lifetime(s) together and the karma between you. *Do not use this exercise together until you both understand the concepts of karma and reincarnation, accept that everyone has been "bad" and "good" in past lives, and are willing to accept and forgive yourself, each other, and others for anything that may have happened in the past.* For more information, see chapter one. Read "Meditation and Regression Preparation" at the beginning of this chapter before using this exercise.

Follow the steps in "Past Life Self-Regression" and then make the following modifications:

1. Decide ahead of time on a regression question/statement.

- You may have been together in more than one lifetime. If your regression question/statement is "Go back to a happy lifetime we had together" or "Go back to a lifetime where we were in love," you may each perceive different lifetimes. If you wish to perceive the same lifetime, make your statement more specific, such as "Go back to the lifetime where we first met each other" or "Go back to the lifetime where our conflict about money/sex/fidelity/etc. first began."

- If you're using the exercise to resolve a specific conflict, an effective regression statement may be "Go back to where the conflict regarding ________ first began between us." Or concentrate on how the conflict makes each of you feel, and then allow those feelings to take you back to explore the root cause. Since everyone perceives events differently, you may return to different times and places.

2. Sit or lay comfortably side-by-side but not touching.

3. Follow the meditation instruction steps A through H on pages 165–167. The deeper you relax through meditation together, the better your results will be.

4. Some additional questions you may want to ask immediately after viewing a past life (or lives) and while you're still in meditation:

- What are we individually meant to learn from this relationship?
- What are we meant to learn together from this relationship?
- What are we meant to accomplish together through this relationship?
- Was our relationship predestined?
- Is there something I owe this person?
- How many lifetimes have we known each other?
- Is this a reward relationship?
- How can we enhance our bond?
- How can we each be a better partner?
- Is our relationship meant to last this entire lifetime? If no, why not?

5. After the regression, wait to share your experience with each other until after you each write down all the details—who, what, where, when, why and how—that you can remember about your experience.

How to Find a Competent Past-Life Regression Therapist

If you would like additional assistance with discovering and releasing the past, use the following guidelines to help you find a counselor or therapist who can best help you.

1. Hypnotists or hypnotherapists who offer past-life regression only as an added service may be able to regress you into a past life, but they may not know how make the session as productive as possible.

- Ask how much experience he or she has with past-life regression.
- Ask what percentage of their clients come to them for past-life regression.

2. Even if they appear to be "spiritual" or "metaphysical," they may not really understand that reincarnation and karma are the foundation of many spiritual and metaphysical concepts, and that reincarnation and karma are part of the reason each of us exist today on this planet.

- Ask what reincarnation and karma means to them.
- Ask if it's possible to dissolve or rise above karma. If so, how? The answer should be yes, through forgiveness, acceptance, and action after discovering the root cause of the karma.
- Ask if they believe that we reincarnate. Surprisingly, not all therapists who offer past-life regression, especially more traditional therapists, believe in reincarnation. A therapist's skepticism and lack of understanding may interfere with your session.
- Ask if they have personally experienced past-life regression. If so, how many times?
- Ask where and from whom they received their regression training.
- Ask for an anonymous example of a client they have worked with and how they used past-life regression to help him or her. Have them define the issue or problem and then provide a brief summary of past-life regression sessions (what events were discovered and what the therapist did to lead him or her through them effectively). *Forgiveness of self or others is almost always an important part of a past-life regression.* Did the therapist help the client do this? If it was appropriate and he or she didn't help the client forgive, they may not be the best therapist to help you reach your regression goal(s).

3. Counselors or therapists with psychological or medical training may have a better foundation to help clients with certain problems, but degrees don't guarantee that they can help you with your past-life regression goals. Pay more attention to their answers to the questions in this section than to their degrees.

4. If they are trained as a psychologist or psychiatrist, they may not believe in going directly to the root cause.

- Ask how many sessions an issue such as yours typically takes to resolve. They may not be able to give you an exact number, especially if they haven't yet consulted with you. However, based on their experience with other clients with similar issues, they should be able to give you an idea.
- Ask if they can take you directly to the root cause, to the lifetime where the conflict first began.

5. Find a therapist or counselor you intuitively feel good about. If you don't feel comfortable with them on the phone or in person, you may not have good results from the session. It's important that you trust the therapist enough to let go and allow the process of regression to work.

If the therapist or counselor doesn't follow all of the above recommendations but you still have a good connection with him or her, you may still be able to experience successful regression sessions. Trust your intuition above all when choosing a therapist or counselor.

Section VI

Putting It All Together

Don't get married until you know
who you are and what you want
in a relationship.

— Jane Fonda

15
Creating a Satisfying and Successful Love Life

In the 1991 movie *Love Potion #9*, Sandra Bullock and Tate Donovan play scientists who create a love potion that makes anyone fall madly in love with whoever has taken it. Such a magic potion doesn't exist, but we do have free will to take the action required to improve ourselves and our love lives. When blocks and interferences are dissolved through awareness and action, love lives really can be almost magically transformed.

As mentioned throughout this book, one of the most powerful and effective methods to discover and release emotional or spiritual blocks is through regression therapy. However, *discovering and dissolving blocks is only part of the equation to success in relationships and other areas of life.* The rest of the equation involves being centered and aware, and then taking positive, constructive, and conscious action at the appropriate times.

The three steps to reaching relationship and other personal goals are:

1. Discover and release blocks.
2. Be centered and aware.
3. Take the appropriate action at the appropriate time.

Love Life Essentials

You're perfect just the way you are, but at the same time, you are constantly changing and evolving. You have the ability to consciously direct your life, change or accept what you don't like, and live your life the way you choose. To become involved in or improve a compatible love relationship, you need to first focus on yourself. Help to attract, improve, or maintain a love relationship by following these reminders.

Invest in yourself

- **Realize that being single is an important part of your love life cycles.** We are programmed to believe that it's not "normal" to be single, and that if you're single for too long, something must be wrong. Being single is a time to get to know yourself, improve and repair yourself on all levels, concentrate on other areas of life, reflect on past relationships, and refine your wish list for a future partner. *Filling your inner void with self-love will dissolve the need to fill it with the wrong person for the wrong reasons.* Learn to love and treat yourself as you would the love of your life. No one will love you until you love yourself.
- **Realize you're worth it.** When you fully realize that you deserve the best life has to offer and dissolve any blocks that may be in your way, it's much easier to reach goals and dreams. Due to programming since childhood, it's easy to subconsciously believe the following "truths": love relationships equal struggle and unhappiness; illness and aging are part of getting older; we only deserve enough money to get by; work equals a lot of effort for a little pay; sex is dirty, bad, and something to hide. Use all the tools presented in this book to discover and let go of old perceptions that aren't serving you. Learn to love and accept yourself.
- **Be yourself.** In our society we are literally programmed to be the person that is expected of us instead of who we really are. Are you doing what you really want to do or what you're "supposed" to do?
- **Being honest with yourself unlocks the door to change.** In order for you or anyone else to help you, it is essential to be *completely honest* with yourself. Being realistic and honest with yourself and about your life will help you identify what isn't working. Digging through to these truths can sometimes be painful, disturbing, or even humiliating, but when you do,

you'll set yourself free by releasing the past and making room for your dreams and goals.

- **Remember who you are.** You have chosen, on some level, to incarnate at this time for specific reasons. Find your purpose in life. Meditation will introduce you to the real you inside and help you express your true self. When you're centered from meditating, you'll know what to do and when to take action to reach your goals. When you're centered, your goals will match your purpose in life.

Let Go of the Past

- **Forgive yourself and anyone who has ever hurt you.** Forgiveness is an imperative part of letting go of the past and moving into the reality you want. Carrying around resentment drains your energy and blocks success. Also, if there are issues from your childhood you haven't yet resolved, they will eventually interfere with your life. If you haven't forgiven a parent, friend, colleague, or anyone else in the past, you'll draw similar people and energies into your life that will "serve" you by recreating unpleasant situations to once again try to resolve the issue. Forgive and release everyone who has ever hurt you, including yourself. Do it for yourself.
- **Discover and let go of the cause of the conflict.** Subconscious fears and misperceptions keep you from being the best you can be. Your subconscious beliefs and fears, which may differ drastically from your conscious beliefs, keep you from attaining your goals. Even if you consciously want to be involved in a happy relationship, make more money, or be successful in your career, you'll fall short of your goal if your subconscious beliefs are not in harmony with what you consciously want.
- **Take total responsibility for your life and yourself.** You and only you are responsible for what you've experienced, are experiencing, and will experience. *There are no victims.* Instead of wasting energy getting angry and blaming someone, consider why you, on some level, have chosen a particular experience. There will always be a hidden lesson. Let go of blame, accept total responsibility, and set yourself free.

- **We are all mirrors for each other.** Every trait (positive and negative) you see in someone else is one that is within you. Use this concept to help yourself. For example, if people who talk more than they listen easily annoy you, maybe you need to become a better listener, or perhaps you aren't listening to your inner guidance. Accept others as they are. You'll be accepting yourself in the process.

Be Good to Yourself

- **Balance the emotional you.** If you feel it would help, find a counselor or therapist with whom you feel comfortable. We all could benefit from good counseling; it's not just for those with severe phobias or other psychological problems. The type of therapy is up to you.
- **Comfort yourself.** We are all children who have learned to act like adults. The five-year-old within you finds change uncomfortable and frightening. Take some time for yourself whenever you feel fear or anxiety. Asking yourself what is wrong during meditation can sometimes shed awareness on hidden fears. Picture yourself giving the frightened child inside you a big hug and allow him or her to give you one too. Being gentle with yourself will make you stronger on all levels.
- **Fill the void within you with you.** You are already a whole person—you don't *need* another (your "other half") to make yourself complete. A healthy relationship consists of two whole people complimenting each other instead of expecting each other to fill a void. Consider what you crave in a partner. What you're looking for in a partner may be related to what you feel you lack. Trace that craving back to its roots. For example, if you feel you have to be involved with someone who has a Ph.D., why is that type of intelligence so important to you? Do you feel, on some level, that you lack intelligence? What you seek outside is within.

Set and Reach Your Goals

- **Decide what you want.** This is the first step to creating a better reality: knowing what direction you want to go in life. Instead of allowing life to happen to you, choose what you want and direct your energy toward your goals. If you remain in touch with yourself through tools such as meditation, your goals will be compatible with your highest path or life purpose.

- **Take the appropriate action.** You'll know when and how to act when you ask for and accept assistance through meditation every step of the way.
- **Affirm that your actions are for the highest good of all involved.** Respect yourself and others while achieving your goals. For every action, there is a reaction. Create only good karma.
- **Concentrate on what instead of how.** The universe can have a funny way of assisting us, and often gives us more help than we realize. Concentrating on *what* you want takes your mind off *how*, leaving you open for guidance which may include better routes to your destination that may have never occurred to you.
- **Reprogram your subconscious and conscious mind.** The most effective way to dissolve blocks is to discover and release them (through forgiveness) with guided meditation/hypnosis or solo meditation.

Use Tools to Help Reach Your Goals

- **Keep asking for guidance.** Ask and you shall receive; God, a guide or angel of the Light, or your Higher Self (or whatever else you want to call the helpful energy that is available to us) is happy to help when you ask. You may be surprised where your answers come from: a newspaper headline that catches your eye, an overheard word or sentence from a stranger, a book given to you by a friend. Pay attention and realize there are symbols and messages for you everywhere, every day.
- **Be in the now, eliminate distractions, and get unstuck.** Meditation keeps you centered and in the moment instead of dwelling on the past or worrying about the future. Meditation calms your mind, which enables you to think, see, and hear clearly so that you always sense the best path to take. When you know that path, your life flows harmoniously and you'll receive assistance whenever you need it.
- **Be grateful in advance and use affirmations**. Words and thoughts are things. After discovering and dissolving blocks,

using positive suggestions that work in harmony with your goals and dreams will help you manifest them. Reprogram yourself for success by repeating phrases out loud or to yourself that work in harmony with your goals: "I am attracting perfect love" or "I improve every day in every way" or "I am doing what I need to do to be the best that I can be." Whenever you find yourself thinking or saying something that isn't in harmony with your goals, say out loud or to yourself "Cancel, cancel, cancel" and then replace it with a thought or phrase that is in harmony with your goals.

Being grateful in advance for what you want sends a message to the universe and your subconscious mind that it already exists. Doing this is also reassuring and helps to erase any fears that you won't attain your goal. Create a phrase and repeat it to yourself or out loud as often as you think of it. It's important to feel the emotion (relief, joy, confidence, happiness, and so on) as if you have already reached your goal. For example, "I am so grateful that/for____________." (Complete the sentence with the following or make up your own.)

- I have a strong desire to be the best I can be in order to create a solid foundation for the right relationship.
- I am doing exactly what I need to do to be the best I can be.
- I have the discipline to do what I need to do to be the best I can be.
- I am creating an existence for myself of pure love.
- Compatible partners are everywhere for me.
- The perfect relationship is easily falling into place for me at the right time.
- I am forgiving and releasing the past.
- I am gentle with myself.
- I am trusting and believing in myself and the clear guidance I am receiving.
- I am accepting all the assistance I am asking for and receiving.
- Everything I need and want to know is revealed to me.
- Everything I need and want comes to me in divine right order.
- Everyday in every way I am respecting my body and mind .

Or you can try a more simplified version of affirmations. State your goal out loud or to yourself and feel the emotions associated with it. For example, as you say "happy, harmonious love relationship," visualize two people together in love and feel what that reality would be like. Do this as often as you think of it. Your subconscious mind will interpret your thoughts as reality and will then assist you in bridging the gap to your goal. Try the same with "wealth," "harmonious family relations," "perfect health," "sleeping peacefully and deeply," "incredible sex," or whatever else you want.

- **Visualize your goal as if it is already reached.** Play the visualization game by yourself or with a friend: Let your imagination fantasize about the reality you want to live. Get really creative and go way past your goal to a vision of a reality you would love to live. *Don't worry about being unrealistic; your mind doesn't know the difference and you'll plant seeds that will grow faster and sooner than you may think.* Talk with your friend or write as if you're living the dream. Become the lead character in your mini-movie and experience the emotion of living your dreams. Have fun with it! You'll be surprised about how effective it can be.
- **Act as if.** Acting as if you have accomplished your goal or are living your dream or have become the person you're creating propels you into your future reality. Your subconscious mind will accept it as a fact and your life will unfold accordingly.
- **Be excited about your goal!** Enthusiasm breaks through fears and doubt and fuels the process of creation.
- **Observe others who have already attained similar goals.** Use the approaches, attitudes, perceptions, and qualities that have worked for others.
- **Say what you mean and mean what you say.** Suppressing who you really are and what you really feel wastes energy and takes away from your goals and dreams. Communicate openly and honestly. Learn to listen well and to express what you really feel.
- **Accept others as they are.** Like you, they are doing the best they can.
- **Trust yourself and the universe.** When you stand up, do you worry that your feet won't support you? Having faith in your-

self and the universe will help bridge the gap to your goal. Being preoccupied with or attempting to force the desired results scatters your energies and sends a desperate message to your mind and the universe that you don't really believe you'll attain your goal, which will interfere. After taking the appropriate action at the appropriate times, let your desire go, relax and be patient for the next clue, and whenever you happen to think of your goal be grateful for what will be.

Become Aware of External Factors That May Affect You and Your Love Life

- **Be aware of spirit possession and attachment.** Well-meaning and not-so-well-meaning entities can interfere with the way you feel, think, and act (see "Spiritual Health" in chapter 19).
- **Watch your diet.** Avoid foods and substances that negatively influence your mood. Give your body what it really needs to feel better, look better, and have the energy to reach your goals (see chapter 19).
- **Realize how the energy of your location is affecting you as** symbolized by astrology of location. Astrology of location considers how a location would affect you (if it is different than your birth place) by relocating your natal chart (see chapter 17).
- **Pay attention to your cycles.** Just as the seasons of the earth have cycles, so does each area of our lives. Go with the flow instead of trying to swim upstream by learning about and paying attention to your love and life cycles. These cycles can be discovered with accurate astrology and numerology charting (see chapter 17).

Stay Aware of the Building Blocks That Influence All Personal and Professional Relationships

- **Character.** Our character and personality are the result of all of the experiences from both our current life and our past lives. They can be clarified through such techniques as advanced numerology, astrology, and handwriting analysis. Once someone becomes aware of characteristics or attitudes that are working against his or her goals, they can then take steps to overcome them.

- **Predestined events and karma.** Predestined events and karma—and the best time to take action to reach goals—can be identified and outlined through such techniques as advanced numerology and astrology.
- **Level of self-actualization.** Self-awareness, acceptance, and forgiveness are imperative to healthy relationships.
- **Free will.** We are ultimately free to choose our actions.

Life and Relationship Formula

How much of our life is determined by free will and how much is predestined? Do we "map out" most of our lives before incarnating, or does our free will determine how our lives unfold? Are our choices on Earth predestined too? As we become self-actualized, do we have more free will or are we just more aligned with our destiny? Do some people have more free will than others? These questions may be impossible to answer, but approximate percentages of how much free will versus how much destiny influences our lives are listed below, based on my personal research. As noted, free will consists mainly of things we can change or accept and destiny consists of situations and events that seem to happen whether we consciously choose them or not.

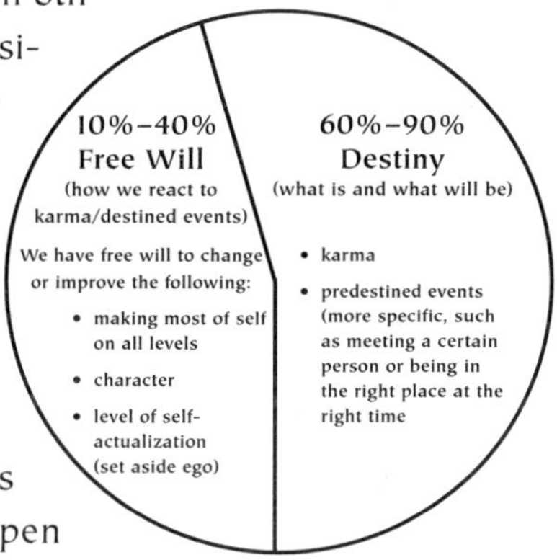

Look at Sex and Sexuality Honestly

Sex. In America an obsession. In other parts of the world a fact.
— Marlene Dietrich (1904–1992)

Sex is an important part of our lives and our relationships. Unfortunately, when blocks develop from sexual confusion or fears, it becomes a problem instead of a gift.

Most of us have been influenced by parents, peers, media, or religion to believe that sex is improper, something to keep secret, to be ashamed of, and so on. What beliefs about sex did you grow up with during your childhood and teen years? If they were negative, those beliefs may still be with you. Even if you feel you're sexually uninhibited, subconsciously you may view sex as society did in the 1800s or even earlier. We really haven't progressed very far with our views and understanding of sex and sexuality, especially those of us in the United States. As a society, we're more sexually liberal than we were in the distant past, but sex still has plenty of negative images attached to it.

- **Examine how you really feel about sex and sexuality.** Are you as comfortable with your sexuality as you think you are? Be honest with yourself. What is your first reaction when you see a provocatively dressed person? "Slut"? "Tramp"? "Whore"? or "Good for them! They feel good about their body." A good example of how uncomfortable our society is about sex and sexuality was the reaction to Madonna's book *Sex*, where she explored her sexual fantasies. By the way she was practically burned at the stake for being honest and upfront about sex and her sexuality, you would have thought she'd committed mass murder.

Our programming about sex often encourages sexual hang-ups, but know that what others say is bad or wrong about sex and sexuality may spring from their own personal inhibitions. Sex is actually a beautiful extension of who we are, and can be used as a tool to understand ourselves and a partner, to connect with a partner, to get in touch with a higher power, and to influence or create our reality. Make it okay with yourself to develop, explore, and experience your sexual self. It's your birthright and no one else's business.

- **Evaluate your situation and resolve any blocks.** You may subconsciously be blocking a more enjoyable and fulfilling sex life. If you feel you aren't enjoying your sex life as much as you could, or if sex or your sexuality cause you stress, you have the option of discovering and dissolving the cause of the problem and setting yourself free.
- **Always practice safer sex.** Besides the obvious hazards, two little-known risks of sexual contact are biological parasites and entity possession or attachment (see chapter 19).

Observe Your Appearance

It may not be the most important part of you, but let's be realistic: we all judge each other by appearance first. This doesn't mean you need to conform to what magazine and TV ads dictate about what is acceptable and what isn't. Simply be yourself and be the best you can be. Would you want to date yourself? Change the characteristics about yourself that you don't like, and accept what you can't change. Learn to appreciate and love yourself. Are you taking care of yourself? Eat only the foods that work in harmony with your body. Make time for exercise. Make the best of your appearance in all the ways available to you.

Journal Your Journey

Tracking your transformation by keeping a journal can be a great tool. You can use a spiral notebook, a computer, or a combination of the two. Pen and paper have the advantage of being portable so you can write anywhere, anytime. Before each entry, write down the day and time. You may also want to begin by writing about how you feel at that moment and why. You can record your thoughts, dreams, goals, traumas, dramas, high points, low points, fantasies, fears, wants, hopes, wishes, anger, resentment, excitement—anything! If you're concerned about your health, record what you consumed during the last 24 to 48 hours and consider how it may be effecting how you feel. Your journal will serve as a silent partner that listens without judgment to all that you express. You'll discover feelings, qualities, and reasons to respect and love yourself that had never even occurred to you. Writing will help you uncover and let go of the past and help you remain in the present. It will help you discover exactly what you want in life. One of the best parts of journaling is reading old entries and realizing how much you have grown.

Love Life Essentials for Couples

- **Identify what isn't working.** See "Relationship Roadblocks," "Love Life Essentials," and "The Wish List" for ideas. Make a list of what you think you and your partner may be doing to weaken the relationship.
- **Consider what you could do to improve, change, eliminate, or accept aspects of yourself** that may be interfering with your love life—without resorting to justifications or excuses. Meditate on how you could improve yourself and your life.
- **Write a list all of your partner's positive qualities on each level:** physical, mental, emotional, and spiritual.

- **Ask your partner to make similar lists** about what he or she feels isn't working about the relationship, and about what he or she likes about you.
- **Make a date to discuss each of your lists** with compassion and understanding and without arguing or expectations. Discuss ways you can work together to improve your relationship.
- **If you're unhappily involved with someone,** you can choose to improve the situation by finding and understanding the cause of the conflicts. Even if your partner isn't interested in improving the relationship, your effort will make the relationship more harmonious for you, which will then affect how your partner reacts to you. You'll also become more clear about whether or not to stay with this person.

Love Life Essentials for Singles

- **Make a list all of your positive qualities on each level:** physical, mental, emotional, and spiritual. How could you make these qualities even more positive?
- **Identify what isn't working.** See "Relationship Roadblocks," "Love Life Essentials," and "The Wish List" for ideas and make a list.
- **Consider how you could you improve, change, eliminate, or accept** what may be interfering with your love life—without resorting to justifications or excuses. Meditate on how you could improve yourself and your life.

The Wish List

Clarifying What Works For You in a Partner

Think about the qualities you like in a partner. Let your mind and heart wander. Which ones are you most attracted to? What makes them so attractive? Which ones are you least attracted to? What makes them so unattractive? Be aware that the negative traits you perceive in others are in some way reflections of you. *This is what relationships are all about: we are all teachers and mirrors for each other.* It would be difficult to perceive something in someone else unless you had possessed that same trait in the recent or distant past or are currently suppressing or expressing the same. Therefore, it's essential to accept others as they are. In doing so, you accept yourself.

You can't expect anyone to be perfect. *Those who expect too much from others are most likely to remain single or unhappy in love.*

Make a detailed list about what is important to you in a partner from the qualities below.

1. Decide what is essential and what you would be flexible with.
2. Don't worry about being too specific, as long as you realize you can't expect a partner to possess *every* item on your wish list (although it is possible) and you meet many of your requirements (be realistic).
3. Consider whether your own qualities and those that are important to you in another person would create a compatible union.
4. Be honest with yourself. You won't attract compatible partner possibilities if you adjust your list to meet the approval and expectations of others and ignore what's important for you.
5. Disregard the qualities that aren't important to you. Add any other qualities not listed that are important to you.

Physical

Age range
Race
Ethnicity
Height and weight range
Build
Attractiveness
Long or short hair
Cleanliness
Style of dress
Other:

Emotional Nature and Personality

More intuitive or more intellectual (right- or left-brain oriented)
Outgoing/warm/friendly or reserved/quiet
Positive attitude
Fun and playful or more serious
Self-confident
Likes alone time, prefers to be with others, or a mix
Accepting or judging of others

Closed- or open-minded to new ideas
Willing to confront issues and problems
Has done work to heal emotional and spiritual self
Aware of self
Emotionally stable
Other:

Spiritual Orientation
Traditionally religious or spiritual (metaphysical/"new age")
Frequency and type of worship if traditional
Beliefs and practices if spiritual
Looks inward or outward for spiritual assistance/guidance
Believes they are here for a reason and has goals to accomplish
Meditation or similar practice (yoga, tai chi, and so on)
Other:

Sex
Frequency and type of sex
Sensual and romantic or more reserved
Affectionate or less demonstrative
Birth control use and preferences
Heterosexual/bisexual/homosexual
Monogamous or interested in non-monogamous alternatives
Discusses or suppresses attractions to others
Other:

Communication Style
Verbal or nonverbal
Intellectual or emotional
Direct or indirect
Passive, assertive, or balanced
Other:

Career Characteristics
Type: entrepreneur, white collar, blue collar, arts, and so on
Importance of career to him or her
Travel for work: frequency and length of time away
Education/degrees
Income range
Other:

Health

Type and frequency of exercise

Diet

Alcohol use: non-drinker; infrequent, occasional, social or frequent drinker

Illegal drug use: none or frequency and type

Prescription drug use: frequency, type, how moods are affected

Habits or addictions: alcohol, drugs, smoking, food, sex, love, work, gambling, shopping, and so on

HIV status

Medical history: ailments, STDs

Interest in alternative medicine

High or low energy

Sleep: how much, how often; morning or evening person

Other:

Activities and Hobbies

Outside activities: type and how often

Sports: type, how often, participate or watch

Reading: subjects, how much, when

Cultural activities: type and how often

TV: kinds of programs and how often

Movie: type and how often

Parties, clubs, bars: type and how often

Dancing: type and how often

Dining out: type and how often

Cooking: type and how often

Political interests: conservative, liberal, or other

Travel: type and how often

Self-improvement workshops and seminars: type and how often

Community service/involvement

Shared interests: what kinds of things would you want to do together?

Other:

Family and Friends

Wants or doesn't want children

How many children, if any

Issues relating to children, such as custody, parenting methods, and financial support

How sociable

Friends: many, a close circle, or just a few

Relationship with family: close, neutral, distant, hostile

Other:

Finances

Financially responsible (bills, debts, savings, investing)

Spender, saver, or mix

Other:

Relationship Dynamics

Always together or alone time

Unconditional or conditional love

Accepts others or tries to change them

Possessive or non-possessive

Same friends, separate friends, or a mix

Equal partnership or one partner more in charge

What else would make you happy in a relationship?

Other:

Other

Pets: number, type, sleep in same bed with him/her, allergies, boarding

Organization and cleanliness of home

Pre-nuptial agreement or none

Arrangements for children (if applicable) should you separate/divorce

Astrological compatibility

Numerological compatibility

Other:

16
Love Life Pledge and Progress Report

Love Life Pledge

I_____________, promise to improve myself and my love life by making a sincere effort to: love myself, respect myself, be gentle with myself, make positive changes in my life, be self-confident, and meditate regularly.

When I'm involved in a relationship, I promise to love and accept my partner unconditionally, let go of any expectations for my partner to change, communicate openly and honestly, detach from anger, and respect my partner as an equal.

When single, I promise to take time to know and improve myself, learn to enjoy being single, be friendly and approachable, accept and let go of the fear of rejection, and take action to meet love possibilities when appropriate.

Signature ________________________________

Date __________________

Progress Report

Copy the following information and record your progress

Date: Time:

Days/weeks/months since last meditation or regression session/entry:

Since my last entry, I have meditated or listened to a meditation/regression recording (circle one):

every day / 6 5 4 3 2 1 time(s) per week / not at all

Since my last entry, I have improved myself (body, mind, spirit) and my love life by:

The results from my efforts have been that I now:

I can improve my efforts by:

My goals for the next ____ days/weeks/months are:

Section VII

Other Resources to Improve Your Love Life

To be happy is to be able to become
aware of oneself without fright.

— Walter Benjamin (1892–1940)

17
Learn and Track Your Love Cycles

Be more aware with ancient practical knowledge

Numerology by Scott A. Petullo

The following information can provide the numerology novice with a beginning and basic understanding of the science and help you gain awareness about life, relationships, and the lives and relationships of others. This awareness will help you more easily understand, have compassion for, and accept yourself and others. However, because of the depth and detail of advanced numerology, the information in this section can't provide a complete analysis. It is not meant to replace a thorough reading by a professional numerologist.

Have you ever felt that you were making a lot of effort to meet potential partners but getting little or no results in return? Have there been other times when relationship possibilities were plentiful without your even trying? These things happen in part because we all have cycles in our lives, just as there are seasons of the earth. By knowing when change and transition are more likely, when the high and low points of your love life may occur, you'll be better prepared to respond out of love instead of fear. You'll be able to ride the waves of opportunity instead of being submersed by them.

Following your intuition is one way to be aware of your cycles. But to achieve the optimum level of awareness, you need the discipline to meditate regularly. "Psychic" readings and other forms of divination and personality analysis can offer additional insights into your timing cycles—although such information is only as good as the psychic or analyst. Some people possess a talent that allows them to see events before they occur; they can unveil the overall course of your life and the general tendency of your fate. More specific information can be found if the analyst or psychic is familiar with your behavior patterns, such as through handwriting analysis. These patterns may indicate how you'll react to circumstances in your life. This choice of action is called free will. Even when you are in a good relationship cycle, if you ignore any love life blocks they will interfere. This is why dissolving relationship blocks and following your love cycles can help you live your best love life possible.

Numerology and astrology are two metaphysical sciences that can accurately outline your personal love and life cycles and the cycles of your relationships. They have been used for guidance since ancient times by scientists, mathematicians, astronomers, philosophers, and even by the founders of the United States of America. Unfortunately, these sciences have been criticized and discredited during more recent times by those who fear the truth or who don't understand how truly valuable this information can be. Horoscope "sound bites" in newspapers and magazines have contributed to a belief that this information is too general and vague to be used for anything more than fun, but even information from supposedly credible sources can be misleading, incomplete or inaccurate if the author has failed to thoroughly study the subject and relay enough information to the reader.

In truth, these ancient sciences are accurate when used correctly and can be incredibly useful tools in our daily lives.

Numeric Analysis

Understanding Human Character and Identifying Cycles of Time

When I tell people I'm a numerologist, those familiar with numerology may say "Oh, I'm a five" (or some other number). The number they usually refer to is their Life Path number, the most important aspect of the several hundred in an advanced numerology chart. What they usually don't know is that this number only gives a glimpse of the overall personality and timing energy. It's similar to trying to describe a person's looks from a picture of the eyes alone. A study of one aspect gives a few insights; a thorough analysis of the whole numerology chart provides much more.

How can numbers describe personality or even future events? The "why" and "how" of numerology is a mystery. A numerologist can't explain why certain types of events transpire time and time again under identical numerological aspects. A numerologist also can't explain how matching patterns of numerological personality aspects (in different charts) repeatedly and accurately reflect human motivations, abilities, or challenges—they just do. The only reasonable explanation as to why numerologists can make predictions and discern personality through numbers relates to the idea that there exists a divine order in the universe and that we are all intimately connected to it.

Numerology is by definition a science, since results are consistently drawn from the same sets of circumstances. Science is based on observation, not theory. Science also has nothing to do with common sense. Much of today's cutting-edge scientific thought appears unusual to the average person. For example, physicists suspect that the universe is somewhat oval in shape, so it's faster to travel in space on a curved line. Psychologists believe that we attract those who have qualities we need for balance or who exhibit our own repressed undesirable personality traits. Their theory is that we are all mirrors for each other to help us resolve our personal issues. How do we "prove" the validity of these types of observations? It's difficult to do, but it's easy to see the truth in them through objective analysis.

Numerology allows you to know more about the meaning of your life, to understand the various levels of your personality, and to identify the why, how, what and when of your relationships. It also allows you to have one of the keys to relationship success: timing. Quantum physicists have long hypothesized that there exists a harmony between all things and that there is order rather than chaos in the universe. We witness the order every single day in how we can predict when the tides will rise and fall, how many months a woman will carry a child in pregnancy, how an apple tree will bear apples and not oranges, and when changes of season are expected to happen. You don't have to be a quantum physicist, though, to identify the strengths and weaknesses of your character or to know about the best times for beginnings and endings. All you have to understand is how numbers symbolize our existence.

Definition of Numerology

Numerology is the philosophical and scientific study of numbers and their connection to human personality and time cycles. It is based on the idea that numbers reflect a divine order in the universe and that everything that is named or numbered is cyclical in nature. Numerology uses the energy of the qualities and characteristics of each of the numbers one through 10: all numbers are made up of these 10 numbers. All dates and times are numbered. Names and places are also numbered through *gematria,* the science of relating words to numbers (each letter of every alphabet is numbered) where words with the same number totals have equal or similar meanings. One of the more well-known and ancient forms of gematria is the Hebraic number system called Qabala (QBLH). Other ancient forms of the science of numbers include Chaldean, Pythagorean (not to be confused with modern or Western numerology), Phonetic and Hindu numerology. Modern numerology is a direct descendent of these sacred codes. The Chinese "Circle of The Heavens," the Indian "Vedas," ancient Egyptian texts and records from Sumeria—this planet's first recorded civilization—all feature coded number systems. The term numerology was created in the early 1900s in response to growing interest in this ancient science.

Advanced Numerology

Numeric analysis—better known as advanced modern numerology—is a body of work that includes most published and many unpublished deeper aspects of modern numerology. These aspects are validated by numeric analysts over years of applying this scientific approach to many subjects. Numerology is a science based on empirical rules; observation is the key to understanding.

The majority of published numerology books in the Western world only scratch the surface of the topic, leaving readers with a nice introduction but failing to provide any thorough depth of understanding. Part of the reason is that advanced numerology isn't considered a best-selling topic—most readers demand lighter subject matter. Perhaps such simplifying contributes to numerology being falsely considered as merely entertainment.

Another reason for the lack of thorough information about numerology is that it takes a certain type of aptitude and desire, perhaps even obsession, to dig deeper into the hundreds of numeric timing and personality aspects in an advanced chart. It then takes months and years to discern which are essential and how to effectively use them. Because of the limited amount of published advanced numerology information, very few people have explored the deeper side of the science, or at least have wanted to make public their findings. Many analysts who have studied numerology in-depth realize that there is a responsibility that goes with the extraordinary knowledge gained.

Regardless of how numerology is presented, any sort of insight can be helpful to the beginning student or lay client. However, it needs to be understood that the shorter the reading, the more incomplete is the information, and therefore the more likely the possibility of someone being mislead or misinformed. A short reading may include two or three different timing or personality aspects, while an extensive analysis can include hundreds of aspects and require hours of interpretation. Additionally, the accuracy of any numerology reading depends on the depth of understanding of the analyst.

Numerology and Reincarnation

The more we know ourselves and the more we understand timing opportunities and challenges in relation to character, the more likely success and goal attainment becomes. Most numerologists believe in reincarnation; they recognize the cyclical nature of life and time and understand how numbers represent universal truths. Numerology, like other metaphysical sciences, indicates that we reincarnate over and over again until we learn and experience all that we need to for our highest growth. According to this philosophy, most of us will be coming back again and again to get it right—if we're here on Earth, it means we still have some lessons to learn.

The key to understanding reincarnation is that a person must take full responsibility for everything that happens in his or her life, and that means eliminating the concept of blame.

We can embrace the circumstances of our lives with compassion and gratitude, or reject them with misery. Karma is our teacher, not our punisher. Reincarnation research indicates that many circumstances in life are predestined, such as who our parents and family members will be, the type of environment in which we begin life, the kinds of personality traits that will likely emerge or be repressed, and the kinds of people we will attract to learn our lessons. Numerology informs us about these and other conditions. It symbolizes the orderly rhythm of the mathematical exactness that permeates all creation. It's unnecessary to believe in reincarnation to benefit from numerology, but the concept does help to explain the why and how of this science. The following information includes some of the more important personality and timing aspects that numerologists use today.

Zero, Qualities, and Fadic Addition

Zero isn't a number; it is a cipher. It is nothing, but it is all. When attached to a number such as 1, the 1 and 0 become 10; the 0 magnifies the 1, making it a more powerful energy than the 1 alone. 10 is more intense than 1 and 100 is more powerful than 10. Consider the 0 an intensifier that amplifies the number next to it. Additionally, numbers represent qualities, as the statement "she is a ten" shows. Figures, far different than numbers, display quantities, as in "party of five." It's easy to see the contrast between these two distinctly different concepts. Numerology addresses the former, giving full meaning to the qualities behind all numbers.

In order to simplify this introduction to numerology, only the numbers one through nine are covered here. For the sake of simplicity, double and multiple digit numbers will not be discussed nor will master numbers (11, 22, 33) or karmic numbers (13, 14, 16, 19). In modern numerology, all numbers other than master numbers and karmic numbers are ultimately reduced to a single digit through fadic addition. This is known as Jaffar, the system of numbers reduction (for example, reducing 17 to 8 by adding the 1 and the 7) that was shared by the Chaldeans, Egyptians, Arabians, Hebrews and by

Moses. Pythagoras then gave this technique of "final digitting" to the Greeks, and it's used today in modern numerology. The single reduced number of any double or multiple digit number is more important than the other numbers, but it's the sequence and the order of the original numbers (from left to right in importance) that makes the full number unique and provides for advanced understanding.

The Life Path

The extent of a rewarding or difficult life in relation to the Life Path is found through a study of the remaining personality and timing aspects. All parts of the numeric blueprint harmonize together to create one's full identity and fate.

Before we move on to the meanings of numbers, I'll help you calculate some of your own numbers to refer to. The most important aspect of a numerology chart is the Life Path. This number is found by adding the numbers of the full birth date together as shown in the following example. Reduce each number to a single digit before adding:

December 5, 1955

12 (December is the twelfth month) + 5 + 1955 =

(1 + 2 = 3) + 5 + (1 + 9 + 5 + 5 = 20) =

3 + 5 + (2 + 0 = 2) =

3 + 5 + 2 =

10 =

1 + 0 =

1

This person has a one Life Path. Volumes of information exist regarding the number found in the Life Path position in the chart.

Different forms of the number one exist. For instance, the number 37 (3 + 7 = 10, 1 + 0 = 1) is recognized as a great deal more fruitful than the number 19 (1 + 9 = 10, 1 + 0 = 1) in most positions in the chart because the number 19 is most often viewed as karmically challenging.

To get an idea of what the number one stands for in the Life Path position, read the summary below and pay particular attention to the overbalanced and underbalanced sections. Of course, the energy is modified by all of the other numbers found in the other positions in the chart, as noted above, and so it's important to get a sense for all the numbers. Until the person is well into maturity, they usually won't be using the most constructive (balanced) energy of the number in the Life Path position on a consistent basis.

The Life Path: What a Person Must Learn

The true definition of the Life Path is that it represents what a person must learn. Correct application of a distinct group of associated energies sets the person free and allows for faster completion of his or her earthly mission. The Life Path also represents the strongest energy in the personality chart, so the focus is on this aspect to identify the person's most significant strengths and weaknesses.

The Main Challenge

Another important position in the numerology chart is called the Main Challenge. Using the same date of birth, it is found in the following way:

December 5, 1955

(1 + 2 = 3) – 5 – (1 + 9 + 5 + 5 = 20, 2 + 0 = 2)

(reduce all multiple digit numbers first, then subtract the smaller number from the larger and place below each pair)

3 – 5 – 2

2 – 3

1

1

The Main Challenge in this example is also a one (the second one is the Fourth Minor Challenge as noted below). Having so much one-type energy in these two powerful positions in the chart, the person will alternate between the underbalanced and overbalanced traits of the number one, but will remain in bondage to one or the other extreme most of the time. For example, if this person has low one-type energy in the rest of the chart throughout the other several hundred aspects (derived from the date of birth and the full legal birth name), he or she will act out the underbalanced energy until the lesson is learned and personal power is gained. In this case, he or she would act dependent, passive, vulnerable and powerless the majority of the time. In contrast, if the rest of the chart had an overabundance of one-type energy, he or she would be so self-serving and aggressive that they would likely do themselves in. This is considering that the other aspects don't soften or modify the hard-core one energy.

The number nine can't be found in the Main Challenge position but the cipher (0) may be found in that position. Generally, zero in the Main Challenge position means that the person has a heavier burden to deal with, but also more potential for reward. Some people incarnate with less karma than others; in these charts the zero can represent lighter challenges.

The Main Challenge: The Secret to Success

The Main Challenge has almost as much intensity as the Life Path in terms of identifying weakness; it is here where the secret to success is found. Once the negative expression of the Main Challenge is overcome, this number represents what the person is capable of in the most constructive manner. At this point, they become a teacher in regards to the energy they have mastered.

The Lessons of The Life Path and Main Challenge

The Life Path number and the Main Challenge number will immediately point to where a person has work to do. Other major indicators exist in the chart, but these two are the most significant. Furthermore, all of the remaining aspects in the chart will either intensify the main energy or reduce it. A numeric analyst must discern how all of the aspects reflect the full personality—and how they relate to timing—through a person's challenges, weaknesses, abilities, strengths, preferences, motivations, and tendencies. Once balanced, the energy symbolized by the Life Path and Main Challenge numbers is one of the most important keys to achievement. Overcoming the difficulties represented by the energy in these positions brings the person that much closer to self-mastery. The following is a concise synopsis of the heart of the lessons to be learned under the Life Path and the Main Challenge numbers for one through nine:

One: Must find, understand, and harness the intense inner power and drive within.
Two: Must create and maintain inner balance.
Three: Must understand their feelings and emotions.
Four: Must use a step-by-step process to create a solid inner foundation (eliminate inner confusion).
Five: Must apply focus and discipline in one or two specific areas to gain true freedom.
Six: Must accept the absolute perfection of their existence.
Seven: Must have faith and trust in self, then in others.
Eight: Must feel the power and sufficiency inside self.
Nine: Must follow the inner voice and discover divine laws inside self.

The Personal Years, Personal Months and Personal Days

Use these calculations and the definitions of each number below to learn more about your love relationship cycles.

More accurate timing interpretation through numerology begins with the long-term cycles such as the Life Path Periods and Pinnacles (see below). However, some of the medium and shorter-term cycles shown below will give you insight about your own relationship cycles.

- The **Personal Year** is figured by adding the month and day of birth to the Universal Year. The Universal Year is the current year. Let's say that the current year is 2013. Using the 12.5.1955 birthday, add the 3 (1 + 2 = 3), 5, and 6 (2 + 0 + 1 + 3 = 6) gives you 14 which is reduced to 5. In 2013, this person is in a five Personal Year. At birth, everyone is in the Personal Year that matches his or her Life Path number. Personal Years move in nine year cycles; a one Personal Year always follows a nine Personal Year. The Personal Year spans from January 1 through December 31 for everyone, and is one of the more popular and important medium length cycles.
- **Personal Months** occurring within the Personal Year are figured by adding the Personal Year to the current month. In October (the tenth month) of 2013, the person with the 12.5.1955 birthday is in a six Personal Month (five Personal Year + 1 (1 + 0 = 1) = 6).

- The **Personal Day** is a useful short-term aspect that is just as easy to calculate. As the following example shows, add the Personal Year, current month, and current day for the same date of birth used above (five Personal Year + 1 (October 1 + 0 = 1) + 7 = 13, 1 + 3 = 4). This person will be in a four Personal Day, a six Personal Month and a five Personal Year on October 7, 2013.

The Numbers One Through Nine Defined: Love and Time Cycles

First of all, there is no such thing as a bad number. All numbers have positive energy behind them. The problem is when there is too much (overbalanced) or too little (underbalanced) of a particular energy. Ultimately, in a spiritual sense, nothing symbolized by numerics is viewed as unpleasant; all situations allow for growth and development. Then again, many occurrences are justifiably interpreted as negative due to the earthly truth that pain—physical, mental and emotional—is unpleasant.

Every number has three main sides: balanced, underbalanced and overbalanced . Each number also has a distinctive set of vibrations linked to it, as described in the following definitions.

In addition to information about the various forms of each number one through nine, insight about how each number relates to time cycles in regards to love and relationships is provided below. The numbers relate to love through the timing aspects such as Life Path Periods, Personal Years, and Pinnacles (described later in this text). Love in connection to personality aspects (for example: Main Challenge, Life Path, and Day of Birth) will not be covered here.

Please note that, for absolute accuracy, all numbers in a timing or personality chart must be interpreted in association with each other, and that some positions in the chart carry more importance than others. For example, if you have a five Life Path, reading the definition for number five below will provide you with a good idea of some of your more important lessons in this lifetime. However, by itself the Life Path number is only a piece of the entire picture and will not give you a complete summary of your personality. Taking into consideration your Life Path, Main Challenge, other personality aspects and timing aspects such as your current Personal Year and

Month will give you a better idea of the general trends and probabilities at this point in time. Even though a seasoned analyst must carefully weigh and scrutinize hundreds of numeric aspects to yield an accurate personality profile and overall direction of present and future time cycles, you will be able to gain at least some important insight by applying the calculations and definitions provided in this chapter. The balanced, overbalanced and underbalanced descriptions of each number relate mainly to the personality aspects (such as a Life Path), but they can also be connected to time cycles.

The Number One

One is connected with new beginnings, independence, new opportunity, inspiration, freedom, originality, success, birth, self-employment, and standing alone. Balanced one energy: initiative, energetic, authoritative, inventive, persistent, creative, confident, ambitious, self-reliant, dynamic, bold, forward looking, assertive. Overbalanced one energy: selfish, vain, impatient, elitist, intolerant, addicted, aggressive, egocentric, self-important, unyielding, impulsive, headstrong, defiant, coercive, self-at-all-cost attitude, arrogant, domineering, possessive, greedy. Underbalanced one energy: passive, weak, fearful, cowardly, dependent, insecure, inferior, submissive, helpless, lack of self-respect, reluctant, changeable, lethargic.

The Number One and Love

Beginning a love affair or getting married during a one time cycle (such as a one Personal Year) is advantageous, especially if you want a long-term relationship. Or course, both partners' time cycles must be considered; if you meet your new love interest while they are in a nine Personal Year, the long-term potential is diminished, at least from their perspective. Also, relationships started under a one cycle can sometimes include a partner struggling with overbalanced one energy. Time alone frequently falls under this number. It can also be a time of new beginnings for existing relationships, such as conception or the birth of a child.

The Number Two

Two is linked to partnerships, marriage, love, divorce, friendships, teamwork, details, public recognition, tolerance, modesty, sensitivity, receptivity and slow growth. Balanced two energy: tactful, sensitive, flexible, diplomatic, helpful, patient, devoted, sincere, supportive, adaptable, modest, cautious, harmonizing, receptive. Overbalanced two energy: scheming, manipulative, faultfinding, resentfully resisting, devious, condescending, unsupportive, sly, disapproving, interfering. Underbalanced two energy: spiritless, unresponsive, cowardly, mentally off-balance, self-depreciating, dependent, inactive, indecisive, unconcerned, overly sensitive, vacillating, disinterested, indifferent, uncaring.

The Number Two and Love

Two is almost always connected to love, or at least friendship. Relationships begun under a two time cycle are usually deep and lasting. This is one of the best numbers for romance. However, if one or both partners enter a two time cycle (such as a two Personal Year) after the relationship is underway, the two has a tendency to symbolize one of two extremes: either strengthening or dissolving the existing relationship.

The Number Three

Three is related to fun, laughter, making new friends, self-improvement, imagination, attracting love, travel, sexual expression, literary and artistic ability, inspiration, emotional expression, good fortune, creativity. Balanced three energy: optimistic, happy, lively, cultivated, amusing, imaginative, tasteful, popular, good taste, gracious, sociable, enthusiastic. Overbalanced three energy: lacks concentration, scatters energy, overconfident, emotionally volatile, temperamental, irresponsible, gossipy, exaggerating, ostentatious, shallow, superficial, boastful, wasteful. Underbalanced three energy: moody, petty, depressed, jealous, unsociable, self-doubting, bored, downcast, envious, fussy, inarticulate, indiscreet, gloomy, melancholy, indecisive, pessimistic, touchy, worrying, dejected, reticent.

The Number Three and Love

Three is one of the luckiest numbers in love matters. Attraction of potential love interests happens in abundance during three time cycles. Unfortunately, indecision is also strongly represented by this number. A person may have more than one option and therefore will have to make a decision. Although fortunate, the three has a tendency to be transitory; love started under a three time cycle (such as a three Personal Year or Month) may not be there next month. Again, several hundred aspects must be considered for the most accurate interpretation. For example, a relationship that begins during two or three very stable long-term timing aspects (such as a four or six Life Path Period or Pinnacle) combined with a shorter term three time cycle (such as a Personal Year) could very well represent a longer-term love connection.

The Number Four

Four is associated with managing money, security, creating foundations that last, work, business success, stable finances, routine, organization, putting ideas into form, efficiency, physical activity, health matters, structure. Balanced four energy: productive, reliable, frugal, cautious, disciplined, economical, integrity, methodical, analysis, serious, constructive, balanced, loyal, patriotic, endurance, prudent, sensible, persevering. Overbalanced four energy: dogmatic, rigid, narrow-minded, pedantic, stubborn, crude, dull, numb emotions, fixed, uncompromising, vulgar, resistant, provincial, obstinate, blunt, lost in detail, straitlaced, contradictory, argumentative. Underbalanced four energy: uncommitted, weak-willed, disorganized, lack of integrity, dishonest, impractical, lethargic, plodding, careless, inefficient, slipshod, uncertain, unfocused, lazy, negligent.

The Number Four and Love

Four is solid and long lasting. Commitment or marriage are very stable when started under the four time cycle. Physical and sexual activity is common under a four time cycle. Existing bonds entering a four time cycle stabilize, but a search for new love under a four time cycle can be limiting; opportunity is often scarce under the four.

The Number Five

Five is related to original enterprises, research, promotion, sales, sensuality, sex, freedom, travel, communication, changes, transformation, flexibility, excitement, marketing, adventure. Balanced five energy: many-sided, free-thinking, questioning, versatile, healthy limits, appropriately dissolving career or personal relationships at the right time, unconventional, charming, curious, adaptable, independent, inventive, original, forward-looking, clever, resourceful, talented, gifted, free, expansive, unprejudiced, natural. Overbalanced five energy: over-indulgent, mercurial, over-sexed, reckless, ending relationships too soon, impatient, thrill-seeking, unpredictable, erratic, inconsistent, extreme independence, insatiable, restless, dissatisfied, outlandish. Underbalanced five energy: fear of change, stagnant, dependent, hanging on to associations that have expired, inactive, conforming, hesitant, fear of risk, out of date, undecided, purposeless, fear of freedom, dull, ineffective, unresponsive.

The Number Five and Love

Attraction of possible love matches is likely during a five time cycle, as is too much of a good thing. Many opportunities will present themselves and the person under the five must use some discretion in decision-making. Like the three, the five isn't stable. However, he or she might just attract a compatible long-term possibility. Chances to enjoy sensuality are high under the five vibration. It also demands healthy limits.

The Number Six

Six is linked to home and family, relationships, marriage, divorce, romance, responsibility, artistic matters, friendships, karma, emotions, slow moving energy, harmony, teaching, healthy balanced living. Balanced six energy: domestic, charitable, advising, friendly, idealistic, tolerant, supportive, appreciative, ethical, peace-making, protective, humanitarian, accountable, faithful, loving, stable, understanding, judicious. Overbalanced six energy: distorted idealism, critical, interfering, opinionated, possessive, stubborn, sacrificing, faultfinding, smothering, over-involvement, martyr-complex, disappointment, complaining, obstinate, unforgiving, disheartened. Underbalanced six energy: uncaring, uncooperative, biased, cynical, unconcerned, disinterested, distant, indulgent, listless, tactless, inhospitable, non-committal, insensitive, inattentive, disillusioned.

The Number Six and Love

The number six is one of the strongest love time cycles. It is the cosmic mother or father energy and, under this number, commitment or marriage is favorable. Like the four, it is solid. The downside of the six in relation to love is that it has a tendency to attract karmic situations. A romance or love initiated under the six time cycle often relates to important lessons, and the lessons are often difficult. At the same time, this hinges on the personality charts of both partners, as well as on the other timing aspects. A relationship begun before a six time cycle will either get stronger or fall apart during this vibration, (at least on the emotional level), similar to what happens in the two vibration.

The Number Seven

Seven is connected to spirituality, intuition, inner growth, analysis, introspection, lowered physical vitality, increased mental activity, conserving assets, planning, attracting unsolicited help, psychic matters, specialization, research, ritual, solitary matters, health issues, travel. Balanced seven energy: metaphysical interests, different wavelength, intellectual, clairaudient, clairvoyant, analytical, perceptive, scientific, faithful, exact, meditative, mystical, occult interests, expert, bookish, poised, telepathic, visionary, deep, dreamer, instinctive, reflective, truth-seeker, studious, technical, wise. Overbalanced seven energy: fearful, nervous, fear of betrayal, non-committal, spineless, critical, paranoid, indecisive, secretive, suppressed feelings, lacking trust in self and others, insecure, hesitant, controlled, guarded, intimidating, fussy, evasive, fanatic, suspicious, self-conscious, secretive, perfectionist, distrustful, impersonal, joyless, pessimistic. Underbalanced seven energy: lack of depth, naïve, ignorant, too trusting, empty-headed, mystified, superficial, unenlightened, lack of faith, inexperienced, undeveloped, uninformed, dense, immature, uncertain.

The Number Seven and Love

Most of the time, seven relates to spiritual and mental matters. It has almost nothing to do with emotional love unless the two who begin a love bond under this time cycle (considering they are both in a seven time cycle) have an abundance of seven in their personality charts and they are living a completely spiritual lifestyle, one where unconditional love dominates. Since this is usually not the case, the person (or both partners) who begins the relationship under the seven vibration ends up with a material or emotional loss—or both. However, if the bond is already established upon entering the seven time cycle, this can be a good number to conserve the love of the relationship if faith is maintained. At the same time, over-sensitivity and a desire to spend time alone may hamper existing relationships. Those looking for love under a seven time cycle may feel as if they are engaged in an uphill struggle; prospects are usually in short supply.

The Number Eight

Eight is tied to power, money, karma, action, business success, business failure, control, material objects, status, influence, loss, gain, administration, management, ego, leadership. Balanced eight energy: prosperous, high-powered, commanding, stamina, self-confident, persuasive, financial awareness, effective, capable, ambitious, businesslike, clear-headed, disciplined, material freedom, systematic, principled, forceful, enterprising, discriminating, authoritative. Overbalanced eight energy: abuses power, cold-blooded, egotistical, overreaction to money, scheming, aggressive, materialistic, corrupt, demanding, lacking trust, militant, threatening, preoccupied with power and money, unsympathetic, bullying, contrary, fraudulent, over-ambitious, lawless, quarrelsome, one-track-mind, undignified, thoughtless, rebellious, coarse. Underbalanced eight energy: timid, passive, vulnerable, fearful, insecure, avoids power and money, poor judgment, gives personal power away, misdirected, inept, non-observant, oblivious, illogical, short-sighted.

The Number Eight and Love

Eight possesses little relationship potential, unless the person under the eight time cycle is looking for status and/or material security through a love bond; people can and do "marry well" under this number. In this way, it does represent "payback." However, the connection frequently lacks the benefits of a close emotional link. At the same time, it is a karmic number, like the six, and the individual often finds that the relationship is costly in more ways than one. This is especially so if the person who enters this bond during the eight time cycle lacks eight energy in his or her personality chart. Divorce can be expensive for those who are learning about the balanced use of the energy behind the number eight. It can also represent a lot of physical activity, like the number four.

The Number Nine

Nine is associated with reward, leadership by example, dramatic endings, emotions, emotional crisis, attracting money, the finest life has to offer, short term matters, conclusions, deep love, compassion, magnetism, travel, idealism, charity, artistic and creative matters, developing spirituality, romance, forgiveness. Balanced nine energy: impassioned, philanthropic, broadminded, affectionate, creative, forgiving, passionate, benevolent, warm, tolerant, sentimental, loving, liberal, generous, enthusiastic, trustworthy, welcoming, devoted, considerate, hospitable, humane. Overbalanced nine energy: deceiving, self-centered, hedonistic, lacking integrity, over-emotional, prejudiced, resentful, bigoted, bad example, wavering, gloomy, depressed, dejected, unbending, vindictive, hateful, forbidding. Underbalanced nine energy: ultraconservative, impersonal, puritanical, detached, blocks intuition, distant, unemotional, mournful, elusive, submissive, drifting, unstable, limited, faint-hearted, victimized, disloyal, vague.

The Number Nine and Love

Nine is the number of unconditional love. No attachments, conditions, or expectations are in order during the nine time cycle because relationships formed during one are often short-lived. Attraction of foreign love is common under this number, as is attraction of deep past-life love. Unfinished business is resolved while transiting the nine time cycle and the person learns to live and let live. Compassion and understanding are necessary under this vibration. Romance has the potential to be wonderful in existing relationships for those entering this time cycle. While it can symbolize a final conclusion for some partnerships, it can also signal the end to problematic issues in others.

Finding a Balance

Until a person reaches maturity (or even much later in life), they often fluctuate between the overbalanced and underbalanced traits as represented by the numbers in their numeric chart. Learning to balance one's personal energy along with appropriate use of willpower is something that comes with age. The Life Path and the Main Challenge are two of the more revealing aspects regarding what the person is likely to be struggling with before they get it right. The keys to anyone's success are predominantly represented by the balanced use of the energy of these personality aspects.

Relationship Compatibility

One of the most beneficial uses of numerology is determining relationship compatibility. The timing and personality aspects of people's numerology charts symbolize the duration and meaning of their bonds with others; all personal bonds have time limits. Some relationships are destined to last a lifetime and some for only a day. Two people may still remain in a relationship or friendship long after the emotional or mental connection has dissolved. Although most people would like to find their "perfect partner" for life, their karmic blueprint and level of self-awareness often dictate otherwise.

Relationship compatibility and timing is an area of study in advanced numerology. Hundreds of aspects must be considered in relation to the entire advanced chart for complete accuracy. For a complete and extensive numerology reading, it's best to consult an expert. However, you can gain valuable awareness about your relationships by using the calculations within these pages.

For Those Who Want To Know More: Advanced Interpretation

The three numbers that comprise the full date of birth are also used to derive more than 100 other personality and timing aspects. In a complete advanced numerology chart using both the full date of birth and legal birth name, more than 400 aspects must be considered for a comprehensive, thorough analysis. This includes the aspects within aspects and cycles within cycles. There are also different levels of each number to read, from the multiple digit number down to the reduced single digit. Each number has similar energies associated with it, but each position in the chart has a different influence. The various aspects in the numerology chart can be grouped into sections such as dominant character traits and timing cycles, modifying agents, "directors" of the overall flow of energy, and outer appearances that, for example, sometimes reflect a facade that is at variance with the true personality. In short, it is best to consult with an expert to get the complete energy at play in the character and timing blueprints for maximum insight.

The Birthday Number

The Birthday Number (the day of birth) is an important aspect of the chart. Although it isn't part of the nucleus, it's one of the top 20 aspects in the numerology personality chart. In personality, it represents a talent a person possesses, a skill they are comfortable with, and, to a degree, how they are seen. In timing, it's a much more important aspect to consider.

There are three Life Path Periods in every person's life; each one spans 24 to 28 years. The Birthday Number is the most important of the three in relation to personal development. The month of birth (first Life Path Period) occurs first, the Birthday number occurs next, and the Year of Birth (third and final Life Path Period) is last. It's the number that represents the "main act" of a person's life. Using the example above (12.5.1955), the subject will have a five Life Path Period representing travel, communication, instability, changes and sensuality during the middle part of the life.

The Life Path Periods

The Life Path is used to map the three Life Path Periods. These periods represent the phases of the Life Path that unfold and form the backdrop of the stage of life. The first of these important long term timing periods (the number of the month of birth) begins at birth and ends when the second Life Path Period begins, somewhere between age 24 and age 33. The second Life Path Period (the day of birth) begins in the one Personal Year that is nearest to the age of 28 years, four months. The third Life Path Period (the number of the birth year) begins in the one Personal Year closest to the age of 56 years, eight months. If the second Life Path Period begins before the age of 28, it will not fully be felt until after the person reaches age 28. To approximate the timing of the three Life Path Periods, just figure that the first will run until about age 28, the second will run until about age 56 and the third covers the rest of the life.

As mentioned above, the second Life Path Period (day of birth) is usually the most important; it represents "prime time," when the person operates in the "main act" of life. Major life changes regularly occur as a person moves from the first or second Life Path Period to the next, especially if the Life Path Period change transpires at the same time as other long-term cycles, such as the Pinnacle (see below). This sudden transition takes place in the life of the person who has a one, two, or three Life Path, as the third Life Path Period and fourth Pinnacle start at the same time (ages 54, 53, and 61 respectively). A sometimes dramatic life shift also happens as the second Life Path Period and the second Pinnacle begin at the same time for those who have the five (age 32), six (age 31), seven (age 30), eight (age 29) or nine (age 28) Life Path. The person with the four Life Path will never see a Life Path Period and Pinnacle cycle change at the same time, but the second Life Path Period spans from age 24 to age 59; it touches all four Pinnacles and the energy behind it is likely to be especially important relative to the person's advancement. Additionally, any timing cycle is always viewed in relation to the personality chart. The higher number of significant personality aspects that match a Life Path Period, or any other cycle for that matter, the more important the Life Path Period becomes. In light of this, though the middle Life Path Period is considered most important for personal growth, one or both of the remaining two (and/or any of the Pinnacles—see below) may have more significance in terms of hardship or compensation.

The Pinnacles

The Pinnacles are another important long-term cycle. Everyone has four Pinnacles that span the duration of life. The first Pinnacle runs from birth to between the ages of 27 and 35. An easy way to figure these cycles is to subtract the Life Path number from 36. The end result is the age of the person during the final year of the first Pinnacle. In the case of the date 12.5.1955 (one Life Path), the result is 35. This means that the person will be 35 during the last year of the first Pinnacle. The last year of every Pinnacle is always a nine Personal Year and the second and third Pinnacles each last nine years. The final Pinnacle lasts from the end of the third Pinnacle to the end of the person's life. Seen below are the Pinnacles for the birthday December 5, 1955.

12. 5. 1955

8 (12 + 5)

7 (5 + 1955)

6 (8 + 7)

5 (12 + 1955)

The first Pinnacle is eight (month of birth added to day of birth), the second Pinnacle is seven (day of birth added to year of birth), the third Pinnacle is six (first and second Pinnacles added together), and the final Pinnacle is five (month of birth added to year of birth). It is simple to figure these long-term cycles, just remember to reduce every multiple digit number before adding. Again, the importance of each cycle is based on the energy of the aspects of the personality chart. Running side by side in timing with the Pinnacles are the Challenges.

The Minor and Main Challenges

The Challenges consist of the Minor Challenges and the Main Challenge. These are already figured using the birthday 12.5.1955 above where the Main Challenge was calculated. The timing of the Challenges is simple; just match the four Challenges with the four Pinnacles, keeping in mind that the Main Challenge is felt during the entire life and the first Challenge is often more important than the second and final. The first Minor challenge, as seen below, is two, (month of birth – day of birth) the second is three, (day of birth – year of birth) the Main and third is one (first Minor Challenge – second Minor Challenge) and the fourth (month of birth – year of birth) is also one. Each Challenge points to what the person must effectively manage during the respective Pinnacle to achieve success.

December 5, 1955

(1 + 2 = 3) – 5 – (1 + 9 + 5 + 5 = 20, 2 + 0 = 2)

(reduce all multiple digit numbers first, then subtract the smaller number from the larger and place below each pair)

3 – 5 – 2

2 – 3

1

1

Timing Cycle Importance

The best way to read the timing in a numerology chart is to start with the long-term cycles to establish a base of energy, add the medium length cycles like the Personal Year, and then follow up with the short-term cycles such as the Personal Months and Days. The long-term cycles form the backdrop of the current life phase, therefore the shorter cycles must be read in relation to them. A three Personal Month in a two Personal Year, for example, is much more likely to include heavy emotions, indecision and troubled relationships instead of enjoyment and harmonious love relationships if they happen in more spiritual longer-term cycles like the nine Life Path Period and seven Pinnacle. Seven and nine are spiritual numbers (as opposed to physical, mental, or emotional) and a seven or nine time cycle often represents occasions when we are forced to turn inward, sometimes through pain and loss. Lighter, less serious times are much more likely when the three Personal Month and two Personal Year combination occurs in less demanding, longer-term time cycles like a five Life Path Period and a three Pinnacle.

Timing cycles must also be read in accordance with the energy in the personality chart. If a person had a tremendous lack of seven-type energy in the personality chart, any cycle of seven would present some difficulty. If a person had a balanced amount of nine-type energy, the nine Personal Year would be rewarding (beneficial endings instead of misfortune or tragedy), especially if the longer term cycles are in harmony with the positive aspects of the nine Personal Year. Beneficial supplemental long-term timing cycle numbers to the nine Personal Year might include three or five (three and five are luckier and relate more to fun and excitement), depending on the personality chart. A nine Personal Year with several nine long-term cycles would include at least some unwanted departures or separations, no matter how positive the energy in the personality chart.

Personality aspects including the Life Path, Birthday Number and Main Challenge and timing cycles including the Life Path Periods, Pinnacles, Challenges, Personal Years, Personal Months and Personal Days comprise an adequate foundation of aspects to begin studying numerology. At least a couple years of serious study, starting with the fundamentals, is required to begin to see the full scope of numerology's validity. An objective disposition and many charts are essential for the process of study, application and observation. If used wisely, the insight provided through numerology allows for significant strides towards self-actualization.

At first glance, numerology may not seem related to your love life or reincarnation. But when you understand that we all move through predictable cycles created in part from our past life karma, and that these cycles can be determined by metaphysical sciences such as numerology, the connection becomes clear. By using the above calculations and then applying them to different periods of your life, you will gain more understanding about your past and present life circumstances. The calculations can also be applied to the future to help you know in advance what potentials your love life may have in store for you. You'll then be able to prepare for and more easily accept change and opportunities.

Scott A. Petullo is considered an expert in numerology, and provides complete and in-depth numeric analyses for individuals and businesses. He can be reached at www.decadcorp.com.

Easy Astrology For A Better Life

The astrology with which most people are familiar is very general. Horoscopes for entertainment are not real astrology. In-depth astrology, like in-depth numerology, takes into consideration the entire birth chart of a person, which is based on the exact time, place, and date of birth. In-depth astrology can take years to learn and understand, but provides a wealth of information for those who take the time to study it. These valuable yet easy-to-use astrological tools can easily be applied to your life without any astrological background.

The American Federation of Astrologers is one source for accurate astrological information. They sell a pocket and wall calendar package for about $25 that will help you get started with astrology. Both provide the exact days and times for moon void-of-course, retrogrades, and other astrological information. The AFA can be contacted at (602) 838-1751 or P.O. Box 22040, Tempe, Arizona, USA 85285-2040. You can also find astrological calendars at metaphysical bookstores. Matrix offers astrological software that also lists moon void-of-course, retrogrades, and other astrological information.

Sun Signs

If an astrology book or column claims that your Virgo Sun isn't compatible with your partner's Leo Sun, this doesn't mean you can't have a compatible relationship. When judging astrological compatibility, you must take into consideration each partner's entire chart. This includes not only what sign the Sun was in at the time of birth, but also where the Moon, Mercury, Venus, Mars, Jupiter, Saturn, Uranus, Neptune, and Pluto were located, along with the aspects between them and what houses in which they each lie. Accuracy increases as you go deeper into a chart or a compatibility analysis.

Moon Void Of Course

The Moon travels around the earth in about 28 days, spending about two and a half days in each of the 12 zodiac signs. After the Moon leaves a sign and before it enters the next sign, it is called void-of-course (v/c).

The Moon rules instinct and intuition. When the Moon is v/c, the energy flow available to all living things seems to slow down and our intuition is temporarily clouded. *During a v/c it's easy to be unrealistic or to perceive things differently than they really are.* During this time people tend to feel scattered and unfocused. Time seems to drag on forever.

Knowing when the moon is void-of-course by checking the times in an astrological calendar can save you a lot of time, money, and effort. Follow them for a couple weeks, then don't look at the calendar for a few days, then look back at those times later. You'll find that even when you didn't consciously know it was a v/c, things were still typical of a v/c. Voids seem to affect everyone.

Moon voids can last from as little as 10 minutes to as long as two days. Moon voids comprise, on average, about eight percent of the standard eight-to-five work week. Of course, it's not always possible to schedule around these times, but it helps to be aware of the difficulties you may encounter.

During a Moon void-of-course, DO:

- Routine work.
- Meditate—this is a great time to go inward. You'll be even more centered after the v/c.
- Break bad habits—if you can refrain during a v/c, it will be easier to do so afterward.
- Creative hobbies.
- Routine cleaning.
- Exercise.
- Relax.

During a Moon void-of-course, DON'T:

- Make important plans—they'll never happen or will happen differently than expected.
- Brainstorm—new ideas never manifest or will backfire.
- Start anything new—things initiated are never finished or take much longer than expected to complete. New acquaintances made are short-lived. If you meet someone during a void of course, the interaction will not be meaningless, but probably different than you expected.
- Buy anything of importance—purchases made will never be used, will break down, or will have to be returned for unforeseen reasons.
- Do anything that requires a lot of concentration—it will require a lot more of your energy. If you have no choice, meditate beforehand so you'll be as centered as possible.
- Schedule appointments: they will have to be changed or rescheduled—or you may get "stood up"!

People who were born during a void of course moon may not be as affected or may be affected differently. Follow the cycles and observe for yourself.

Mercury Retrograde

The planet Mercury rules transportation, communication, and perception. Mercury moves in the same direction as the Sun (direct motion). When Mercury is closest to Earth, it appears, because of an optical illusion, to reverse its direction for about three to four weeks (retrograde motion). This happens about three times each year.

During a Mercury retrograde, DO:

- Reevaluate, reconsider, renew, recharge, rewrite, repeat: most things with a "re-" prefix are appropriate.
- Be aware that things begun during a Mercury retrograde often end during one and tend to be more temporary.
- Double-check and confirm details and plans. You may be focused but a second party may not have been.
- Have more compassion in relationships—misunderstandings are common.
- Expect delays or changes in plans.

- Meditate more. Retrograde is also a time when perception and communication can go deeper.

During a Mercury retrograde, DON'T:

- Start businesses you want to last. An exception may be businesses that deal with Mercury ruled things, such as communication and transportation.
- Make major purchases.
- Have any major surgery performed.
- Sign any contracts: the contents may later prove to be inadequate or unclear.
- Expect any major plans to manifest as expected. Stay open and make final plans and decisions after Mercury retrograde.

Most astrological calendars list the days Mercury goes retrograde and direct, but there is also a "shadow" period before and after the retrograde of about 15 to 20 days. *Therefore, Mercury retrograde affects us for about two months, then we are free of its influence for about two months, then it effects us again for two months, and so on.*

If you were born during a Mercury retrograde, these times may affect you in different ways. For example, Madonna was born during a Mercury retrograde. Her career deals with communication and she has had tremendous success.

Venus Retrograde

Venus retrograde occurs every 18 months for about six weeks. Since Venus rules love, friendships, and money matters, Venus retrograde is an unreliable time for these areas. Still, a Venus retrograde doesn't mean you should avoid new love relationships or friendships. Keeping your expectations in check is recommended, though. Sometimes Venus retrograde is a time when past-life lovers or friends come back into your life to resolve issues. Don't expect relationships or friendships started during these times to be long-term, although it does ultimately depend on each individual's astrology chart.

Location Astrology

Your location affects all areas of your life. A certain area of the world may be great for your career goals, yet counter-productive for your love goals. Location astrology can give you more insight into how your current location is affecting you. There are different approaches to this science: I have found that using the relocated astrological birth chart (if the location you want to know about is different than your birth city) is most accurate. If you're interested in exploring location astrology, find an astrologer who analyzes the entire relocated birth chart, not just a relocation map, to the city of interest. Or, have your relocated birth chart printed out, buy the best astrology books you can find, and determine for yourself how life may be like in your city of interest.

18
Successful Dating

After you have worked on yourself and when you're in a favorable cycle to become involved with a compatible partner, where and how do you meet that special someone? When someone is truly ready to meet the right person and the timing is right, it often happens without much effort. Still, there are many ways you can improve your chances. If you're not truly ready or if you ignore your relationship cycles (see Chapter 17), your efforts to become happily involved will most likely result in frustration and heartache. For example, you may meet love possibilities during unfavorable cycles, yet things may never seem to get off the ground or you may encounter more relationship challenges.

Where Can You Meet Potential Love Possibilities?

- Friends of friends
- Singles groups and events
- Classes and seminars
- Spiritual or religious groups
- Gyms
- Sporting events
- Volunteer work
- Dating services
- Art gallery shows and other cultural events

- Grocery stores (try an organic produce/natural product grocery store if you're into health and wellness)
- Personal ads
- Anywhere when you're least expecting it

Be creative! There are many more places and methods to meet people. See "Making Contact: How to Flirt" below for more information about how to connect with someone who makes your heart race.

The Reality of Personal Ads

You've answered someone's ad or they have responded to yours. You haven't actually met face to face yet, but he or she seems perfect! It's finally happening for you! You have so much in common that you even wonder if this person may be a soul mate. Before you make wedding plans, know that this person is probably not what you want them to be.

If your hopes are too high with a new personal ad possibility, you don't have many requirements in a partner, you're not perceiving the person as he or she really is, you have unrealistic expectations, or all of the above. It's difficult to know if someone is a soul mate or even if you would like each other in person until you actually meet and spend time together.

The main problem with personals is that you get to know him or her initially only by what he or she writes or says. Everyone is afraid of rejection, so even though they may not intend to lie, words can sometimes be presented in a way that is misleading. For example, a man who says he values monogamy may fail to mention that he just can't seem to actually be monogamous; three wives have left him because of his infidelities. Or how about the woman who says she loves romance? Did she mention that her idea of romance is receiving plenty of expensive presents?

Moreover, it is easy and common to project what you're looking for in a mate onto the person and ignore danger signs. Fantastic! He likes the same authors, food, and vacation spots that you do! But what about the fact that he will not tell you his age and has no picture to send you?

In addition to your hopes and desires clouding the situation and the illusions he or she may have about themselves, there are people who lack integrity and will lie about important details without even a second thought or caring about the consequences. Someone who lacks integrity often believes their own lies because of their justifications. Until you really get to know him or her, you'll not know for sure if he or she has told you the truth about age, career, relationship history, marital status, STDs, or other important information.

Though there are risks involved, answering or placing personal ads can be a great way to meet a partner, especially when you follow the recommendations below. They will greatly improve your odds of success.

- Know what you want in a partner. When writing an ad, be specific enough to attract compatible possibilities, but not so specific that no one responds. In addition to stating information about yourself and what you're looking for, add personality or humor to your ad. Make your ad stand out from the rest.
- If using on-line personals, post a recent picture of yourself.
  - Consider taking the time to take some good photos of yourself, either with a friend or with a tripod and a mirror.
  - Try to use a picture that will portray you accurately. If your picture makes you look significantly better than you do in person, either from the angle it was taken, lighting, makeup, or how long ago the picture was taken, those you meet may be disappointed face to face. Or post the exceptionally good one in your ad and then make sure to send several other pictures in your initial correspondence with the person to give them an accurate idea of your appearance.
  - You may want to keep your photos "G" or "PG" rated, as posting, sending or requesting nude photographs may imply or initiate short-term sexual relationships rather than longer-term love relationships.
  - If you don't have a scanner, most copy shops can inexpensively scan pictures onto a disc.
- Most don't intend to lie, but in an attempt to market themselves they may exaggerate. Some have illusions about their appearance and personality that aren't even close to the truth. Request a picture from those who respond to your ad and be leery if they refuse. Do you really want to spend time and energy interacting with someone online and then find when you

meet them that they look and behave nothing like their description? What else are they being misleading about?

- Read between the lines: "I want someone who can make me laugh" may seem like an innocent statement, but sometimes it can mean that the writer expects their date to entertain them. Or it may indicate the writer is depressed, bored, or boring. "I want someone to stick with me no matter what" may indicate that the writer has something to hide (that will be discovered by you later). "I love to be spoiled" may indicate a gold-digger or a taker. "I'm looking for a permanent relationship" may indicate a fear of being alone. Love is forever, but most relationships are not.
- Even if you are, don't describe yourself in your ad as "very good looking." This will scare away good possibilities who may be more modest about their opinions of themselves and who may assume you only will date very good looking people. Stating this in your ad will also encourage others to have higher expectations of you and cause them to look more closely for your faults.
- If you've ever read, placed, or responded to personal ads, you may have noticed that most think they look younger than their age. A question one may want to ask is, "You look younger compared to whom?" Granted, most may look younger than people their age did 20 or more years ago. This is mostly due to updated clothing and hair styles and a little exercise. One's perception of looking younger may come from what people have told them, sometimes in response to "How old do you think I am?" or "How old do I look?" Most will guess younger so as not to hurt anyone's feelings. It is possible to maintain a healthy and youthful look well into your 50s, 60s and beyond if you do the things that truly work and avoid the things that age the body and mind. This goes way beyond "eating right" and "exercise." When you achieve a truly healthier state, you'll feel better and look younger than you have in years (see chapter 19).
- Don't fool yourself by saying that "looks don't matter." This implies that you have absolutely no preferences as far as appearance and most of us do. If you make the most of your

appearance and prefer someone who does the same, this doesn't mean you're vain or shallow. People who accuse you of this may be jealous or too lazy to make the most of their appearance. Love relationships in our society usually begin with appearance; it is what we see first.

- Screen possibilities carefully. Be direct. Ask questions to confirm their age, weight, height, marital status, intent, and so on. If necessary, explain that you prefer to be cautious to save both of you time and energy. In light of the dangers associated with personal ads, anyone who tells you that you need to trust them more is either naïve about the reality of personal ads or is trying to manipulate you.
- Be honest, but avoid disclosing too much personal information initially or answering questions that you don't feel comfortable about.
- People will show their true colors by the way they communicate online: do they answer your (reasonable) questions or do they ignore them? Do they willingly answer the same questions they ask of you? Do they ask about you or do they just write about themselves? Do they capitalize the first letter of your name or even write your name in responses? If not, this may indicate a lack of respect. Do they type their name as a signature in all caps? If so, this may indicate selfishness or an inflated ego.
- Have no expectations of more than a friendship with personal ad possibilities. Expectations cloud your perception. If you have visions of love and then there is no chemistry face to face, you'll be disappointed every time.
- Limit your interaction before meeting face to face. If you spend too much time typing or talking on the phone with each other, you'll regret it if there's no connection in person. Your mind will create a perception of the person derived from your dreams, hopes, desires, their words, and their photos which will usually be different than what you'll perceive face to face.
- Stay detached. Emotions can cause you to miss danger signals.
- Use your intuition. Consider everything he or she tells you. Don't assume they're honest. Trust their actions more than their words.

- No matter how much interaction you've had by phone or online, always meet for the first time in a public place and provide your own transportation.
- If someone is relatively compatible and you feel good in their presence, give him or her a chance! Your ideal mate may be slightly different than you envision him or her to be.
- Follow the Dating Tips below for any face-to-face meetings.

Dating Services

There is a common misperception about dating services: only "losers" or desperate people need to pay money for a date. While it is true that most dating services have a variety of members, some of whom may be desperate, it is also true that a reputable dating service can be a great way to meet compatible people.

If you look in the phone book of any medium to large size city under "dating services," you'll usually find that prostitution or escort services use this name as a cover. It's usually pretty easy to tell the difference between an escort service and a dating service, either by their name or hints in the ad such as "by the hour" or "lovely ladies."

Authentic dating services—meaning a fee is paid by all members to meet potential love mates—range in price from $25, to $25,000. The most basic and least expensive type of dating service typically costs between $25 and $100. These often use "state of the art" computer matching. Unfortunately, these are usually a waste of money as they don't meet with members to validate the data and *most answer the questionnaire as they want to be perceived instead of how they really are.* Furthermore, unless this type of service has thousands of *active* members and their questionnaire is extremely detailed, your matches will seldom be even remotely compatible. Due to the popularity of Internet personals, computer dating services are no longer as common.

Most dating services meet with each of their members. They range in price from about $150 to $5,000+. They may use extensive interviews, videos, pictures, personality tests or a combination of these approaches. Each have their advantages and disadvantages which are discussed below. These services often have a range of packages and prices, depending on the length of time you are active as a member, how many introductions, and whether or not you want the option to "freeze" your membership.

So why pay money to meet potential love possibilities when you can do it other ways for little or no cost? There are many advantages to a good dating service (some dating services, like other businesses, promise a lot but a deliver a little). Most importantly, all members are screened. This is done by requiring potential members to show identification, usually two forms, to confirm name, age and address. Some services do credit checks and background checks on all or questionable members. Some services even use private investigators. Liars usually will not pay $1,000 to $5,000 for a service like this, especially since the contracts members are required to sign often state membership will be revoked with no refund if they misrepresent themselves about age, marital status, HIV status, or any other important information. In addition to screening members, a good dating service gets to know each member through a thorough interview. Relationship history, career, financial stability, family, health, goals, interests, hobbies, and more are either touched on or covered extensively. As a result, a good dating service provides quality, compatible dates to members. Knowing detailed, truthful information about someone new ahead of time is one of the best advantages as it saves a lot of time and frustration. Moreover, those who pay this much money are serious about meeting compatible people. They truly feel they are ready to meet and get involved with the right person. Therefore, your chances of meeting like-minded people are greatly increased.

How to Find a Good Dating Service

What to look for and questions to ask:

1. How long have they been in business? If they have more than one location, how long has the location where your matches would come from been operating? If less than a year old, unless they've done extensive marketing and promotion, they may not have enough members to match you compatibly yet. Request a lower rate if they are not taking this into consideration. A package of a certain amount of quality matches with no time limit would be best in a situation like this, since you may have to wait months in between compatible matches.

2. How do they screen members? If they don't meet face to face with each member, it isn't going to be any more effective than a personal ad.

3. How many *active* members are available at this time? The number they give you may be the total they've had come in the door or that are currently in the files, not how many are available to date. Most heterosexual dating services have more women than men. The opposite is true for homosexual dating services.

4. What percentage of the members would be compatible with you? This percentage is figured by such factors as the appropriate sex, age range, income range, religion/spirituality, looks, location, and so on *and* the factors important to those who may be matched with you. After asking this question, ask how many of these potential matches are available and would find you compatible? They may not be able to give you an exact number, and may have a policy of not spending time and effort matching people until they are paid members. The person(s) responsible for matching should be able to tell you whether there is a high, medium, or low number of members who may be compatible with you. This question is more appropriate for an in-person interview, after their sales pitch and before you join. If there are few currently on file who would be compatible with you, request a lower rate, unless they are willing to work with you to help make you more marketable or even market you separately.

5. What techniques are used to match members? Photo dating is only good for those who photograph well. Video dating is better, but unless the service and videographer do a superb job of helping people present themselves well, members may not be perceived as well as they would be after the second or third date when they would be more relaxed and confident. If no photos or videos are used, who does the matching? Does this person actually meet the members? If not, is the interview information recorded *in detail* so the matchmaker can use it to provide compatible matches?

6. What is the fee range? Most services will not disclose their rates over the phone. This is because most people don't understand the reason for their higher rates. If the service has a good reputation and you're making an effort to be your best, you'll get your money worth. *If you don't know yourself, have unrealistic expectations in love, and expect the service to solve all your love life problems by introducing*

you to Mr. or Ms. Right, you'll be disappointed. Even if the service does introduce you to ideal matches, since they can't control your behavior or personality, they can't guarantee that any match will lead to even a second date.

7. What kinds of packages are available? Length of time? Number of matches? Options?

8. If you do join a dating service, follow the Dating Tips below when you begin meeting other members.

Making Contact: How to Flirt

Someone captures your interest. You immediately feel attracted to him or her. Your heart rate increases. You feel light-headed. Now what? How are you going to connect with this person without scaring him or her away? Here is one approach:

1. Discreetly observe him or her and and "tune in" to perceive everything you can.

2. If you have a good feeling about the person, make and hold eye contact and smile. Smiling is an important part of flirting. Smiling helps the other person realize your intentions. Practice smiling whenever you think of it. Keeping a happy look on your face will invite others to approach you, too.

3. Know that there is a fine line between flirting innocently and offending someone. Never stare at someone's private parts, unless of course it is obviously mutual. Take a hint if they don't respond to your advances. If you're attracted to him or her, don't assume you're their type. At the same time, if the other person is shy and you wait until you're absolutely sure they are interested, you may miss an opportunity. Simply be friendly, polite and respect other's boundaries. This way, even if they are not interested in you romantically, you may make a new friend.

4. If the person returns the eye contact and smiles back, approach and say hello. Talk casually.

5. If there isn't time to make eye contact, casually begin a conversation: comment on something he or she is wearing, holding, carrying, or doing; ask a question that is related to where you are or what you're doing. It is okay to be obvious, as long as you remain polite. If he or she continues the conversation, they may be interested or they may just be being polite. If he or she doesn't continue the

conversation, they may be shy, they may have no interest, or they may not even realize that you're flirting! Be assertive yet don't overstep your boundaries. You may increase your chances of being flirted with wherever you go by carrying or wearing something others can easily use to start a conversation.

6. If the circumstances make it difficult to approach him or her and you have received clear signals they are also interested, write on the back of your business card, "I can see you're busy. Please call me—I would love to talk with you" (or something similar), and smile as you hand him or her your card. If at a restaurant, have your waiter give him or her your card.

7. Feel if the interest is mutual. Sometimes it is easy to misinterpret someone as being interested in you, when they in fact are just being friendly. Occasionally, when flirting with someone who isn't aware of themselves and what they want, you may get mixed signals. This can be confusing. Their words don't match what they are really feeling or what they really want. They may say words or give many signals that indicate they are interested, then say or insinuate, "No, I'm married/involved" or "No, I'm supposed to be heterosexual/homosexual" or "No, I'm not interested in a relationship/casual sex." They give many indications they are responding to your flirting or advances, but would deny doing so. Other times, you may encounter someone who appears interested in you too, but may only be attracted to your attraction to them. This may happen more often to overly assertive people. They may like you, just not the same way you like them. They may be interested in the attention, communication, or interaction from you, but are not physically attracted to you or are not available.

8. If someone who you're not interested in flirts with and asks you out, be direct and polite: "Thanks for asking, but no." It may be difficult to be direct if you're not used to this type of communication, but it will save you hassle and him or her heartache.

9. If it feels appropriate and you feel there is a connection, say that you'd love to get together for coffee or lunch sometime. Ask him or her for their business card or a number you can reach them at (but don't ask for a home number). Give them yours too. Keep in mind that some who are afraid of hurting your feelings or who find it difficult to be direct may lie, say they are interested, and agree to

meet you for a date, even if they don't intend to follow through. If this happens, don't take it personally. Let it go and move on.

10. If you call to follow up and ask for a date and you feel they are preoccupied or not interested, say, "I've probably caught you at a bad time. I'll give you my number and you can call at a better time."

11. If they don't call back, don't take it personally. There could be a thousand different reasons: they may be interested in you but they just ended a relationship and don't feel like dating yet; they may already be involved; they may be shy and didn't have the courage to call you back, and so on. If you happen to see the person again, smile and say hello. If they approach you, they may or may not be interested. If not, let it go.

12. If you happen to be rejected, don't take it personally. The person did you a favor by keeping you available for someone who is more compatible. The worst thing you can do is become angry at the person. This is pointless, especially since the reason for rejection may have nothing to do with you. You can't expect everyone you like to like you back.

13. If the person returns your interest and agrees to a date, don't assume they have the same intent as you.

14. When someone flirts with you who isn't your type, either ignore them or be polite yet firm. Don't give them mixed signals. When you refrain from getting offended when someone you're not attracted to hits on you, you'll have more confidence to flirt and to be more assertive in the future. In other words, those who automatically react with disgust or anger if someone who isn't their type approaches them, they may fear rejection and miss opportunities because they are afraid to flirt. Flirting becomes easier if you accept the possibility of rejection and if you don't take it personally when rejected.

15. If you're involved in a monogamous relationship and are flirting behind your partner's back, reconsider your actions. Besides eventually hurting your partner when he or she finds out and displaying a lack of integrity, it is also frustrating to singles seeking singles. Perhaps it is more difficult for you to be monogamous. Still, this isn't a valid excuse to have an affair. See chapter 13 for more information about responsible and honest non-monogamy.

Dating Tips

- Keep an open mind and be realistic. It's okay to be particular about your requirements as long as you meet the majority of them yourself. However, if you wait for someone who fits your ideal image completely, you may be single for a long time and miss compatible possibilities.
- Meeting for coffee/tea/juice for the first time is recommended. Sitting through a long meal with someone you don't know can be uncomfortable, especially if there is no immediate attraction.
- Give each person a chance. Try to concentrate on what you like instead of what you don't. Everyone is likely to be a little nervous, so focus on the feeling you have when you're with the person instead of what they did or didn't say or do.
- Try not to analyze every new possibility as if you're going to spend the rest of your life with the person. If you do, you'll find something wrong with everyone you meet. If you meet each new possibility with an open mind, you'll enjoy yourself more and may be pleasantly surprised.
- Even though love and romance may be on your mind, perhaps you were meant to meet each other for other reasons: a friendship, a business relationship, to receive a message or advice, or to learn more about yourself.
- If you're talking about something for more than five minutes and the other person has not responded, the subject may be of little interest to that person. Talk with, not at. Ask questions (not too personal initially) to get the conversation rolling.
- Don't judge a person if he or she has not had a long-term relationship or had negative experiences in love. Your experience in love with the person may completely different. Besides, a long-term relationship isn't always a sign of stability; it could indicate fear of change or dependency.
- Don't dwell on previous relationships.
- Don't say "I'll call you" as an easy out if you don't intend to. "It was nice meeting you" will do.
- Have self-confidence and faith in yourself.
- Have fun!

- It can often take months to discover if someone is compatible. More singles today are choosing to date more than one person at a time before making a commitment. If your first date leads to more dates and you're dating more than one person, you may want to consider being up front about it. When it feels appropriate, mention that while you really want to get to know him or her, in the meantime you aren't ready to fully commit to one person and would like to have the freedom to date others. As long as you're sincere, honest and are okay with he or she doing the same, your honesty should make the situation less complicated and less stressful. If your new date isn't comfortable with this kind of arrangement, especially if you have only been dating for a short time, he or she may have issues with dependency or jealousy that may become a problem in a relationship.
- Since dating eventually may lead to sex, always practice safer sex. See chapter 19 for information on two rarely discussed additional risks of sex and how to avoid them.
- Pay attention to your love cycles when making an effort to improve your love life. This will help you to go with the flow and avoid frustration (see chapter 17).

Your past-life loves are out there. If you follow the above recommendations and use your intuition, you'll eventually reunite with the right ones at the right times. Meanwhile, learn to enjoy being single and love yourself first.

If you want it, you'll find a way.
If not, you'll find an excuse.
— Sunjay Gupta

19
Stepping Stones to True Health

The following information is provided for educational purposes only, and isn't to be interpreted as an endorsement, recommendation or approval of anyone, any product, or any treatment. This information isn't to be considered complete, nor does it contain all medical resource information that may be relevant, and therefore isn't intended as a prescription, replacement or substitute for anyone seeking medical treatment and/or appropriate care. The information isn't meant to replace the advice of a qualified medical practitioner. Consult with your physician or other health care provider.

What Does Health Have to do With Your Love Life?

Your state of health affects how you live, feel, and love. When you look and feel your best, your partner will appreciate you more. If you're single, you'll attract more partner possibilities. When you're truly healthy, you feel calm and centered. This will enhance your love life. Here's another reason for better health: If you don't care about longevity or how you feel, do it for a better sex life! There's a direct link between what you feed your body and your sexual drive and performance.

Most of the information reported in mainstream media about health seems to stem from the marketing arm of the medical industry and whomever else they are in bed with. The key word is industry. It isn't in their best interest to help everyone prevent all disease.

If they accomplished this, they would make no money. Of course, there are many well-meaning people involved in the medical industry, but these people may not be the key players. It's great news when we learn that a certain food or supplement may help prevent cancer, for example, but we would all be better off if scientists would focus their time, energy, and money on the true causes of disease instead of bandage remedies.

Health and Resistance to Change

Your customs, habits and routines have been formed over many years. Though you may be consciously aware of how much you could benefit by making some changes in your life, your subconscious mind may create countless excuses to stay the same. The more you resist, the more you may benefit from taking the action required. If you really want to reach your goals, you'll ignore your inner critic and "just do it."

If you do feel yourself resisting change, know that this is natural. Diet, especially, is a stumbling block for almost everyone: much of what we want to eat is motivated by emotional reasons. There are hundreds of articles in medical literature which show a correlation between nutritional deficiencies and disease. Scientific studies have definitively linked nutrition to mental and emotional health. Everything from depression to eating disorders, anxiety, stress, psychosis, and personality changes can be fundamentally impacted by nutrition. Therefore, starting with the physical body when re-creating your reality is ideal. When you're balanced physically, it is much easier to "see" and think clearly. At the same time, spiritual imbalances create physical imbalances, so working with all levels by also addressing the subconscious mind through guided meditation and/or meditating on your own can also make change easier.

Here are some basic guidelines to achieving a healthier lifestyle:

1. Look at yourself and your life realistically. Do you feel the way you want to?

2. Visualize your ultimate health goals. What steps must you take to achieve them?

3. Identify and change what isn't working. Learn about your body and what it needs.

4. Discover any hidden causes of poor health. Don't overlook the need to resolve underlying issues (root causes) from this lifetime or previous ones.

5. Reprogram your subconscious mind through hypnotherapy, guided meditation, or affirmations. Choose suggestions and ideas that work in harmony with your goals.

6. Eliminate distractions and get "unstuck." Meditation and exercise calm and balance the mind, body, and soul, making it easier to do the things necessary to be in perfect health.

7. Take action. Ask for assistance from God, your guides and angels of the Light, and/or your Higher Self every step of the way and you'll know when and how to act so that you may reach and maintain your goal.

8. Know that true health is a conscious choice that you can achieve.

A Note About Drugs

Do you want to live your highest path? If so, you need to avoid all drugs and learn how to feel good without them. There is no room for street drugs in your life if you want to be the best you can be—or prescription drugs unless absolutely necessary. There's often a more effective natural alternative to prescription drugs, and getting to the root cause of the problem can sometimes eliminate the need for them.

I have noticed that clients who do drugs seem disconnected from their intuition. Drugs keep you in a haze, making it impossible for you to see clearly. When your reality is distorted you make the wrong decisions in life, making it impossible for you to reach your goals or even to know which goals are for your highest good. Drugs make life's problems seem 10 times worse and throw off your entire balance—physically, mentally, emotionally and spiritually.

"In moderation" is fine if you want to be moderate instead of living up to your potential. But be aware that drugs, even in moderation, will lead to problems. Drugs lower your energy level, which enables spiritual parasites to feed off you. See through the hype and glamorization of drugs: some people claim that some drugs induce a "spiritual" experience. This may or may not be true. In the process, however, the user risks physical, mental, emotional, and spiritual damage. Drugs create blocks to true spiritual awareness and understanding. If you want a spiritual experience, learn to meditate.

Health "Outside the Box"

Consider alternative options to stay healthy and avoid disease. Conventional/traditional medicine and health care is just one approach. Another is holistic/alternative medicine and health care, which addresses all levels of the body: physical, mental, emotional, and spiritual. Find and treat the cause of disease, not just the symptoms. To find a physician who uses the best of conventional and alternative medicine, contact the American Holistic Medical Association, (919) 787-5181, or the American Association of Naturopathic Physicians, (206) 323-7610.

The Two Rarely Talked-About Risks of Sexual Contact

Any discussion of health issues in a relationship book is bound to lead to talking about sex. Most people think of safer sex as the use of condoms, dental dams, gloves, and so on, to avoid unwanted pregnancies and STDs such as HIV, chlamydia, herpes, hepatitis, gonorrhea, syphilis, genital warts, and shigella. However, anyone having sex will benefit from being aware of two additional, seldom-talked-about risks of sexual contact: biological parasites and entity possession or attachment.

Biological Parasites

No one wants to talk about parasites. The truth is that they are transmitted quite easily. Yes, we have positive bacteria in our system that is supposed to attack the negative bacteria. That's a best-case scenario if the system is healthy and strong to begin with. In our society, where foods, alcohol, chemicals, and prescription drugs that work against the body are quite popular, many people are not as healthy as they want to believe they are. According to *The Cure For All Diseases* by Dr. Hulda Clark, there are many different forms of bacteria and parasites, and it's more of a problem in our country than most realize. Once these foreign bodies enter your system, they eventually can cause many different types of diseases depending on which organ they settle in. Some of these parasites are easily transmitted through bodily contact and saliva. Kissing is generally assumed to be safe, and it is if you want to avoid most STDs, but not if you want to avoid parasites that could cause disease. Furthermore, tests performed by the medical industry to detect parasites are notoriously inaccurate. Parasites burrow into organs and the contents of the intestines. Unless a purge is done of the entire intestines—which is difficult—parasites may go undetected.

It turns out that these little critters are easy to get rid of by using the right herbs for about 15 days and then once a week for maintenance, since we are constantly picking up bacteria and parasites through the food we eat and through other ways. Other more stubborn parasites may require medication. It's all explained in Dr. Clark's book. Try the parasite herbal cleanse and other cleanses that are recommended in the book and see for yourself.

Spiritual Health: Entity Possession or Attachment

Even though I risk a fearful or critical reaction about this section from some readers, I have included it because I feel spirit attachment and possession are important issues to be aware of as they can greatly interfere with relationships.

The idea of entity possession or attachment causes some people to think of the movie *The Exorcist*. While the subject of possession was greatly exaggerated in the movie for dramatic effect, entity possession (when an entity or energy seems to control its host) and attachment (when an entity or energy seems to influence its host) can and do happen. Sometimes the symptoms are subtle and go unnoticed; sometimes a person can literally be taken over, even from birth or before.

There are several books on this subject, including *Spirit Releasement Therapy* by William J. Baldwin, D.D.S, Ph.D., *Remarkable Healings* by Shakuntala Modi, M.D., *Remote Depossession* by Irene Hickman, D.O., and *The Unquiet Dead* by Dr. Edith Fiore. All of these authors explain that after people die, they usually go to "the Light," as written about in many life-after-death books. Some souls, however, don't go to the Light and remain earthbound. This is especially true in cases where someone dies angry, was a sex addict, alcoholic, or substance abuser, or if they died a violent or sudden death. These souls resist the white light for various reasons and instead seek out and merge with someone in a physical body who can feed their addiction or has similar feelings of anger, depression, or other fears. They may also be motivated to stay in close proximity to loved ones they knew while in a physical body. The intense feelings at the time of death are often experienced by whomever the entity attaches to or merges with. Even entities who don't mean any harm can cause fatigue and depression or confuse their thoughts and desires with those of the host.

How do you know if there is unwanted or uninvited energy interfering with your life?

The following are possible symptoms of possession or attachment:

- Emotional or physical reactions to the idea of spirit attachment/possession.
- Physical/ emotional/ mental/ spiritual feelings of being blocked.
- Drug or alcohol abuse.
- Sudden onset of alcohol or drug abuse (especially if there are distinct personality changes while under the influence).
- Addiction to sex.
- Sudden unexplainable onset of sadness, depression, anger, fears, guilt or anxiety.
- Reckless behavior.
- Poor memory and concentration.
- Hearing inner voices (especially with negative messages).
- Sudden change in personality.
- Feelings of being followed.
- Feeling drained.
- Sudden unexplainable physical problems.
- Recurring dreams or nightmares.

Some therapists who help clients release entities believe that 85 percent or more of the population may have entities interfering to some extent with their lives. But while the subject of entity attachment can seem frightening, there's really nothing to fear. It is simply energy that needs to be directed to the proper place.

How does one acquire unwanted and uninvited energies? It's surprisingly easy: by lowering the energy field or aura with alcohol, drugs, extreme emotions, sexual abuse, surgery, or illness.

Unwanted, uninvited energy can also attach before birth, during birth, and during childhood.

You may be more susceptible to entity attachment by:

- Using some prescription or any street drugs (even once) or overusing alcohol.
- Walking through or near a cemetery or hospital, especially while under the influence of drugs or alcohol.
- Using drugs or excess alcohol in a bar.
- Being under the influence of drugs or alcohol in a sex club.
- Having sex with someone while under the influence of drugs or alcohol.
- Having sex with someone while feeling strong negative emotions such as fear or anger, especially if you're more spiritually sensitive.
- Walking through a crowd while feeling depressed, angry, or other strong emotions, especially if you're more spiritually sensitive.
- Consuming too much of any food, or foods to which you're allergic or intolerant.
- Practicing ancient Wicca spells. While there are many good and well-meaning people who practice Wicca or witchcraft, and while the Craft is (in most cases) a positive method to harness and direct energies that are available to us all, using certain ancient Wicca spells can potentially bring forth, all the way back from ancient times, fear or entities that were associated with these spells. If you do choose to practice Wicca, do your homework. Make sure you know what you're doing. Since casting spells can open up the aura and lead to possession or attachment, utilize the white light of protection before attempting any spells. Remember that what you put out will come back to you.
- Practicing black magic or satanic worship.

How to avoid picking up entities, especially if you're spiritually sensitive:

- Avoid drugs and alcohol.
- Avoid sugar, especially if you're sensitive to it.
- Avoid overeating.

- Avoid negative people.
- Avoid Ouija boards and séances that potentially risk exposure to malevolent entities.
- Mentally surround yourself with white light daily. Picture a bright light shining out from your solar plexus, surrounding and protecting you. Ask for assistance from God and/or guides of the Light.
- Mentally fill your home and office daily with white light.
- Burn sage to help clear your home and energy field.

If you feel it is necessary, use an "entity releasement script" such as the one provided in *The Unquiet Dead* by Dr. Edith Fiore. This script is directed toward human entities who were once in their own body, who are now confused, and who need to be directed to the Light. The help of a spirit release/depossession professional may be needed for the release of dark or more stubborn energy/entities.

Appendix

"Do you really believe in this stuff?"

There are many misconceptions about reincarnation and metaphysics in general, though it is natural to question such topics. Those who adamantly and sometimes ferociously resist these ideas generally do so for two main reasons: they are influenced by what others have told them about metaphysics (which may involve religious dogma), or they react out of fear, which is often the result of misunderstandings or erroneous assumptions, or from being persecuted in past lives for either practicing or being accused of practicing something related to metaphysics. Fortunately, in such cases, the root cause of these fears can be discovered and dissolved through past-life regression therapy.

Some may feel angry because they have resisted taking responsibility for their actions in this life or in past lives. They may blame others or perceive themselves as a victim, and may feel threatened by the concept of karma.

Extreme skeptics who have allowed me to regress them have discovered forgotten events from the distant past about which they still subconsciously feel intense guilt or resentment. Some didn't do anything wrong but felt responsible nonetheless. Before obtaining the awareness in a past-life regression of why they so strongly rejected the concepts, it was easier to blame or condemn. Denying the past allowed them to escape guilt or resentment. After regression, assuming they allowed the process to work for them, they found their negative opinions about these concepts falling away. They began to understand the importance of compassion and forgiveness, especially with themselves. They began to realize that we are all in this world together; we are all connected. After a successful regression, the need for physical proof of metaphysics seemed less important. Instead, they tended to focus on the awareness that came from rising above and beyond their personality and ego and connecting with who they really are—our soul or Higher Self. Though they weren't able to bring forth conclusive evidence from any past lives, they came to realize that the awareness and compassion acquired through the process was more important.

Reincarnation and Traditional Beliefs

There are those who interpret the Bible figuratively, believing it contains wonderful stories from which we can learn. Their reasoning may be that those who wrote the Bible were human just like us; the material may have been translated or written based on the rules and beliefs of the society at that time. Conversely, there are those who interpret the Bible literally, as if everything written is "the word of God," and believe that the guidelines of the Bible should be followed strictly.

Both sides are at times guilty of interpreting the messages of the Bible to fit their personal beliefs. Both sides can find information to "prove" their beliefs, including whether or not reincarnation and karma are true. The fact is that we may never be able to prove that reincarnation or anything else in the Bible is true or false, and it hardly matters. However, each individual has a right to believe what he or she chooses.

Whether the Bible is to be taken literally or figuratively, there are those who claim that reincarnation was once discussed and accepted. According to *Edgar Cayce on Reincarnation* by Noel Langley, the Byzantine Emperor Justinian (483–565 A.D.) "summoned the Fifth Ecumenical Congress of Constantinople in 553 A.D. to condemn the Platonically inspired writings of Origen." These writings apparently referenced the pre-existence of the soul.

Furthermore, according to *The Christian Conspiracy* by Dr. L. David Moore, the Bible was edited for more than 500 years for political reasons after the crucifixion of Jesus Christ:

> Although it may be somewhat difficult for some to believe, the Bible in its present form didn't always exist. In fact, there is a lot of historical evidence which states that the old Testament, in its present form, didn't exist until some 60 years after the death of Christ; and the New Testament in its present form didn't exist until almost 300 years after that. The major point to be understood is that the Old Testament upon which so much of early Christianity depended in order to have a historical basis and to become legitimized, didn't officially exist until well after Christianity had been established and even after much of what later became the New Testament had been written. In addition, one major reason for establishing the Old Testament as canon was because during the first century C.E., Christianity was distorting the historical record in order to enhance their own new religion.

In addition to the extensive editing and rewrites of the Bible, there was the influence of the Inquisition or the Holy Calling (1231–1820). This was established by the Papacy to punish anyone who expressed a belief in reincarnation or practiced anything metaphysical that would threaten the universal control of the Church. They proclaimed these beliefs as the work of the devil and any believers were sent to dungeons, tortured, or burned to death.

Countless people have died because their beliefs (or beliefs of which they were accused) went against those of the Church, including the millions put to death for "witchcraft" from 1484 to 1775. *Fears of persecution may remain in the subconscious minds of many alive today. We are conditioned to believe that anything metaphysical is invalid in part because "inquisitional viewpoints" still exist.*

Organized religion continues to provide support and structure for those who choose to use it. However, some organized religions, which may be based on fear and guilt, continue to openly condemn and spread misinformation, intentionally or unintentionally, about metaphysics. This is unfortunate, since many have found that both their metaphysical viewpoints and their traditional religious background can exist together peacefully.

"Do you believe in God?"

I often hear this when I mention what I do for a living. Usually those who ask are religious or grew up with religion. Somewhere in their past, someone told them that metaphysical subjects are not part of God or that they are evil. They may have accepted this without question and without doing their own exploration or research. Perhaps this false belief stems from the Inquisitions, when the Church executed millions for practicing or believing in metaphysical subjects, whether or not the accused were actually doing so or not. My usual answer is: "Yes, I do believe in God, but not as a man in a white beard who judges and punishes us. I believe God is a force that is in all living things. This force is part of us and we are part of it. I believe God loves and accepts us all unconditionally."

"Doesn't the Bible claim that reincarnation and karma don't exist?"

It is debatable exactly what the Bible contained before it was extensively edited over a period of 500 years for political reasons. Some claim that references to the pre-existence of the soul and reincarnation were among the deleted passages. Others claim that reincarnation was taught by Christians during the time of Jesus.

"What about Judgment Day? If a soul has lived in different bodies, which body is judged? Who will be punished?"

"Judgment day" is a human, earthbound idea related to the concepts of heaven and hell that have been taught by religions for centuries. Some say its purpose is to enable the Church to control its followers. But when you sift through the dogma and discover the deeper spiritual meaning, you'll find that the concept of a judgment day, while distorted, is actually rooted in truth. We judge ourselves after each life from the perpective of our Higher Self, usually with the help of guides or elders in the spirit world. That awareness of our actions and their consequences is used to determine what kind of experiences are needed in future lives. There isn't one judgment day but many, one for each soul after each lifetime.

Furthermore, it's our personalities that are judged, not our bodies. Our bodies are only temporary containers holding who and what we really are so that we may exist and interact on this physical plane. As far as punishment, we only punish ourselves. For example, if we purposely hurt someone in one life, we may choose, on a soul level, to experience the situation as the one being hurt in another life. The reasons we choose what happens to us vary. Often they are to help us understand the importance of treating ourselves and everyone else with respect, love, and compassion (see Recommended Reading for sources about research regarding "life between life").

"If there really was a God, why would he or she allow all the violence, poverty, and suffering that is so prevalent in our world?"

This question implies a belief that God is only good and that some anti-Christ is behind all our problems. If we could only get rid of this anti-Christ, we would live in a utopia of never-ending peace and perfection. In reality, we are responsible for everything that happens to us and we all have free will. We all can react to situations any way we choose. This isn't God's responsibility; no one "did this" to us. Because of the laws of karma, your words, thoughts, and actions in the past have created your reality in the present, whether or not you remember them, and whether or not your current personality chooses to accept this. You do have the option, however, of taking responsibility, thus setting yourself free.

Questioning the Validity of These Concepts

"Only gullible people believe in that stuff."

Some people may accept metaphysical theories, without much consideration, but unfortunately, blind acceptance doesn't usually lead to complete comprehension. Most of those who understand metaphysical concepts don't automatically accept any new theory. For many, including myself, accepting an idea that can't be proven, like reincarnation, involves questioning, considering various explanations, applying the idea to their own life and the lives of others, and discussing other possibilities. Only then, after finding no good reason to discount it, will the theory be accepted. With an unbiased attitude, diligent research, and intuitive awareness, people will discover the truth. Ironically, it is sometimes those who condemn others for accepting metaphysical concepts who display gullibility, believing misinformation all too readily without bothering to do their own objective research.

"If past lives really do exist, why hasn't there ever been any verifiable evidence discovered during a past-life regression?"

In fact, there have been many cases of past-life regression where people received names, dates, locations, addresses, and other information that later checked out to be accurate. There have even been cases of people receiving information that wasn't yet publicly known, such as about cities and cultures before they were discovered by archeologists.

However, even though this may seem like proof of reincarnation, it still doesn't prove that the person who received the information through past-life regression or meditation actually lived as that person. There could be other reasons that someone has access to such facts; perhaps we have the ability to "tap into" the past, which allows us to remember experiences, emotions and details about a life. Perhaps our brains have some unexplainable ability that science isn't yet aware of to view the experiences of those in ancient civilizations with incredible accuracy. Other possible explanations include spirit attachment/possession and genetic memory. However, genetic memory doesn't explain how someone can recall incarnations where he or she lived as a different race.

It's also quite common for psychics, astrologers, numerologists, and other metaphysical readers to give past-life descriptions that match what someone has seen through a past-life regression. Still, this doesn't prove the existence of reincarnation. The reader may have picked up on what the person was "tapping into" or projecting.

Whatever the reason, verifiable evidence is beside the point. What is most important with past-life regression is that you use the awareness gained to help yourself accomplish the ultimate goal: learning to love and accept yourself and everyone else unconditionally.

"Why should anyone believe the year, clothing, culture, events and other information received from a past-life regression if there is no investigation of documented history to check the accuracy?"

While I usually don't focus on details such as these during my past-life regression sessions unless the client wants to, many therapists do. Dr. Ian Stevenson has done extensive research about such details and has documented his findings in his books. Much information received through regression has been proven to be true through research.

Rather than attempting to validate the information received during or after regressions, I prefer to help each client make the most of the session by focusing on more important aspects of the experience such as relationship dynamics, lessons learned, forgiveness, acceptance, and overall theme. I feel this is far more productive and beneficial.

"You can't prove any of this."

We can't disprove it, either. Before you automatically discount metaphysical theories in this book or elsewhere, try to consider the information objectively. If you don't, you may miss opportunities to help yourself. What is significant is the awareness that can be gained and the fact that problems can be released and overcome through the process of past-life regression, without drugs and without side effects.

"If you really want to add validity to the concepts of reincarnation and karma, why don't you have scientists attempt to prove that we have lived before?"

Although there have been studies about reincarnation (see Recommended Reading), who is going to fund such a project? Major scientific studies are often funded, directly or indirectly, by corporations interested in creating more profits. Since there is no money in proving or disproving reincarnation or karma, it is difficult to get financial support for such a project.

Second, until the scientific community recognizes and accepts that we are more than just physical bodies, and that physical, emotional and mental "diseases" and problems often begin with the spiritual body, they will consider such projects a waste of time.

Third, until the scientific community understands and accepts the concepts of karma and reincarnation, they will not even begin to consider or want to understand how to measure or validate the spiritual body.

Fourth, how many times have you read or heard about a new scientific study that "proves" something, only to read or hear months or years later that science has disproven the same thing? Scientific studies can be biased or incomplete, yet we place a lot of significance on them.

Lastly, validating the concepts seem less important when taking into consideration how the process has helped so many people significantly improve the quality of their lives—inexpensively, in little time, and with no side effects.

"If past-life regression therapy is such a cure-all, why has the media ignored it?"

Occasionally there are stories about past-life regression in the mainstream press. Due to the skeptical reactions so many people still have regarding such therapy, these accounts are unlikely to make headlines. Furthermore, this type of therapy is a threat to certain people and industries: if everyone realized how they could use the power of their mind to improve their health, relationships, finances, career and more, a lot less money would be spent on the less effective but more popular traditional approaches.

"If past-life regression is as effective as you claim it is, everyone would use it."

While past-life regression therapy has a higher success rate than conventional chemical and talk therapy, it is less popular because we are conditioned from birth to disbelieve that we have lived before. Furthermore, some people subconsciously want to keep their problems. Since past-life regression can help, they will avoid it and anything else that really works. As the truth spreads about the effectiveness of past-life regression, this type of therapy will become more popular.

"If past lives really do influence our present life so profoundly, why don't we remember them?"

We do have the ability to remember our past lives, but most of us are programmed from birth to forget. Children, when encouraged, can often describe their past lives in detail without a past-life regression. Unfortunately, most parents dismiss or even discourage such memories. If as children we were encouraged to perceive and explore past-life memories instead of being told "it's just your imagination," we may be able to develop this ability. Additionally, if we remembered all the things we did and all that happened to us in past lives, it would be too difficult to concentrate on and deal with all the issues of our present life, which is more important. However, the actions of our past do influence our present lives, whether we remember them or not.

"How could people who give a B.C. date during a regression possibly know it's B.C.?"

The subconscious mind stores memories of all our experiences, from this life and other lives. The superconscious mind is our link to all that is. During regression, individuals access the subconscious or superconscious mind. Some are confused by a question such as "What year is it?" They may be deep in meditation or trance and engrossed in the past-life regression. Since there may not have been a calendar system during that time, they have no idea what the question means. Or they may have been uneducated in that past life and weren't aware of the calendar system. Most individuals, however, have a heightened intuitive awareness about what they are perceiving and can switch back and forth between the past life they are perceiving and their present day reality. When asked a question during regression about what they are perceiving, they often will intuitively know the answer.

"How do people know during a past-life regression that others they perceive in past lives are their current lovers, friends, relatives, or enemies?"

Like most experiences, you need to go through it to understand it. Since individuals are in a meditative state during regression, they often have heightened intuitive awareness that accompanies the past-life perceptions. For example, they may visualize a Native American wearing a full headdress, but they intuitively know that this person or soul is now their uncle John. Sometimes individuals will see images of the present day person flowing in and out of awareness along with the past-life character. Some will look into the eyes of a past-life figure and just know it's someone they know now. Others are able to feel the past-present connection.

"What about evil spirits? Couldn't this explain past-life recall, especially with the people who seem to become the past-life person through regression?"

When approached correctly, possession or attachment by entities during the process of past-life regression is highly unlikely. Most past-life regression therapists take precautions to prevent this from happening, such as utilizing the "white light." Some ask guides of the Light before the regression for guidance and protection. Some burn sage and white candles, or use Reiki or other forms of energy healing.

The hypnotic, meditative, or reflective state needed for past-life regression to work is similar to the state everyone enters when falling asleep or just waking up in the morning. The risk of possession during regression is about the same as it is during sleeping or daydreaming—remote.

Spirit possession or attachment is actually fairly common outside of regression therapy. Most of these "evil spirits" are not evil at all; they are souls or fragments of souls who aren't occupying a body of their own at this time. For various reasons, after their physical body died, the soul remained on the physical plane instead of entering the Light or the spiritual world. Some spirits who remain earthbound and feed off the energy bodies of others have no relation to their hosts. Others are friends or relatives who wish to remain close after they have died. Some of these spirits have good intentions, and others have not-so-good intentions. All can potentially interfere with your life. However, they are usually easy to release using the correct techniques. Those who are more at risk for possession include alcoholics and drug users; these substances weaken energy and attract spiritual parasites (see Recommended Reading and "Spiritual Health: Entity Attachment" in chapter 19).

Sometimes a past-life regression subject who has been experiencing spirit possession or attachment before the session will view a lifetime that he or she has not lived but one associated with the attached spirit. Either way, regression therapy will be beneficial as such attaching spirits are often drawn to people who have similar conflicts or karma.

"The past doesn't matter; what is most important is the present. Why waste time on past-life regression when the problem could have started in childhood?"

Past-life regression research indicates that most current problems are *influenced* by pre-natal, birth, or childhood experiences that were caused by past-life experiences. *The past doesn't matter until you realize it is affecting your present.* You have the option of improving your life by discovering and releasing the root cause of any problem. Your subconscious mind is aware of this root cause. Your conscious mind often isn't. Past-life regression is an effective tool to access subconscious memories. When the statement "go back to the root cause of the conflict" is used during a regression, it allows the person to perceive where, when, and how a conflict started, and whether it originated in childhood, in the womb, or a in past life.

"Past-life regression seems like fantasy; so many people have seen themselves as someone who was wealthy or famous."

This is a common misconception, perhaps encouraged in part by somewhat unscrupulous psychics who tell clients how important they were in their past lives. When people are regressed and see their own past lives, it's common to perceive experiences as being both rich and poor, male and female, powerful and powerless, productive and unproductive, and so on. If people perceive themselves as a famous historic figure such as Cleopatra, Joan of Arc, one of the Disciples of Jesus, or even as Jesus himself, there are four possible explanations for this:

1. The person really was the historic figure in a past life.
2. The person is identifying with personality patterns associated with the historic individual to such an extent that the person believes he or she was that individual.
3. The person's ego is adding to the session. For example, perhaps he or she is perceiving through regression the ancient civilization of Egypt and a woman who looked like Cleopatra, or they may have been associated with Cleopatra, but the regressed person wasn't actually Cleopatra.
4. The person is somehow connecting to the energy or consciousness that was once part of the historic figure.

"People who believe in concepts such as reincarnation don't have the courage to face the fact that death is the end of life."

It actually takes more courage to accept and live the concepts of reincarnation and karma because it means you have to take responsibility for *everything* you do, say, intend, and feel—for all that happens to you. There is no such thing as a victim and you can't blame anyone for anything. Furthermore, physical death may be the end of our body, but we are far more than just a body. Our soul consists of energy or life force. Science has proven that energy never dies and can't be destroyed; it just takes a different form.

"Why do accounts of past lives through regression sometimes seem so simplistic and clichéd? They seem made up."

Information from past lives travels from the subconscious or superconscious mind to the conscious mind, from where it will be perceived and described. If the participant isn't relaxed or is especially skeptical of the process, he or she may only receive partial information and may even interpret what is received based on the present reality instead of the time or life from which it came. Moreover, past-life explanations or the root reasons behind current problems often *are* simple. Because we are programmed to disbelieve reincarnation and because we're often caught up in our dramas, it's sometimes difficult to perceive the truth. Regardless of the details perceived, the most important part of the process of past-life regression therapy is the awareness obtained and how the person chooses to use that awareness.

"How do you know that what people perceive in past-life regression isn't simply some fragment of their imagination based on a movie, picture or book they remember?"

Of course that is possible, but why are they seeing *that* fragment instead of a fragment from the trillions of other sensory information bits we are bombarded with during our lives? In accordance with the theories of reincarnation and karma, nothing is by chance, including information perceived through past-life regression. Whatever one perceives in past-life regression, whether it's from a past life or a movie viewed 10 years ago, the information almost always relates to the issue at hand. The intense emotional response that many feel during regression indicates that what they perceive is more than just a fantasy or daydream; fantasies and daydreams don't provoke such responses.

We receive messages every day in many ways from our higher consciousness, our guides, our Higher Self, God, or whatever else you choose to call this energy. You can try to prove the validity of these messages or choose to heed them and benefit from their wisdom.

Other Common Questions

"I've spent a lot of time and money on therapy but the sessions didn't solve my problem."

Each therapist, both those who use past-life regression and those who don't, relies on different approaches. In my opinion, depending on the problem and willingness of the person, it's almost always more beneficial for the client when the focus of a session is on discovering and releasing the root cause of a problem through regression. Furthermore, it's important that the therapist guide the client in such a way that as much can be accomplished in each session as possible. *A regression session is often more beneficial when forgiveness issues are included, along with questions that help the person become aware of the karmic reasons for the current life problem, conflict, or situation.* With this approach, it's possible to help a client solve a problem in less time than more traditional therapy. Having a client talk out the problem from the current life perspective in session after session may help. This approach is sometimes more for the benefit of the therapist (see "How to Find a Competent Past-life Therapist" in chapter 14).

"If they really wanted to help others, those who perform spiritual services wouldn't charge money for them."

Providing spiritual services is an occupation just like any other. Clients pay for the time of the therapist, healer, or reader. With no income, he or she wouldn't be able to continue providing the service. In addition, clients often gain more from a service or product when it costs money. If it was free, they might not recognize it as having value.

"How can you say that people 'choose' to experience illness, unhappiness, suffering, and unpleasant ways of dying? To imply that my husband who died from cancer chose to leave me is upsetting."

The soul chooses, before each lifetime, major events from which we can learn. Often our path includes our method of death, though our current personality may not be aware of these choices. Your husband's soul agreed to accept that body, knowing that part of the contract was that the body would die rather young. He accepted the body (and you, as a soul mate, probably accepted those conditions) for reasons *that may have had no relation to his dying young of cancer.* People everywhere die young and yet their souls derive much karmic benefit from those lives. Your husband may not have consciously wanted to experience cancer or leave you, but his time and method of death was what you both may have needed to experience for your highest good.

"I find it hard to believe I/my friend/my wife was a prostitute in a past life."

While I'm not endorsing prostitution, this statement may imply a belief that a prostitute is less of a person than someone who isn't. We are all equal, no matter our profession, race, age, bank account balance, sexual orientation, social status, body type, or other factors. Try to accept and have compassion for those who are different than yourself. Besides, considering that prostitution may be the oldest profession in our world, and that many of us may have lived hundreds of lifetimes, the idea isn't so hard to believe.

"I find it hard to believe that someone who is so nice could have been cruel in a past life."

Those who are exceptionally "nice" now may have learned the value of compassion, consideration, and love from lifetimes where they were the opposite. Who we are today, including our personality characteristics, skills, likes, and dislikes, is the result of experiences from both our current life and our past lives.

Recommended Reading and Sources

Astrology

Avery, Jeanne. *Astrology And Your Past Lives.* New York: Simon and Schuster, Inc., 1987.

Bloch, Douglas and Demetra George. *Astrology For Yourself.* Oakland, CA: Wingbow Press, 1987.

Devlin, Mary. *Astrology and Past Lives.* West Chester, PA: Para Research, Inc., 1987.

Forest, Steven. *The Inner Sky.* San Diego, CA: ACS Publications, 1989.

Forest, Steven. *The Changing Sky.* San Diego, CA: ACS Publications, 1989.

Goodman, Linda. *Sun Signs.* New York: Bantam Books, 1971.

Murray, Rose. *When Planets Promise Love.* St. Paul, MN: Llewellyn Publications, 1999 (originally published as *When Will You Marry,* 1995).

Pottenger, Martha and Zipporah Dobyns. *Planets On The Move.* San Diego, CA: ACS Publications, 1997 (astrology of re-location).

Flirting and Dating

Wolf, Sharyn. *Guerrilla Dating Tactics.* New York: Penguin Group, 1994.

Reincarnation

Cunningham, Janet, Ph.D. *A Tribe Returned*. Crest Park, CA: Deep Forest Press, 1994.

Cunningham, Janet, Ph.D. and Michael Ranucci. *Caution: Soul Mate Ahead! Spiritual Love in the Physical World*. Columbia, MD: Two Suns Press, 1999.

Fiore, Edith. *You Have Been Here Before*. New York: Ballantine, 1978.

Goldberg, Bruce, D.D.S. *Past Lives Future Lives*. New York: Ballantine, 1982.

Langley, Noel. *Edgar Cayce On Reincarnation*. New York: Warner Books, Inc., 1967.

Lucas, Winafred, Ph.D. *Regression Therapy: A Handbook for Professionals, Vol. 1*, Crest Park, CA: Deep Forest Press, 1993.

Lucas, Winafred, Ph.D. *Regression Therapy: A Handbook for Professionals, Vol. 2*, Crest Park, CA: Deep Forest Press, 1993.

MacLaine, Shirley. *Out On A Limb*. New York: Bantam Books, 1983.

Moody, Raymond, M.D. *Coming Back: A Psychiatrist Explores Past-Life Journeys*. New York: Bantam, Doubleday, Dell Publishing Group, 1990.

Moore, David L. *The Christian Conspiracy: How the Teachings of Christ Have Been Altered by Christians*. Jasper, GA: Pendulum Plus, 1994.

Sprinkle, R. Leo, Ph.D. *Soul Samples*. Columbus, NC: Granite Publishing Group, 1999.

Steiger, Brad, and Francie Steiger. *Discover Your Past Lives*. Atglen. PA: Schiffer Publishing, Ltd., 1987.

Steiger, Brad, and Lorin Williams. *Other Lives*. Phoenix: Esoteric Publications, 1985.

Steiger, Brad. *You'll Live Again*. Nevada City, CA: Blue Dolphin Publishing, Inc., 1996.

Stevenson, Ian, M.D. *Twenty Cases Suggestive of Reincarnation*. Charlottesville, VA.: University Press of Virginia, revised and enlarged edition, 1974.

Sutphen, Dick. *You Were Born Again To Be Together*. New York: Simon and Schuster, 1976.

Sutphen, Dick. *Predestined Love*. New York: Simon and Schuster, 1988.

Sutphen, Dick. *Past Lives, Future Loves*. New York: Simon and Schuster, 1978.

Todeschi, Kevin J. *Edgar Cayce on Soul Mates: Unlocking The Dynamics Of Soul Attraction*. Virginia Beach, VA: A.R.E. Press, 1999.

Todeschi, Kevin J. *Soul Development: Edgar Cayce's Approach For a New World*. Virginia Beach, VA: A.R.E. Press, 2000.

Weiss, Brian L., M.D. *Many Lives, Many Masters*. New York: Simon and Schuster, 1988.

Wambach, Helen. *Reliving Your Past Lives*. New York: Barnes and Noble, 2000.

Life Between Life

Newton, Michael. *Journey Of Souls: Case Studies of Life Between Lives*. St. Paul, MN: Llewellyn Publications, 1997.

Newton, Michael. *Destiny Of Souls: New Case Studies of Life Between Lives*. St. Paul, MN: Llewellyn Publications, 2000

Moody, Raymond A., Jr., M.D. *Life After Life*. New York: Bantam Books, 1975.

Future Life Progression

Snow, Chet B., Ph.D. *Mass Dreams Of The Future*. New York: Doubleday, 1989.

Spirit Attachment/Possession

Baldwin, William, Ph.D. *Spirit Releasement Therapy: A Technique Manual*. Terra Alta, WV: Headline Books, Inc, 1992.

Fiore, Dr. Edith. *The Unquiet Dead: A Psychologist Treats Spirit Possession*. New York: Doubleday/Dolphin, 1987.

Modi, Shakuntala M.D. *Remarkable Healings*. Charlottesville, VA: Hampton Roads Publishing Company, Inc., 1997.

Hickman, Irene, D.O. *Remote Depossession*. Kirksville, MO: Hickman Systems, 1994.

Scientific Studies Involving Reincarnation

Journal of Scientific Exploration, Allen Press, Lawrence, KS. Has published various articles about reincarnation studies.

Journal of Regression Therapy, International Association for Regression Research and Therapies (IARRT), Riverside, CA. (909) 784-1570, http://www.IARRT.org.

True Health

Airola, Dr. Paavo. *How To Keep Slim, Healthy and Young With Juice Fasting*. Health Plus, Sherwood Oregon, 1971.

Anderson, Richard N.D., N.M.D. *Cleanse and Purify Thyself*. Part of the Arise and Shine Herbal Cleanse program, 1988.

Calbom, Cherie and Keane, Maureen. *Juicing For Life*. Avery Publishing Group Inc., Garden City Park, NY, 1992.

Clark, Hulda Regehr, Ph.D., N.D. *The Cure For All Diseases*. San Diego, CA: New Century Press, 1995.

Crook, William G., M.D. *The Yeast Connection*. Random House, Inc., New York, 1983.

D'Adamo, Dr Peter J. with Catherine Whitney. *Eat Right For Your Blood Type*. G.P. Putnam's Sons, N.Y., 1996.

Gates, Donna with Linda Schatz. *The Body Ecology Diet*. B.E.D. Publications, Atlanta Georgia, 1996.

Hay, Louise L. *Heal Your Body: The Mental Causes for Physical Illness and the Metaphysical Way to Overcome Them*. Carlsbad, CA: Hay House, Inc. 1994.

Hay, Louise L. *You Can Heal Your Life*. Carlsbad, CA: Hay House, Inc. 1999.

Hippocrates Health Institute, 1443 Palmdale Court, West Palm Beach, FL 33411. (305) 471-8876. (800) 842-2125. Spa, classes and clinic.

Griffin, Edward G. *World Without Cancer: The Story of Vitamin B17*. 1997.

Lynes, Barry. *The Cancer Cure That Worked: 50 Years of Suppression*. Queensville, Ontario, Canada: Marcus Books, 1987.

Mendelsohn, Robert S., M.D. *Confessions of a Medical Heretic*. Contemporary Publishing, 1990.

Meyerowitz, Steve ("Sproutman"). *Food Combining and Digestion*. Great Barrington, MA: The Sprout House, Inc., 1987.

Meyerowitz, Steve ("Sproutman"). *Juice Fasting and Detoxification*. Great Barrington, MA: The Sprout House, Inc., 1984.

Responsible and Honest Non-Monogamy

O'Neill, Nena and George O'Neill. *Open Marriage*. New York: M. Evens and Company, Inc., 1984.

Easton, Dossie and Catherine A. Liszt. *The Ethical Slut*. San Francisco, CA: Greenery Press, 1997.

Nearing, Ryam. *Loving More*. Web site and magazine: www.love-more.com.

Numerology

Avery, Kevin Quinn. *The Numbers of Life*. Garden City, NY: Dolphin Books, Doubleday and Company, Inc., 1974.

Barratt, Rodford. *The Elements of Numerology*. Rockport, MA: Element Books Inc., 1994.

Buess, Lynn. *Numerology for the New Age*. Sedona, AZ: Light Technology Publishing, 1978.

Bunker, Dusty and Javane Faith. *Numerology and the Divine Triangle*. West Chester, PA: Whitford Press, 1979.

Campbell, Florence. *Your Days Are Numbered*. Marina del Rey, CA: DeVorss and Company, 1931.

Deaver, Korra. *The Master Numbers*. Alameda, CA: Hunter House Publishers Inc., 1993.

Decoz, Hans. *Numerology Key To Your Inner Self*. Garden City Park, NY: Avery Publishing Group, 1994.

Goodwin, Matthew Oliver. *Numerology: The Complete Guide Vol I*. North Hollywood, CA: Newcastle Publishing Company Inc., 1981.

Goodwin, Matthew Oliver. *Numerology The Complete Guide Vol II*. North Hollywood, CA: Newcastle Publishing Company Inc., 1981.

Hitchcock, Helyn. *Helping Yourself with Numerology*. West Nyack, NY. Parker Publishing Company, Inc., 1972.

Hulse, David Allen. *The Truth About Numerology*. St Paul, MN: Llewellyn Publications, 1996.

Javane, Faith. *Master Numbers*. Atglen, PA: Whitford Press, 1988.

Jordan, Juno. *Numerology The Romance In Your Name*. Marina del Rey, CA: DeVorss and Company, 1965.

Sepharial. *The Kabala of Numbers*. North Hollywood, CA: Newcastle Publishing Co., Inc., 1974.

Index

About the Author

Stephen Petullo has been studying metaphysical concepts (in this life) since the early 1980s and has a liberal arts degree that includes a minor in psychology from the University of Arizona. During the 1990s, Stephen owned and operated an upscale introduction service for those seeking compatible love relationships. He uses a variety of techniques to help clients fulfill their potential: hypnotic and non-hypnotic inductions, guided meditation, metaphysical counseling, pre-natal, birth, and past-life regression, spirit release, and Reiki. Stephen maintains a private practice in southeast Florida, and is available for individual sessions, group sessions, workshops, and presentations.

If this book helped you improve your life, if you have a personal story you would like to share with Stephen, or if you would like to contact him about his services, please write:

Stephen Petullo
c/o MetaPublishing
3741 NE 163rd Street, #314
North Miami Beach, FL 33160

Stephen@howisyourlovelife.com
www.howisyourlovelife.com

About the Contributor

Scott A. Petullo has a liberal arts degree from the University of Arizona and has been exploring metaphysics since the early 1980s. He has been a serious student of advanced numerology since 1992 and is considered an expert on the subject. He uses advanced numerology (numeric analyses) to determine timing cycles, personality traits and compatibility. Scott is also a master handwriting analyst. He received his Certified Master Graphologist designation from the Institute of Graphological Science in Dallas, Texas, a state-licensed and accredited institution. Scott maintains a private practice and provides personality, compatibility and timing analyses for individuals and businesses.

If Scott's numerology section helped you improve your life, if you have a personal story you'd like to share with him, or if you'd simply like to contact Scott about his services, please write:

Scott A. Petullo
c/o MetaPublishing
3741 NE 163rd Street, #314
North Miami Beach, FL 33160

decad@msn.com
www.decadcorp.com

Whether past lives are real
or your imagination, and whether
you're a believer or a skeptic,
past-life self-regression can help you
reach your love life goals.

Quick Order Form

Toll-free fax orders: (866) 375-7217. Fax this form.

On-line orders: www.howisyourlovelife.com

Toll-free telephone orders: Call (866) 375-7222 and have your credit card ready.

Postal orders: MetaPublishing, 3741 NE 163rd St. #314, North Miami Beach, FL 33160, USA. Telephone: (305) 947-5100

Or visit www.howisyourlovelife.com for descriptions and current product offers

Please send me the following:

❑ *Your Love Life and Reincarnation* (book)
$17.95 Quantity ____

❑ *Past Life Self-Regression: Discover and Release the Root Cause; Couples Past Life Self-Regression; Singles Past Life Self-Regression* (CD)
$15.95 Quantity ____

❑ *Forgive and Release Meditation; Relationship Meditations* (CD)
$15.95 Quantity ____

❑ *Love Potion Meditation For Singles* (CD)
$15.95 Quantity ____

❑ *Love Potion Meditation For Involved Individuals or Couples* (CD)
$15.95 Quantity ____

Name: ____________________

Address: ____________________

City, State, Zip: ____________________

Telephone: ____________________

E-mail address: ____________________

(your information will not be shared with anyone)

Sales tax: Add 6% + any applicable county rates for products shipped to FL addresses.

Shipping and handling: orders are shipped priority mail
US: $4 for the first book or CD and $2 for each additional product.
International: $9 for first book or CD; $5 for each additional product (estimated).

Payment: ❑ Check ❑ Visa ❑ MasterCard ❑ American Express ❑ Discover ❑ Optima

Card number: ____________________

Name on card: ____________________ Exp. Date: ____________

Card Holder Signature: ____________________

Quick Order Form

Toll-free fax orders: (866) 375-7217. Fax this form.

On-line orders: www.howisyourlovelife.com

Toll-free telephone orders: Call (866) 375-7222 and have your credit card ready.

Postal orders: MetaPublishing, 3741 NE 163rd St. #314, North Miami Beach, FL 33160, USA. Telephone: (305) 947-5100

Or visit www.howisyourlovelife.com for descriptions and current product offers

Please send me the following:

❑ *Your Love Life and Reincarnation* (book)
$17.95 Quantity ____

❑ *Past Life Self-Regression: Discover and Release the Root Cause; Couples Past Life Self-Regression; Singles Past Life Self-Regression* (CD)
$15.95 Quantity ____

❑ *Forgive and Release Meditation; Relationship Meditations* (CD)
$15.95 Quantity ____

❑ *Love Potion Meditation For Singles* (CD)
$15.95 Quantity ____

❑ *Love Potion Meditation For Involved Individuals or Couples* (CD)
$15.95 Quantity ____

Name: ____________________

Address: ____________________

City, State, Zip: ____________________

Telephone: ____________________

E-mail address: ____________________

(your information will not be shared with anyone)

Sales tax: Add 6% + any applicable county rates for products shipped to FL addresses.

Shipping and handling: orders are shipped priority mail
US: $4 for the first book or CD and $2 for each additional product.
International: $9 for first book or CD; $5 for each additional product (estimated).

Payment: ❑ Check ❑ Visa ❑ MasterCard ❑ American Express ❑ Discover ❑ Optima

Card number: ____________________

Name on card: ____________________ Exp. Date: ____________

Card Holder Signature: ____________________

Quick Order Form

Toll-free fax orders: (866) 375-7217. Fax this form.

On-line orders: www.howisyourlovelife.com

Toll-free telephone orders: Call (866) 375-7222 and have your credit card ready.

Postal orders: MetaPublishing, 3741 NE 163rd St. #314, North Miami Beach, FL 33160, USA. Telephone: (305) 947-5100

Or visit www.howisyourlovelife.com for descriptions and current product offers

Please send me the following:

❑ *Your Love Life and Reincarnation* (book)
$17.95 Quantity ____

❑ *Past Life Self-Regression: Discover and Release the Root Cause; Couples Past Life Self-Regression; Singles Past Life Self-Regression* (CD)
$15.95 Quantity ____

❑ *Forgive and Release Meditation; Relationship Meditations* (CD)
$15.95 Quantity ____

❑ *Love Potion Meditation For Singles* (CD)
$15.95 Quantity ____

❑ *Love Potion Meditation For Involved Individuals or Couples* (CD)
$15.95 Quantity ____

Name: ____________________

Address: ____________________

City, State, Zip: ____________________

Telephone: ____________________

E-mail address: ____________________

(your information will not be shared with anyone)

Sales tax: Add 6% + any applicable county rates for products shipped to FL addresses.

Shipping and handling: orders are shipped priority mail
US: $4 for the first book or CD and $2 for each additional product.
International: $9 for first book or CD; $5 for each additional product (estimated).

Payment: ❑ Check ❑ Visa ❑ MasterCard ❑ American Express ❑ Discover ❑ Optima

Card number: ____________________

Name on card: ____________________ Exp. Date: ____________

Card Holder Signature: ____________________